# THE DAILY LIFE.

# THE DAILY LIFE;

OR

# PRECEPTS AND PRESCRIPTIONS

FOR

# CHRISTIAN LIVING.

BY THE

REV. JOHN CUMMING, D.D., F.R.S.E.,

MINISTER OF THE SCOTTISH NATIONAL CHURCH, CROWN COURT, COVENT GARDEN, LONDON.

"Not slothful in business; fervent in spirit; serving the Lord." — ROM. xii. 11.

"A servant with this clause
Makes drudgery divine:
Who sweeps a room, as for thy laws,
Makes that and the action fine."
GEORGE HERBERT.

BOSTON:
PUBLISHED BY JOHN P. JEWETT AND COMPANY
CLEVELAND, OHIO:
JEWETT AND PROCTOR.
NEW YORK: SHELDON, LAMPORT AND BLAKEMAN.
1855.

CAMBRIDGE:
ALLEN AND FARNHAM, STEREOTYPERS AND PRINTERS.

# PREFACE.

THE following reflections are intended to act on the minds and hearts of those who are very busy by day, and very weary at eventide. Every Christian must descend from Tabor and its bright radiance into the low level of every-day life. We need more religion in such circumstances, and less theology. We require not arid dogmas, however orthodox, but warm joys — sustaining strength — cheering hopes, and inspiring expectations. We need also direction, guidance, encouragement. What so powerful a check to evil, or so comforting an assurance of peace, as a sense of a presence that encourages us in the paths of righteousness, and encompasses us with a ceaseless defence? True spiritual religion will enter into every relation, transaction, toil; and not only regulate them, but give energy of heart and strength of hand to fulfil them. Instead of crushing by stern law, it attracts by beautiful example. It keeps us free from the sour asceticism that caricatures the world and corrodes the temper; and no less so does it remind us of the enthralment of indulgence, and the danger of pampering the mind. It enjoins temperance, moderation, forbearance; and these are elements of strength. In sorrow, which enters, sooner or later, every heart — in sickness, or at seventy — in bereavements, and vexatious trials, and bitter disappointments, which are the shadows on the dial of daily life, we need the sweet sunshine of the blessed gospel. The perfect character would be a composite of Martha and Mary — the industry, and hospitality, and domestic management, that never wearied; and the piety, and teachableness, and love, and lowliness of heart, that sat at the feet of Jesus, and drank in the truths of everlasting life.

To many a Martha these pages may give warning of being overanxious about many things, and that "one thing is needful;" and to many a Mary, that the highest spirituality is not incompatible with an active and laborious life. The apostles retired from Calvary, and Gethsemane, and the garden of Arimathea, to their accustomed labors on the sea, and Jesus met them there and blessed them. Daily life may be richly charged with divine life, and the air and hopes and joys of eternity inspire and invigorate the toils and trials of time. Prayer and praise and thanksgiving are not peculiar to the Sunday; they are for every-day living. May we so pass through the things that are seen and temporal, that we finally lose not those things that are unseen and eternal. May the daily life of time merge in the sabbath life of eternity, and this little work be as useful in the age that now is, as it will be useless in the age to come.

# CONTENTS.

# THE DAILY LIFE.

---

## CHAPTER I.

### REJOICE EVERMORE.

"He is the happy man whose life even now
Shows somewhat of that happier life to come;
Who, doomed to an obscure but tranquil state,
Is pleased with it, and were he free to choose,
Would make his fate his choice; whom peace, the fruit
Of virtue, and whom virtue, fruit of faith,
Prepare for happiness; bespeak him one
Content indeed to sojourn while he must
Below the skies, but having there his home."

"Rejoice evermore. Pray without ceasing. In every thing give thanks: for this is the will of God in Christ Jesus concerning you. Quench not the Spirit. Despise not prophesyings. Prove all things; hold fast that which is good. Abstain from all appearance of evil." — 1 THESS. v. 16–22.

THE words "rejoice evermore," are the first of seven prescriptions that occur in succession, describing the completeness or the perfection of the Christian character. Principle should or will always flower into practice. Life will show itself in living. Every Scripture truth has a directly practical tendency. Christian doctrines are not abstract dogmas, to be retained in all the clearness, and with all the coldness, of moonlight in the head; but warm, prolific, practical truths, like the grace of God spoken of by the apostle, tending and teaching us to live soberly, and righteously, and godly in this present world, looking for that blessed hope, the glorious appearing of Jesus Christ our God and Saviour. We cannot suppose that the vital truths of Christianity received into the heart fail to bear fruits. No Christian doubts their fruitfulness. We feel it to be true; in our practical experience and history we know it to be true; but there are persons who think and say, "Christians are always proving doctrinal truths, and rarely do they attempt to show us the blossoms these should bear as the ornaments of Christianity, and the fruit that should ripen upon them as its practical growth before God and all mankind." The beautiful prescriptions, seven in number, given by St. Paul, contain, as carried into practical life, the plastic influences that generate a holy life, and ripen into the fruit, the fragrant fruit, of the Christian character. However, we need not argue that doctrinal truths are practical. We never can admit that a cause is without an effect; or that the sun at mid-day sheds down no splendor. We cannot suppose a person in his senses speaking of a fire, but regretting that it has no heat; or of the sun at noon, but lamenting there is no light. In the same manner it is absurd, and equally absurd, to speak of great, broad, doctrinal truths, and yet to regret they have no practical value. They are living, and therefore fruitful. A truth is meant for telling not only with the lips, but on the life, the character, and the conduct. Great truths we admit may be taken into the head, where they may lie cold, magnificent abstractions — for they never part with their magnificence even when thus received, but there they produce no proper fruit. But we are in such a case to blame not the truths, but the subject that imperfectly receives them. If one were to scatter seed-corn upon the pavement, or on the hard stones, we could not reasonably expect a harvest; not because the seeds had no vitality, but because the hard stones were not receptive soil. So when these truths produce no practical fruit of whatever things are pure, and just, and lovely; do not blame the truths, which is the common thing, but blame yourselves, which is the difficult, and, we admit, the painful, but, nevertheless, the right thing. The tendency of man is to lay the responsibility upon the truths, and say, "I am not what I should be because these truths leave not the power which the preacher says they have;" but the real duty is to lay the guilt upon himself. We have in all likelihood taken the truths into the head and left them there, instead of taking them into the heart and giving them hospitality there, where by their constraining and sanctifying energy you would be adorned by all the fruits of practical and true Christianity. It is important to show that vital truths have all a directly personal and practical effect; and to do so not simply by quoting instances in actual life, but by quoting such prescriptions as are given by the apostles, and thus showing how they regard them, and what they hold to be, logically, their precious fruits.

The seven or eight prescriptions in the very short, but extremely suggestive, passage, in 1 Thess. v. 16–22, contain the perfection of the Christian character. They are Christianity not in portrait on the outer page, but in living sculpture and in living men. It is the perfect man in Christ Jesus. The whole seven have a most intimate connection, being linked together in sweet and blessed harmony. If you wish always to rejoice, the way to do so is to "pray always." And if you want to pray successfully for new blessings, the way to do so is "to give thanks" for old ones; and if you desire "always to rejoice," always to pray, always to give thanks, take care you "quench not the

2

Spirit," who can enable you to do so. And if you wish not to quench the Spirit or to grieve him, but, on the contrary, to cherish him, despise not these declarations of God's word, which are here called "prophesyings." And in order not to despise prophecy, "prove all things." And in order not to live as a mere controversialist, always proving, but never practising, "hold fast that which is good." So that you can see throughout all a binding and beautiful connection, the one woven into the other; and the whole in practice constituting the perfection of Christian character.

In reading these Divine prescriptions, let us notice their universality or endurance — or if there be any other word better fitted to express my meaning. It is, "Rejoice evermore;" not to-day and to-morrow, but evermore. It is, "Pray always," or continually. It is, "In every thing" — not in some things, but "in every thing give thanks." It is, "Despise not prophesyings" — in the plural number, that is, any part of God's word. A negative like this in the Bible is a strong positive, it means, revere them profoundly. "Prove all things" that are submitted to you as being from God. And, finally, "Abstain from *all* appearance of evil." There is an all-embracing universality in these prescriptions, teaching us that there is no age in which any of them is unseasonable, that there is no year in the threescore and ten, or month in the year, or day in the month, in which these prescriptions are impracticable. In sunshine and in shadow, in life's bright spots, and in life's bleak and desert ones, when the heart is bounding and when the heart is breaking; in all time of your wealth, in all time of your tribulation, rejoice always, pray continually, quench not the Spirit, abstain from all appearance of evil.

We cannot help noticing, what is no less interesting, the intensity of each prescription. We do not mean simply their connection, nor merely the universality of their application, but the intensity in each. All real life is earnest. Wherever there is a professing Christian who is not thoroughly in earnest, it is want of Christianity that makes him so. It is impossible to believe what this book teaches, and be apathetic or indifferent. It is, "Thou shalt love with *all* thy heart;" and the constant opposite of that is, Thou shalt hate with all thy heart; but any thing between is neither cold nor hot, and it will be rejected utterly of God. Not only "Joy," but "Rejoice always;" not only "Pray," but let your prayer culminate or blossom into praise. "Despise not," means study and deeply reverence. And not only prove, but approve; and not only hold, but hold fast that which you have proved to be good. There is therefore the intensest force in each prescription. Thus there is, first, a close connection subsisting among all the graces of the Christian character. There is, next, the applicability of every prescription to every phasis of the Christian life. And, lastly, we see the intensity of all that characterizes the Christian, and marks him out as separate and distinct from the world.

Let us now, after having traced the connection that subsists among these prescriptions, ponder and try to explain the first prescription of all; namely, "Rejoice evermore." What a glorious prescription, "Rejoice evermore!" Christianity is not a sepulchral thing, a gloomy life, a depressed condition of social existence. It is impossible that it can be so, as the world brands it with such a prescription as this from an apostle's lips, "Rejoice evermore." True, the Christian has his sorrows; but these are not unsweetened. True, the Christian life has its shadows and its showers; but these are not unmingled with bright beams of heavenly light; and the saddest aspects of a Christian's daily life are but the April showers of spring that usher in the approaching bright and beautiful summer, — the everlasting and the heavenly sunshine. Christian life is not a penance as the Romanist thinks it, but a privilege, as God describes it. It is not a reluctant sacrifice wrung from us, but a joyous and freewill offering gladly and gratefully rendered by us. And therefore the light of our life is not a dim, but a bright religious light. The injunction of our apostle is, "Rejoice always;" and the prayer of the apostle's Lord, "That my peace may remain in you;" and again, "That my joy may abide in you, and that your joy may be full." And Peter, catching up the thoughts of his Lord still shining with undiminished lustre on the leaves of memory, answers in his Epistle, "Whom having not seen, we love; in whom, though now we see him not, yet believing, we rejoice with joy unspeakable and full of glory." And the Apostle Paul, echoing the same grand sentiment, says, "We joy in God. Rejoice; and again I say, Rejoice." This shows us, that of all happy men upon earth the Christian should be happiest. His sorrows come from sin, his griefs spring from evil; his sunshine, his gladness, and his joy are the spontaneous and normal elements of his true Christian and holy life.

Unless our hearts are filled with the joy that the gospel imparts, our life must become gloomier the longer that it lasts. Unless a Christian feels the joy that this blessed book makes known, his life will grow sadder the nearer it draws to a close, and the most aged man will necessarily be the saddest. I appeal to experience. Do we not feel that, as we grow older, we become less susceptible of impression from the joys that once shone so brilliantly and struck us with such force before? You now look at the child playing with his baubles, and wonder how the little child can be pleased, perhaps forgetting that kings are only playing with baubles more splendid, but no less empty, as seen by angels and the inhabitants of higher spheres. Do not those who have reached the middle of life, and look back on the march they have left behind, notice that the procession of those who are no more with us grows longer every day; and scenes, that made the heart bound and set the feelings all on fire twenty years ago, now cease to produce the least effect when repeated and even radiant with more than their former brilliancy. Do we not find that, try as we like, we cannot recall the romance of childhood, or rekindle the dying embers of departed youth, or restore to the canvas the bright colors that have faded, and gone forever and ever. But here lies the charm of Christianity, — here is the preciousness of the gospel of Christ, that as natural joys ebb away and are spent, heavenly ones rush into their forsaken channels. As the past ceases to impress, the future and the heavenly begins to shower down new and better pleasures. As the old heart dies to the excitements that thrilled it once, the new heart begins to come under the influence of those brighter and better joys that come from the future. As earth ceases to attract, heaven begins, if we be Christians, more powerfully to draw us. We cease to look backward to a world that cannot give us any real delight, and begin to look forward to a brighter and a better world, that, like a distant star, grows lovelier the nearer we approach it. Old age without religion loses two worlds at once; the world that has past is gone, and it has no future world to go to: but old age, inspired by living religion, only exchanges the old world, that is ready to perish, for the new, the brighter and more glorious world, that begins to burst upon it. Of all beings upon earth, we pity an old man without living religion. We pity the young that have not that which can sanctify their joy; but still more do we pity the old whose hearts are the dry and empty channels of streams that have evaporated, and are not replenished with the living waters that flow from the fountain of God and of the Lamb. Thus we see how precious religion is, even if for no other reason than that it takes the place of those joys that have withered, and cheers us as we go down the other side of the hill towards the valley of the shadow of death; so that, as the pleasures of memory fade, the pleasures of a sure hope shall become brighter every day.

Having seen the excellence of this joy, and the importance of religion as inspiring it, let us try to ascertain why we should rejoice; and then, in the next place, what is meant by rejoicing evermore. Why should we rejoice? There is every thing in the Bible to make a Christian rejoice; there is nothing to make a Christian, *as such*, sad, dejected, and sorrowful. God has undone all that should grieve us, and he has done all that should make us exceeding glad. He has undone all that should distress us. "There is no condemnation to them that are in Christ Jesus." Glorious truth! "There is no condemnation to them that are in Christ Jesus." The curse of the law has been borne and exhausted by our Substitute; it cannot scathe me. The blessing of the law that I forfeited has been repurchased by my Saviour; it cannot escape me. All that I deserve as a sinner he endured; all that I owe as a creature he paid. In him there is no condemnation. On the other hand, he has done all that could be done to make me happy. He so loved me that he gave Christ to die for me. He has given me his word to guide me, his Holy Spirit to teach and to comfort me, and the bright promise of an inheritance, incorruptible, and undefiled, and that fadeth not away. And as if to make me sure of all he has said, "All things are yours, Paul, or Apollos, or Cephas, the world, things present, things to come; life or death—all are yours;—*because* ye are Christ's." In what sense are all yours? All the world's troubles and trials are mine, to keep me from presumption—all the world's joys and blessings are mine, to keep me from despair or doubt—all things that are in the world work for good to them that love God, and are the called according to his purpose. I see nothing in the law that can alarm me — nothing in the Bible that can depress me — but much in every page, more in every providential arrangement of heaven, to cheer me, and to make me respond with joyous utterance to the prescription of the apostle, "Rejoice always." His ordinances are mine also, and for my benefit. What a blessed fact that God should bow his ear to listen to a sinner's prayer. I believe the simplest privileges that are revealed in this book we may absolutely miss the weight and meaning of by not dwelling upon them. Would not this make us happy, that we have access in this world to the fountain of honor, of power, of influence? How much more so, if we were what we should be, that we have access to the fountain of living waters! Hence prayer in a Christian's experience is ever delightful. There is not only joy in his conscious privilege, but there is joy in the use of that privilege. When the mere worldly man prays, he prays as a Romanist, — namely, as a penance. And hence a mere professor *performs* prayer, a true Christian *prays* prayer. With the one it is a sacrifice to propitiate God; with the other it is a child's expression of his lowest and his loftiest wants in the ear and to the heart of a listening and loving Father. Hence to a Christian, prayer is not only privilege in itself as well as a right, but it is enjoyment in the exercise of it. A Christian, too, *should* rejoice and *may* rejoice in full assurance of faith. We do not say that every true Christian has full assurance. The Bible does not teach the absolute duty of full assurance of faith, or that if not fully assured we have not faith at all. But unquestionably many a Christian can say with no feigned lips, "I know in whom I have believed, and that he is able to keep what I have committed to him against that day;" and another can say, "Whom have I in heaven but thee? and there is none upon the earth I desire beside thee; and when heart and flesh faint and fail, thou wilt be the strength of my heart, and my portion for ever and ever." Faith believes in Christ for salvation; assurance, which is a step higher, believes that in Christ we already have salvation. Both are saving. The first is saving only, the second is saving and comforting too. And an apostle writing, says, "These things we write unto you"—wishing them to have full assurance—"that your joy may be full."

A Christian rejoices in the knowledge of God. What music is to the sensitive and susceptible ear, what beauty is to the eye, what health is to the frame and sweetness to the taste—all this, and more than this, the knowledge of God, through apprehension of the everlasting gospel, is to the true Christian. Isaiah expressed the blessings of Christians, not of a prophet only, when he said, "How beautiful upon the mountains are the feet of them that bring glad tidings of good things!" And to a Christian whose mind is enlightened, all, not only all that God has *written*, but all that God has *made*, is perfectly beautiful. Earth is clothed with new verdure, because he sees it was his Father who clothed it. All Providence is full of new blessings, because it is God's action in the midst of the world; and even thistles and thorns are welcome to a Christian, because they urge him to quicken his pace through time, and to hasten to that "city which hath foundations, whose builder and whose maker is God." A Christian rejoices in prayer, in the Bible, in the knowledge of God; and the more he mingles in all this prescription of the apostle, the richer the joy that is poured into his heart.

But there are other ways in which our joy is increased and strengthened. A Christian rejoices, and has his joy increased, by giving for Christ's sake. If you wish to be happy, begin, if you have never begun before, liberally to give to what is good. This is not said at random, but on the strength of our blessed Lord's own assertion, "It is more blessed to give than it is to receive." In all you give to the widow, in all you distribute to the orphan, in all that you lay upon the altar in response to the claims of Christ and his kingdom, you have no ground for boasting, but you have much ground for increase of joy and rejoicing evermore. By a great law, the larger you make the amount of your beneficence the richer the harvest you will reap in the end. He that gives most enjoys most. Every cup of cold water that you give to the thirsty, every kind look that you reflect on the needy, every morsel of bread that you impart to the hungry, every helping hand you hold out to the downtrodden, every text of truth you whisper in the ears of the dying, every page of the Bible you send forth to the distant ignorant, comes back to yourself in waves of swelling joy, and by a beautiful reaction you reap whilst you sow, and taste the blessedness whilst you exercise the beneficence of giving to them that need your sympathy and your assistance. It is a grand and blessed law in God's holy providence, that if you try to increase your own joy by gratifying your desires and appetites, you find that you stimulate them by indulgence, and the more you give them the more they necessarily crave. But, on the other hand, if you wish to increase your joy by denying your own desires and appetites, and giving as a ministry to the wants and necessities of others, you will find that, though your desires and appetites are thus unstimulated, yet will your gratification increase, and the more you give the more you will swell the current of your happiness, and multiply the joys of your own heart. To rejoice always, therefore, give always. "There is that scattereth and yet increaseth." It is recorded of a man who had made an ample fortune and had retired to a country-seat to enjoy it, that when he had nothing to do he became absolutely wretched; so wretched that he formed the horrible idea of committing suicide. Going to drown himself he met a poor woman who had not tasted bread for four and twenty hours; cold — ragged — wretched — starving. She implored aid, he gave her a shilling; and the grateful smile reflected from that starving woman's face arrested his career, and he returned a wiser and a better man, saying to himself, "If God makes me the instrument of giving happiness by the gift of a shilling, I think he must have more work for me to do in the world." If any do not know what to do, and therefore cannot find happiness in the world, let them apply at the nearest Sunday school for work as teachers. Visit the first day school and take an interest in it. Follow a city missionary in his laborious, and arduous, and excellent toil; and you will reap blessings in that poor man's footsteps. If you want to be happy, do good; if you wish to rejoice, begin to be beneficent. This is a law that God has made. In every age, in every circumstance, in every sphere, it has been proved to be practically true; make the experiment, and you will find it is so still.

We may increase our joy and rejoice when we cannot give, by the expression of sympathy with those that suffer, or coöperation with those that do good. The apostle says it is one of the Christian duties to "rejoice with them that do rejoice, and to weep with them that do weep." To refuse to do so must spring from envy, or from jealousy, or from ill-will. The sorrow that a brother feels, which finds a resounding echo in my heart, leaves a sense of satisfaction there. If you have no wealth to give, you have a tear to shed — a helping hand to extend — a kind word to say; and you will find that these will return in streams of happiness into your own bosom. And wherever therefore we see the cause and kingdom of Christ promoted really and truly, we should rejoice; if we do not rejoice, let us ex amine ourselves; there is something wrong in our character. If you see a rival party — another church — spreading the gospel more successfully than yours, to be envious is human, to rejoice is divine. And just in proportion as you hail good done, by whomsoever it is done, and rejoice in blessings distributed, by whatsoever hand they are distributed, will your own joy be increased and multiplied in all directions.

We have seen, first, that joy is the true state of a true believer; secondly, that without the increasing joy of the gospel old age must only be increasing sorrow; thirdly, that God has undone all that could obstruct the entrance of joy, and that he has done for us all that can communicate true joy. We have seen next that he has left us prescriptions that under his blessing multiply and increase our joy — such as sympathy with them that suffer — giving to them that are needy. Let us now try to show, and as briefly as possible, that the joys which spring from these cisterns, or rather from the fountain of life, ought to be exercised not only *everywhere*, but *always*. "Rejoice evermore." The word translated "evermore" is πάντοτε, which means literally "at all *thens*" — "at every then" — at all times, on every occasion, — rejoice. If we open the Bible we find that joy and rejoicing is the experience of Christians in the worst of circumstances. In a truly beautiful passage of the prophet we find a striking instance: "Though the fig-tree shall not blossom, neither shall fruit be in the vines; the labor of the olive shall fail, and the fields shall yield no meat; the flock shall be cut off from the fold, and there shall be no herd in the stalls" — that is, famine, desolation, pining, and pinching poverty — what shall I do? The stoic would say, I will be insensible — that is, I will turn granite. The mere man of the world will say, I will destroy myself, that is, I will commit suicide; and the mere philosopher will say, I will submit to it; but the Christian can triumphantly exclaim, "I will" — notwithstanding — "rejoice in the Lord, and joy in the God of my salvation." Paul says, "As sorrowful, yet always rejoicing" — his life like an April day — sunshine and showers, tears and smiles, intermingling in rapid succession. James says, "Count it all joy when ye fall into divers temptations." And, again, it is said of the Christians, in the Epistle to the Hebrews, "Ye took joyfully the spoiling of your goods." We are therefore taught in all these passages, that in that hour when, according to this world's wisdom, a Christian should weep, he may "rejoice evermore." There is no night that falls upon our hemisphere in which there are not some intermingling rays. There is no sorrow in which there is not some compensatory spring of joy and thankfulness. Have you lost your property? Has some storm, unexpected — and it may be, undeserved — swept away all that your industry had accumulated? Is not that ground, the world would say, for sorrow? It is, no doubt, ground for sorrow; and if you look at the loss in itself, you must weep; or if you regard the loss as an accident, you cannot but grieve. But if you can look above the loss, and see it was a Father that took it from you, because you made it a substitute for him; or that it was infinite love that snatched it from you, because your heart was there instead of being where Christ your treasure is; then the loss of earth may be the gain of heaven, and the departure of the riches of this world may leave you a deeper hold of the unsearchable riches of the Lord Jesus Christ. It is thus, that amid the losses of this world you may feel in the knowledge that God sends them, and that a Father's love is in them, what will make you, like the early Christians, "take joyfully the spoiling of your goods." The mere man of the world says, "I am afflicted, I have lost my property; *therefore* God hates me." But the Christian be gins at the other end, and says, "God loves me, therefore my loss of property must be the expression of that love." The natural man argues from the physical effect below, up to the moral feeling that is in God's bosom above; but the Christian begins his creed, — as he begins his prayer, — with "Our Father," and then he argues downwards, "the heaviest blow is from his hand, the sorest loss is his will, the bitterest disappointment is only the expression of his infinite and inexhaustible love."

But, perhaps, you have suffered a severer trial than this: you have lost those that you loved on earth; you are bereaved and left forlorn and alone; and you ask, Can I hear or respond to the words of Paul, "Rejoice evermore," whilst I gaze on the pale face of the beloved dead? Can I rejoice when my tears flow so fast and so bitterly? Yes, even there, when dust goes to dust, and ashes to ashes, a Christian may hear an undertone of gladness, and feel an undercurrent of joy in his deepest and his bitterest sorrow; for if the lost was a Christian he is not lost, he is only gone before, — the preoccupant of the everlasting rest, — the inheritor of the better land. You feel a new detachment from a world that is perishing, and a new attachment and attraction to a world that lasts forever; and, instead of burying your heart in the grave of the dead, you will lift it to the home and the habitation of the living, knowing that "absent from the body is present with the Lord," and that departure from you was to be "with Christ, which is far better." Thus the palm rises where cypress grew, and joy springs from the scenes of grief, and the grave rings already with the accents of a coming and a joyous resurrection.

But there is another hour, — that hour that comes to all, and must come to the oldest and the youngest; the hour when "the dust shall return to the earth as it was, and the spirit shall go to him that gave it." In that hour Christians

3

have rejoiced — and Christianity teaches us to rejoice; and if we have felt its blessed influence in our hearts, a dying hour will be to many of us our brightest and our happiest. When God says to the Christian, "Come up hither," he invariably gives him a robe of willingness to put on for it. We often anticipate what we shall feel when dying by what we feel now. We are now in full health and strength, and we do not wish to die. Quite right; there is nothing sinful in that; it is altogether natural. It is unnatural to die. But when God lays us on the last bed, and the heart, "like a muffled drum," indicates it is "beating" its last "march to the grave" — then and there God gives us — what he has not given us yet — a willingness to "depart and to be with Christ which is far better." We shall discover at that hour, inspired by God, and "willing in the day of his power," that the body we are leaving is only the broken up and ruined temple in which Divine service is now ended; and that the holy and immortal Levite that lived and officiated within, begins his ascent through the veil into the holy of holies, to serve God without imperfection and without suspension. Death comes to the Christian, clad in no robes of terror, but with a bright and joyous welcome. The Greeks made it a rule never to mention the word θάνατος, death — the Romans rarely mentioned the word *mors*. They would not even say that a man was dead; they were frightened at death; and I do not wonder at it. A Roman would say of a person that died, not, he is dead, but, *fuit*, that is, he was; meaning he was once, but he is not now; the word death being so terrible to an heroic Roman, so repugnant to an accomplished Greek, that neither used it when they could escape the necessity of the employment of the sad word. It is Christianity that has made death familiar, that has clothed it in robes of beauty, that has disclosed in it, not the foe that comes to smite, but the messenger of Christ that bids us welcome to our everlasting home. And why should not a Christian rejoice at death? It is being lifted from the field of conflict into the everlasting rest; the soul goes at that hour to join the companionship of them with whom we took sweet counsel upon earth, and to wait till the rest of the saints are gathered to their everlasting home. One wonders that a true Christian, who has half his family, his relations, and his friends in the great continent of heaven, should not long to cross the sea that separates this distant isle from it, and so to be, not only with Christ whom he loves, but with them who have preoccupied the many mansions, years and months before him.

Thus, "in all time of our tribulation, in all time of our wealth, in the hour of death, and," I may add, "in the day of judgment," a Christian may rejoice, "rejoice evermore:" rejoice that God reigns, rejoice that not a hair of his head can fall without his permission, rejoice that there are no accidents; that "a mother *may* forget her infant, that she should not have compassion on the fruit of her womb; but I will not forget thee: I have engraven thee upon the palms of my hands; thou art continually before me."

Thus Christians may rejoice now — rejoice exceedingly; joy entering into us here, as a tiny rill, we enter into joy there as an illimitable sea; the joy of heaven beginning upon earth, and the joy of earth expanding and unfolding itself in heaven. That Christians dying thus rejoice, I think we have a very beautiful instance in the very remarkable words of the late Dr. Payson, an eminent American divine, who says, writing a letter, as he was able to do in his dying moments, "Were I to adopt the figurative language of Bunyan, I might date this letter from the land of Beulah, of which I have been for some weeks a happy inhabitant. The celestial city is full in my view. Its glories beam upon me — its breezes fan me — its odors are wafted to me — its sounds strike upon my ears — its atmosphere is breathed in my heart. Nothing separates me from it but the river of death, which now appears but as an insignificant rill, that may be crossed at a single step whenever God shall give permission. The Sun of righteousness has been gradually drawing nearer and nearer, appearing larger and brighter as he approaches, and now he fills the whole hemisphere, pouring forth a flood of glory in which I seem to float like an insect in the beams of the sun, exulting, yet almost trembling, while I gaze on the excessive brightness, and wondering with unutterable wonder why God should deign thus to shine upon a sinful worm. I want a new heart to love him, a new tongue to celebrate his praise."

This is not fanaticism, it is the enthusiam of a love refreshed and strengthened with the joy of the Lord, not the fanaticism of one who knows not what he says.

Are we branches of the vine? Are we members of the body of Christ? Have we abjured every name but his? Have we ever felt in its pressing force the vast importance and value of the soul? Have we ever asked, under deep depression, "what must I do to be saved?" Have we found Him in whom alone is everlasting life? Are we Christians? There is joy like a river for the humblest Christian; there is no joy for the most illustrious personage who is a stranger to the gospel of Christ. If you be Christians, rejoice. You owe it to God, to show to the world that he makes his own happy; you owe it to the world, to draw it to that spring from which your heart is filled; you owe it to yourselves. Rejoice, for the Lord is your strength. Rejoice evermore; rejoice, and again I say, Rejoice.

# CHAPTER II.

## PRAY WITHOUT CEASING.

"Man's plea to man is, that he never more
Will beg, and that he never begged before.
Man's plea to God is, that he did obtain
A former suit, and therefore sues again.
How good a God we serve, that when we sue,
Makes his old gifts the examples of his new!"

"Pray without ceasing." — 1 THESS. v. 17.

SEVEN more practical, compressed, and sententious prescriptions, for daily life, could not be selected, than those which begin at the 16th verse, and end at the 22d verse, of the 5th chapter of 1 Thessalonians. We have seen the intimate connection of one with the other. Do you wish to enjoy all the sweetness of the first — "Rejoice evermore" — you must "pray without ceasing." Do you wish to pray without ceasing, you must give thanks in every thing for what you have, as the best preface to asking for things which you have not. Do you desire to pray without ceasing, and in every thing to give thanks? Then "quench not," or grieve not, him who inspires all prayer — the Holy Spirit. And do you long to know how to think of this blessed and Divine Being, and not to quench the Spirit? Then "despise not prophecy." And do you long to be sure that you are right? Then "prove all things." But do not stop there, but "hold," and not hold only, but "hold fast that which is good." And do you desire in all respects to appear what you are? "Abstain," not from all evil only, but from all constructive evil, "from all appearance of evil."

In our last chapter we endeavored to unfold the meaning of "Rejoice evermore." We now proceed to open the spring from which that joy must flow, and to exhibit the root on which its pleasant fruit must ripen. There is no true joy in a Christian's heart unless there be living and real prayer in a Christian's practice. The two are inseparable. God will not give privilege without duty; and, blessed be his name, he never gives duty without the accompaniment of precious privilege.

"Pray without ceasing." Prayer is the spring of joy, the secret of emancipation from trouble. "Is any man afflicted? Let him pray." The Pentecost of 1800 years ago was an answer to prayer. And what a change that made! the timid, cowardly, vacillating Peter becomes the intrepid champion of the truths which terrified him even by their utterance before. The obscure became the teacher of nations; reserve burned into eloquence; and he that was once afraid to confess his Master before a servant-maid, now confronts kings and royal cabinets, and, like Paul, reasons, unabashed, of righteousness, and temperance, and judgment.

The very first inquiry suggested by the apostolic prescription is, What is prayer? I do not know that I can answer that question in language more succinct or more expressive than that which is given in a document of far greater value than some are disposed to set upon it at this day — a document that many have known in youth, and, I doubt not, have not forgotten in riper years — the Shorter Catechism. The question is asked in that beautiful formulary of sound doctrine, What is prayer? and the answer given is, "Prayer is an offering up of our desires to God for things agreeable to his will in the name of Christ, with confession of our sins and thankful acknowledgment of his mercies:" a very beautiful and a very comprehensive definition. It is the offering up of our desires to God. In Scripture prayer is scarcely defined. Its meaning is assumed. It is an instinct; it was born of the first want; it was understood in the human heart at its first ache. Man needs not a definition of that which the deepest instincts of his nature explain, the moment that he knows what it is to be hungry, and thirsty, and naked, and in need of any thing. Prayer is hunger's appeal for food; it is thirst's cry for living water; it is sin's yearning for forgiveness; it is death's last look for everlasting and glorious life. We need not a dogmatic definition; we feel what it is. The duty and necessity of prayer belong to this present dispensation; in the future dispensation there will be no wants, and therefore no prayer. In the present there are nothing but wants without ceasing, there must must be therefore prayer without ceasing. The psalmist says very beautifully, "Whom have I in heaven but thee?" heaven is the place of having; "and there is none," he adds, "upon the earth I desire beside thee." Earth is the place of desire. That is heaven, where all is having and must be all praise; that is earth, where all is desire, and must be all prayer or asking.

This sense of the duty and necessity of prayer, which we all more or less feel, is plain proof that none of us are at home. Our inmost and deepest wants and longings, our sorrows, our griefs, and our bitterness, that rise and fall, and come and go, like the successive waves of the ocean in their rise and ebb, and roll like these across the human heart, all tell us unmistakably, what indeed we cannot but feel, that this is not our rest, and that there must still remain a rest for the people of God. On the other hand, those deep yearnings that we all feel, those longings that we never can express in prayer, — and the humblest peasant has had thoughts that the most gifted orator never uttered, so that the unwritten wants of the human heart would form the richest and the deepest poetry, — those desires after satisfaction and rest, tell us either that the tide that once covered the world with its light and joy has ebbed away, and left us; or that an ocean fulness is yet to roll inwards, and to cover heaven and earth with perpetual and unbroken happiness. Our wants are prophecies of their satisfaction; our sorrows are presentiments of everlasting comfort. Nature is as it is because there is a day of restoration before it. Man is said to be vanity; he would be so absolutely were it not that he can feel it. The fact that man feels he is vanity, is evidence that beneath all the vanity there underlies a grand nature that looks forward to a glorious destiny.

Prayer is less a duty we are commanded to fulfil, and more a heavenly privilege we are invited to enjoy. The real question is not, *Must* we pray? but, *May* we pray? The true question is not, Ought we pray? but, Will God hear us when we pray? There is great evil in regarding prayer as mere duty. The moment we regard it as a duty we begin to perform it. Very justly, and not oftener than true, it is said — "Service was performed." Yes, it was *performed;* it was a performance from beginning to end; and so the consequence of regarding prayer as a duty is, that we go forth to perform our duty, and having expressed our wants in prayer, we conclude our duty has been done. But this is a great mistake; this is accepting the means as the end. You go to the well deeper than Jacob's well; you draw water — living water; but, instead of drinking the water as you should, you are satisfied with having raised the bucket to the ground, and you retire, having done your duty. The end of drawing living water is to drink it; the meaning of praying is to reach something beyond it. Prayer is not a religious duty, but the means of attaining religious blessings. By its very nature it is the instrument of religious progress, comfort, and peace.

As prayer is not a duty, so it is not a penance. It is not an expiation of any sin we have ever done, or an atonement for any deed that cleaves to our memory. Prayer is not an effort to prevail on God to diminish his claims on us, or an attempt on our part to make an atonement to him for the transgressions of which we have been guilty. You may repeat "Pater Nosters" twelve hours without ceasing, and yet you may never have prayed at all; and when you have prayed with all the fervor of a saint, and all the fulness of the apostolical description — without ceasing — you have not made an atonement for a single sin, nor is it able, nor was it meant to do so. Prayer is not the expression of a love we feel; it is not the expiation of a sin we have committed; it is not the payment of a debt we owe; it is not in any sense the performance of a duty that devolves upon us; it is something far better and nobler than all these. We must regard prayer as a means, not an end; as a precious and great privilege; not as a provision for God, but a provision for us. And hence one earnest "Our Father" on the beaten streets of London, rises to heaven with infinitely more acceptance than all the "Pater Nosters" that were ever offered on the encausted tiles and consecrated pavements of the cathedrals of Europe.

Prayer is not — and our Lord warns us against this — a display or an exercise to be seen of men. Often and again he warns his disciples against imitating the practice or accepting the prescription of the Pharisees. They made long prayers at corners of the streets and the highways, expecting to be seen of men. Our Lord says, "In this respect be not ye as them." But in our days it may be possible to imitate them, if not in letter, yet substantially. When family worship in the home is superseded by early service in the chapel, or *matins* at morning and *vespers* at night, we have in these last the ancient Pharisee clothed in the garb of a modern priest. To make long prayers in public, to be seen of men, is the very essence of Pharisaism. But so to pray that none but God shall hear, so to kneel that none but God shall see; and to show how truly we have prayed by how purely we can live — that is Protestantism, that is the religion of the Bible.

As prayer is not to be made to be seen of men, neither is it meant to inform God. Very beautifully it is said, "He knoweth what we have need of before we ask." And hence long prayers, that tell God in most eloquent language what he is, and in very picturesque language what we are, seem altogether inappropriate, and in fact are miscalled prayer. We do not need to tell him what he is, nor to proclaim or to persuade him to believe what we are. True prayer is the deep expression of our deepest wants in the simplest and the tersest Saxon, and in the hearing of him who knows all our deepest wants before we tell him the uppermost of all. Of all things truly shocking, grandiloquent language in prayer is not the least so. Watch a person who loses his temper on the streets; when he speaks we hear no fine phrases, no beautifully rounded sentences; he takes the nearest, shortest, tersest words; and he makes them the vehicle of his deep feeling. Read the greatest of dramatists, and you will find the very same thing. Study our Lord's prayer — how simple! "Our Father which art in heaven." Or take the nearest to it, some parts of that magnificent composition, the English Liturgy — how beautiful its opening confession! all monosyllables, no fine language. "We-have-done-those-things-we-ought-not-to-have-done." How very simple, and yet how expressive of deep want, how appropriate as the vehicle of it! Would that such a model were universally followed; it is the nearest approximation to the beautiful and perfect model set by Him that spake, and prayed, and lived, and died, as man never did.

Prayer is not designed or meant, as some have mischievously construed it, to alter the designs and purposes of God. Some have said, "God is omniscient, and knows all things. God has his sovereign purposes, and decreed all things. Is it therefore," they say, "possible that your prayers can alter the purposes of heaven; or that he whose plans have been chalked out from everlasting can be moved to turn aside from it by the earnestness or eloquence of your entreaties?" The objection that has been often made to prayer, is practically such as this — "God is omniscient, therefore he knows what you want. What is the use of telling him?" The answer is plain. God is omnipotent. He can give you harvests without sowing. What is the use of sowing? But nevertheless you sow, and nevertheless we pray; and your common sense tells you that it is truer and more Scriptural than the metaphysics of the schools. It will be told us God is immutable in all his plans and purposes and acts; therefore why try to make him change? God is immutable in the principles of his government, but he is not immutable in his acts. For instance, God did not create once, God did create once, and now he has ceased from creating. Here are three distinct and different acts; yet God is the same yesterday, to-day, and for ever. God therefore may be immutable in the principles of his government, but not in the modes in which he carries those principles into development. But, you say, we see that God governs the world by second causes. If there be a frost, fruits will be nipped; if there be no rain, the earth will be parched; and we shall find this law

Father which art in heaven;" and the less of criminal deprecation, and the more of filial confidence in our prayers, the more we exhibit the characteristic spirit of the gospel of Christ. But when all is deep and earnest deprecation of wrath, without one single expression of filial trust, such a litany or prayer sounds more like the wild wail of despair, than the hopeful cry of the still beloved, though long a prodigal, son, seeking bread from his father's stores, and a shelter under his father's roof-tree. For what did the prodigal say, at his greatest distance from home, in the depth and bitterness of his worst estrangement? "I will arise and go to my father." That was the last lingering tie or link within him, and that thought thrilled, in blessed vibrations, through his soul, awakened in his lonely heart all the music of the blessed, and made him arise, and with delighted hopes go to his father, and seek — what he found there — a blessing, and bread, and a joyous welcome.

We are to pray to God not only as a Father, but also evermore in the name, and through the merits, and relying on the intercession of our Lord and Saviour Jesus Christ. The name of Christ is not, as some seem to regard it, a musical close to a beautiful collect; nor, as others view it, the signal to the congregation that the prayer is done. That is not the meaning of praying in the name and for the sake of Jesus Christ. It is no decent peroration; it is no accustomed *finale* to our prayer. His name is the very ground on which we kneel, it is the very right of our approach, it is the very channel through which we address God, and by which God can send down blessings upon us. It matters not where we pray if we pray in that name. It may be in the house, in the temple, on the hill-side, by the sea-shore; it may be on the streets. Prayer offered by God's child in the name of God's Son has the pledge and promise of acceptance always and everywhere. And, on the other hand, cathedral, church, oratory, chancel, sacred carpet, or solemn floor, in no degree, in no shape, even the very faintest, contribute to the efficacy, or add to the acceptance, of prayer. Whether it be upon the street, or upon the sand, or upon the sea; or whether it be in the cathedral, or the chancel, or in the oratory, these things are the mere accidents and incidents of prayer; its essence and its efficacy is, that it is offered in the name and through the merits of the Lord Jesus Christ. Nor does it matter in what language we offer up our prayer. It is not true, as they assert in the Western church, that there is one holy language in which all prayer must be offered. The incarnation consecrated all space for prayer, and Pentecost consecrated all tongues for its utterance. There is therefore no place intrinsically more holy than another, there is no tongue more sacred than another. But the mischief of attaching sacredness to places and tongues — I mean efficacious sacredness — is this, that what we add to them we practically detract from Christ. We depress him thereby as the only Saviour, and we invest these with a false and factitious value, as if they contributed to the acceptance of our prayers in the sight of God. His name alone should be engraved upon every prayer; his name alone must be the chord in every petition; his name alone must give fragrance to all our confessions, our wants, and our petitions; and by the utterance of his name we not only declare our utter destitution of the blessings that we need, but we also declare our utter unworthiness to ask them. We are humbled in the dust as having no right when we use Christ's name; and express our wants and our sins through it and by it, and obtain, according to God's promise, great and effectual forgiveness.

We must pray by the aid and teaching of the Holy Spirit of God. The Spirit inspires the prayer, the Saviour presents it. Many have started the very difficult inquiry, Can a natural man pray? Is it possible to pray unless the Holy Spirit has directed the heart? Let us not pause to discuss it. Pray; and the very first feeling that you have that you ought to pray, is proof that the Holy Spirit has come to you as the Spirit of prayer. And when that Holy Spirit inspires prayer you will not need — what I was deprecating before — fine words; nay, you will not need a form, words will spontaneously come. In the family many cannot do without a form. True Christians who truly pray, cannot pray with two or three without a form. If so, let them use it. If a man cannot walk without a crutch, let him use a crutch. If you cannot pray without a form, then by all means adopt the form. Many a spiritual prayer is breathed from a form; many a formal prayer has been uttered extemporaneously. But the essence of prayer does not lie in these things. We may say prayers all day, and yet we may never pray at all; and the heart often prays most fervently when the lips are dumb or wholly inaudible. It is not the eloquent tongue that we want, but the humble and the anxious heart. We do not care about a praying place, nor do we care much about a praying book. If we have deep wants felt within, the heart will speak should the lips be dumb. And God hears heart prayer; he is not dependent upon its outward and eloquent expression. In his ear the publican's first cry, the Magdalene's first tear, the thief's last word, rose with infinite and perfect acceptance, and brought down an answer exceeding abundant above all that they could ask or think.

We may pray for all that we feel truly and sincerely that we need. Not a few true Christians make a sad mistake here; they say, Well, I would ask God to give me such a mercy if I thought it was according to his will, or to give me relief from this overwhelming difficulty, or to send me a little money to enable me to get over that great obstruction, or to grant me a little health — but *may* we ask God for these? Unquestionably we may. But am I sure it is according to God's will? We have no business with this; it is God's *prerogative* to decide what is good for us, it is our *privilege* to tell him all our wants — the deepest, the greatest, the worst, and the oldest. He asks me, as his child, to unbosom every want that I feel, and to leave with him the prerogative of giving what is best, or of withholding what is wrong, or of judging what is most expedient for me. Do not go into God's presence with a cold and distant reserve, or with a suspicious heart; but with all the filial confidence of an affectionate child; tell him what you want, tell him what you think is good for you; leave him when, where, and how he pleases to answer your prayer. He will not always give you what you ask — and we are thankful that it is so; — if he had given us all we asked we should have been ruined long ago. But this we know, that if he do not give us what we ask, he will give us an equivalent; he will answer us either in kind, or by equivalent. If, for instance, we are under a heavy burden, let us pray to God that he would be pleased to remove it. He may not be pleased to take away the load, but he will do what is the same — he will perfect his strength in our weakness, and help us to bear it. So Paul prayed: he felt some thorn, whatever it was; some pain, or trouble; he prayed to God that he would take away the thorn. God refused to do so, but he did what was as good, he gave him this equivalent — "My grace is sufficient for you." You must leave God to give the answer in what shape he pleases; he only asks you to put confidence in him, and be satisfied that the answer will be given in some shape or another. But, at the same time, we must admit there is an order, and a proper order, in our prayers. For instance, the great prescription that is to regulate all the departments of social and conventional life is, "Seek first the kingdom of God and his righteousness, and all other

in bondage you are to pray; for prayer, we are told, threw open the prison doors in the case of Peter; it is said that when Peter was in prison, "prayer was made without ceasing by the church of God for him;" and the prison doors were opened, and Peter came forth. Prayer shut the jaws of the ravening lions in Daniel's den. And, therefore, in each of these things, prayer was offered; in each of these things, prayer was answered. In all things, it is said, we are to pray. Now, what are the things? The Apostle Paul tells us. He says, "In all these things we are more than conquerors." But in what things? Affliction, distress, persecution, famine, nakedness, sword, Rom. viii. 35. These are the things. Well, in every one of these things we are to pray to God. There is no depth to which the Christian's soul can be depressed in which he may not pray. There is no load of grief that can bow it down under which a Christian heart may not pray. Dumb lips may have yet a praying heart; and no doubt more fervent prayer has been offered on the stones of the Royal Exchange in the agony of loss, disappointment, trial, grief, bitterness, sorrow, than ever was offered in the noblest cathedrals of mediæval Europe. Prayer lies in the intensity of our feeling, the sense of our want, the full conviction that God hears, and that we have only to ask and he will send down an answer exceeding abundantly. In each thing pray; in every thing let your wants be made known to God.

The apostle gives another element of the "without ceasing," in such a phrase as this; "at all times." By night and by day; in all time of your tribulation, in all time of your wealth. But a Christian will say — "We can well understand praying in all time of our tribulation; but, to pray in all time of our wealth is surely unnecessary! — this is surely the time for praise." You are mistaken. The man that has an empty cup may pray, and should pray, that it may be filled; but he that has a full cup, ought to pray that he may hold it firmly. It needs prayer in prosperity, that we may have grace to use it; as truly as it needs prayer in poverty, that we may have grace to bear it.

There is no day in the current of the years on which it is unseasonable to pray, inconvenient for God to answer, or impossible for him to give. What a blessed truth is this! There is no year, day, or month, in the currents of time, in which it is inconvenient for the King of kings to hear, or unseasonable for us to ask, or impossible for him to grant.

The next element of "without ceasing," is "everywhere." There is no place on earth — the east, the west, the north, or the south — where man may not pray. In the deep coal-mine half a mile beneath the surface of the globe; on the loftiest Alpine crag; on the quarter-deck on the Baltic, and on the Euxine, the sailor may pray; and I have heard that there are hundreds of praying soldiers and sailors in both of these places. And, depend upon it, God can hear the sailor's prayer as he is rocked on the giddy mast and upon the restless wave as easily, and answer it as quickly, as he can hear our prayer in the great assemblies of his people. It is not the praying place or the praying book, but the praying heart, that is true prayer in the sight of God. And are there not times when prayer is your only relief? In those night seasons of the soul, when the dark and desert side of nature is uppermost, when the toys that we chased have lost their gilding, and the excitement that we once felt has only proved by its results that it was vanity and vexation of spirit; when weariness, chill and dreary, creeps into the heart and over us, and we feel that this is not our rest — oh! what a blessed privilege, that we can lift up our hearts to our Father in the skies, and know that we are not orphans, that we are not in a forsaken world — that this is the school of our holy discipline, and that a home, bright as heaven and boundless as infinitude, awaits us beyond it! And in those painful emergencies which happen to all, when skill has no resources, when the tide of life will not cease to ebb, and when no power upon earth can put the shadow ten minutes back upon life's dial — not to speak of ten years — how delightful the blessed privilege that we may be careful for nothing, but lift up our hearts to God in prayer! How delightful to a Christian the thought that all space is holy and all time is canonical for prayer; and that many a blacksmith has offered purer prayers by his anvil than consecrated priest has offered by his altar. It is our sense of want, our deep and full persuasion that our Father will supply it, and our approach to him in Christ's name — be it on the deck, on the field, or on the mountain side, or on the sea-shore; be it in the shop, in the parliament, the palace, or anywhere — it is the heart that prays; if it be there, there is prayer; if it be not there, we have but the splendid trapping of exhausted formality, not the expression and the breathing of a living and responsible soul.

And, lastly, says the apostle, you are to pray "with all perseverance." The expression "without ceasing" means "with all perseverance." Now many will pray fervently to-day, and cease to pray to-morrow. But mark what God's promise is. It is absolute that he will answer prayer; but *when* he will answer it he reserves to the disposal of his own sovereignty; it is for us to wait for the *when* and persevere in prayer. And are we not encouraged and confirmed in this even by the analogies of the streets? As you come to the sanctuary day after day, you should watch the boy at the crossing soliciting alms. Study his conduct. Our Lord uses the sparrow, and the ripe ears of corn, and the pebbles in the brook, and the flowers in the field, as lesson books for us; let us also take the modern facts that occur to us in our way, and see if there are not still left in these lessons for us. Watch the beggar boy. He asks alms first gently; then louder, if he fears a chance or a possibility of refusal; and when you seem to turn away he will follow you; and when you have gone to a distance he will keep his keen eye upon you — never giving up hope, never despairing that the hand will reach the purse or the pocket and fling an alms to him. What is that? Perseverance in begging. Why should there not be equal perseverance in prayer? He for an earthly, we for a heavenly. Because we do not persevere, what is the frequent result? We asked blessings in the year 1853, with all the fervor and the earnestness of conscious want; we ceased from asking under the impression that we should never obtain. The blessings we asked come down in showers in the year 1854, we forget that we asked in 1853, and therefore we are unthankful for the blessings when they are given. If we waited for an answer, and watched, and waited, and watched again, we should learn to believe that prayers that have been offered like seeds sown in tears, will never rise to heaven without bringing down an abundant and a glori ous harvest.

Then let us, in the language of the apostle, "pray without ceasing." Do not think that any want that you feel is too trivial for God to hear, to answer, or to grant. He hears the cry of the wild raven, he listens to the appeal of the sparrow on the housetop; and why should he not hear you, O ye of little faith?

"Seek, and ye shall find — knock, and it shall be opened — ask, and ye shall obtain." It is God's will that you should pray always — in every thing — everywhere; with the deepest conviction that God will grant what we need. Or to sum up all in the beautiful words of a poet who has lately gone to his rest — I mean the late James Montgomery —

"Prayer is the soul's sincere desire,
Unuttered or expressed;
The motion of a hidden fire
That trembles in the breast.

Prayer is the burden of a sigh,
The falling of a tear;
The upward glancing of an eye,
When none but God is near.

Prayer is the simplest form of speech,
That infant lips can try;
Prayer the sublimest strains that reach
The Majesty on high.

Prayer is the Christian's vital breath,
The Christian's native air;
His watchword at the gates of death,
He enters heaven by prayer.

Prayer is the contrite sinner's voice,
Returning from his ways;
While angels in their songs rejoice,
And say, Behold! he prays.

The saints in prayer appear as one,
In word, in deed, and mind;
When with the Father and the Son
Their fellowship they find.

Nor prayer is made on earth alone;
The Holy Spirit pleads;
And Jesus on the eternal Throne
For sinners intercedes.

O thou, by whom we come to God,
The Life, the Truth, the Way;
The path of prayer thyself hast trod;
Lord, teach us how to pray."

## CHAPTER III.

### IN EVERY THING GIVE THANKS.

"Not thankful when it pleases me,
As if thy blessings had spare days;
But such a heart whose pulse may be thy praise."

"A blessing given to those who 'll not disburse
Some thanks, is little better than a curse.
Great Giver of all blessings, thou that art
The Lord of gifts, give me a grateful heart,
O give me that, or keep thy favors from me,
I wish no favors with a vengeance on me."

"In every thing give thanks: for this is the will of God in Christ Jesus concerning you." — 1 THESS. v. 18.

Now we enter upon the third prescription — "In every thing give thanks;" a prescription that will need explanation in order to convince us that in every thing — on every occasion, and at every circumstance — we are to give thanks. We are not only to pray to God for blessings, but we are also to praise him as the necessary sequel when we obtain those blessings. If we only expressed our wants, there would be something in that extremely selfish; but if while we express our wants we praise him who satisfies them from his fulness, there is something in this extremely Christian. Prayer without praise, is a constant craving for possession; but the absence of praise when we have that possession will soon make it take wings and fly away; for the man who is an unthankful possessor — whether of a pound or of a million, will not be a long or a happy possessor. Praise is the tribute that God exacts for his gifts; and if we refuse to render the little tribute, which does not diminish the excellency of the gift, we cannot expect that we shall long continue in the possession of it. The blessings that God gives, are only deepened and endeared to us when we lift our hearts to bless him for his beneficent and unmerited mercies. To be always praying, is to be a Christian when we are in need; but to be never praising, is to be atheists when we have got what we asked for. And therefore very justly is it remarked by an apostle, "Is any man afflicted? Let him pray. Is any man merry? Let him sing psalms." Our afflictions bring us to God, — our blessings bring us to God; and thus all things that betide the Christian, whether they be prosperous or adverse, impel him in the same blessed direction; they bring him near to that God who hears his prayer and satisfies his wants; who makes welcome his praises and redoubles his blessings. Gratitude to man is an expression of feeling that most people would be ashamed to be without. Ordinary courtesy will teach us to thank a benefactor; and if we select from the masters of poetry in the English language their opinions upon gratitude, we shall find that the natural man even reprobates ingratitude as one of the basest and the most deforming vices.

> "I hate ingratitude more in a man
> Than lying, vainness, babbling, drunkenness,
> Or any taint of vice, when strong corruption
> Inhabits our frail blood. —
>
> How sharper than a serpent's tooth it is
> To have a thankless child!"

The great dramatist justly says, if we call a man ungrateful we brand him with the severest and the most ignominious epithet. But what is this gratitude? It is the responsive or joyous tribute that a man pays for disinterested or unexpected kindness. It is the fragrant incense that a good deed bestowed upon you kindles in the censer of your human heart. And never does that heart appear so beautiful, or exhale so fragrant perfume, as when, acknowledging the good it has received, it praises and thanks its benefactor. If we be ashamed to be unthankful to man, how is it that we can muster courage — no, not courage — atheistic daring to be unthankful to God? There is scarcely an individual on earth that will not thank a human benefactor for a blessing; are there as many who can stand up on the proper occasion, and thank God for health, strength, and daily bread? Few feel ashamed in being found thanking a benefactor for a blessing. Shall any be ashamed if found out thanking God for their daily bread? Why should it be thought strange to thank God? Surely, surely! if we bless the cistern we cannot be indifferent to the fountain. If we are not ashamed to thank man, shall we fail to be ashamed of the omission of thankfulness to him who enables man to help and be beneficent to us? "In every thing give thanks." It is not only duty, it is our glory. A thankful heart is one of the choicest gifts, and not the least happy. And very beautifully therefore does the poet say in one of the hymns, at the end of the Psalm Book —

> "Ten thousand, thousand precious gifts
> My daily thanks employ;
> Nor is the least a thankful heart,
> That tastes these gifts with joy."

Gratitude is not only duty, it is beauty. We find this illustrated in the very analogies of the world. The deserts of the earth, that receive into their bosom the dews of heaven and the sweet sunshine, but bear no golden harvests, are always to the outward eye bleak and repulsive; fields that receive the showers and the sunshine, and express themselves in responsive tributes of bountiful harvests, ever look the most beautiful and joyous. In other words, barren lands are unlovely; fertile lands, that wave with corn and with the kindly fruits and fragrant flowers, are to the outward eye all beautiful and full of laughter. They shout for joy, they also sing. What is the song of birds, the lowing of cattle, the bleating of sheep upon their pastures, the hum of bees, the fair foliage, the fragrant flowers, the beautiful blossoms, but the earth thanking God, in her many voiced psalm, that he clothes her every spring with verdure, and forsakes her not in the depths of winter; and giving token of that day, when all earth shall ring with gratitude not only to him who made her, but, when she had unmade herself, redeemed her by his blood, and put her in her right orbit again. While all things praise God, it seems strange that man should fail to do so. Are we thankful? Do we recognize God in mercies? It is too true that true Christians oftener pray than praise. It is too true that the mass of mankind neither pray nor praise. What is the reason that even Christians should oftener pray than praise? In heaven there is nothing but praise, because all is ever accumulating possession; on earth there must be prayer and praise both, because there are wants to be felt, and blessings to be received. But what reason may there be that many do not thank God for the blessings which they enjoy as they ought to do? The first reason we must assign, and one many are conscious of, is pride. It is an odd thing that a human being should be proud. There is much in man to admire; there are remains of his pristine magnificence that show what a noble being he was, and what a noble being he may yet be; but there is nothing in himself or in his history that should make him proud. His sins should humble him, for they are his own; his virtues should humble him, for they are not his own; and every thing he looks at should only lead him to God in order to give him the glory, and take nothing to himself. But, notwithstanding this, man likes to see his own dear image reflected in the possessions that he has; he loves to say, My own right hand won this; my own sword clave my way to this; my own power got me that; I have nobody to thank but myself. He likes to hear his own sweet voice, ringing in echoes of self-praise from the blessings that God gives him; he does not like to be obliged to another; he would rather not be a humble recipient of mercies, he would prefer to be able to say, I did something; if God did much, I did little; if he gets glory, I ought not to be without praise. But God will not allow us to be recipients and possessors of his blessings on such terms. He says, I give you all the blessings; but I ask of you all the praise. And the blessing is not diluted in your possession by the praise you render to him that gave it. The wild bee, that feeds upon the fair and fragrant flowers, it has been remarked, nourishes the flower and adds to its fragrance, while it takes away for its own stores what will feed it and its infant brood, and not impoverish any. So it is with the blessing that God gives: we render to him the tribute of praise, which pleases him, and does not impoverish us. Let us lay aside vainglory; let us guard against that pride which would give to our own genius, wisdom, or worth, praise that belongs to him who alone is worthy. But there is another reason for this absence of thankfulness to God. It originates very often in practical atheism. There is no such phenomenon, perhaps, in this present world as a thorough atheist. The man who is, by intellectual conviction, an atheist, is only fit for a lunatic asylum. It is impossible that his can be a sober and logical and deliberate conviction. Atheism is that freezing gap, that horrible, freezing void, in which no wing can soar, and no heart can beat, and no soul can breathe. No man can come deliberately to such a horrible conviction. But whilst this is true as looked at intellectually, yet practically there are many kinds of atheism. The good we receive, in which we do not thank God, or recognize his presence, gives token of atheistic feeling. We are delivered perhaps from shipwreck; we say, It was that clever pilot, it was that nice reach into which we got, it was that lucky wind, that saved us. Or, if raised from a sick-bed, we say, Oh, it was that new and powerful medicine — it was that very talented physician — it was this new system — Homœpathic or Hydropathic, or some other *pathic;* it was both, or any thing, or every thing. We try to see and to praise some thing of our own, instead of looking above the pilot, above the physician, beyond the means, and resting only upon God, that gave wisdom to the pilot's head, firmness to the pilot's hand, and a blessing to the physician's prescription. Not that we should ignore such things — this would be folly. Common sense is not dislodged by Christianity. There are second causes, and we very properly act upon them. We know that caution, or care, or precaution, guards against many an incident — I will not call it accident, but rather incident — that flesh is heir to. All we require is, whilst we recognize the second causes; whilst we thank the physician, and we ought to thank him; whilst we thank the pilot, and we ought; yet that we should lift the heart far above the pilot in the storm, and the physician by the sick-bed, and give the full and swelling tribute of our praise to that Pilot who sleeps in no storm, and forsakes us in no trial; to that Physician who watcheth over Israel by night and by day; and thus, whilst thankful to the instrument in the instrument's place, still raising, far beyond the instrument and far beyond the horizon, thanksgiving, praise, and glory, unto Him in whom we live and move and have our being.

Let us examine ourselves — let us take a retrospect. Some of us have been raised from sickness, saved from shipwreck, spared on the field of battle, or on the quarter-deck. Well, we have done right in thanking all the instruments — thus far most properly have we acted; — but have we omitted thanking God — praising him — have we had a tribute for everybody, but none for God — have we sung our hymn to hundreds, but never yet one to him? What is this but to construct a pantheon in the 19th century, and to fill it, not as the ancient Romans did, with marble, and wood, and silver statues, but with the new gods, called "second causes;" and to give to the second causes the glory that belongs to Him who alone should fill the pantheon with his presence, and to whom alone thanksgiving and praise are emphatically due.

We have contemplated gratitude as one of the most beautiful *traits* in man, when paid from man to man; — but so often and so painfully omitted where it is so justly due — to God. We have tried to show two sources of its omission; first, self-righteousness; and, second, by our practically living as if there were no God. This prescription is most comprehensive, "In every thing give thanks." In all the blessings that a believer tastes — in every one of them in detail, in every thing in detail, we are to give thanks to God. God's power is as much displayed in one atom as it is in the everlasting hills; his presence is as much reflected from the dew-drop that dances upon a rose leaf, as it is from the all-encompassing and girdling sea; and so God's beneficence may be as truly in the least beat of a healthy heart as in the long life of a venerable patriarch. God's goodness may be in every-day mercies as well as in anniversary blessings; his goodness may be in little things, so minute that by the vulgar eye they are unnoticed, as well as in those magnificent things that no one can fail to take notice of. In the little rill of comfort that flows into individual and solitary hearts, as well as in the great streams of mercies that flood a vast nation, God's goodness may be. But alas! such is our strange perversity, that the very commonness of God's mercies is in some degree the cause of our unthankfulness for them. For instance, there is not a greater mercy upon earth than health. One day of good health is worth many days of splendid excitement; and there are few, if soberly expressing their convictions, who would not say that a healthy body, or good health, is worth the brightest coronet and the weightiest crown. But why do we not thank God oftener for it? Because it is so common, that we cease to feel it is a blessing. And yet, of all human blessings, it remains the very richest and the choicest. Do we thank him for it? If we have not perfect health, do we thank him for as much health as we have? In every thing — surely in this great thing, though it be a common thing — we ought to give thanks to God. But alas! the more common our mercies are the less we value them. Spring water is a far richer treat than all the wine in the East and in the West: yet, peradventure, we would thank God for rich wine — but how little do we thank him for the bubbling fount and the sweet streams that we can drink of, as of the stream that makes glad the city of God, without money and without price. But, because it is so cheap, we cease to value it, or rather we undervalue it. And when we think, moreover, that we have forfeited all by the fall, how thankful should we be for the very least mercy or blessing that we enjoy! The light of day — rising and setting suns — peaceful slumbers — protection in our rising up and in our lying down — all these are common, but they are choice mercies notwithstanding; and the best way to be very humble, as well as to be very thankful, is to reflect more how little we deserve, how much God has bestowed upon us.

But all will admit, no doubt, that when we are prosperous and full we ought to thank God. But the expression of the apostle is, In *every thing* we are to thank God. We are enjoined to thank God, not only when full and prosperous, but when we are poor and empty. In our gains and in our losses — in health and in sickness — in prosperity and in adversity — in peace and in war, the prescription is neither spent nor diluted — thank God. And this is a very important prescription; and also a very searching test. When Satan looked upon the patriarch Job, he told God, "Doth Job serve God for nought?" — meaning that he was thankful because he had every thing that was calculated to make him thankful. But, "Take away from him these mercies, and he will curse thee to thy face." Well, we read that God said to Satan, "Job is in thy hand — every thing except his life; you must not kill him." Satan, let loose under the permissive power of God, tempted and tried the patriarch in every way. And what was the result? The patriarch thanked God when his sons and his daughters were taken away from him; he thanked God when his riches were snatched from him; he thanked God when he was the suffering victim of disease; and at the end of his bitterest trials he said, "The Lord gave, and the Lord hath taken away," — and for his giving and his taking away, his goodness and his afflictions, "blessed be the name of the Lord." In every thing give thanks — in affliction as in prosperity. But it is objected, this is so difficult a prescription that it needs explanation. It does need it; but the explanation is easy.

There is no state in which the sufferer can be placed,

deep and sorrowful as Job's, in which, if he will only look with an unprejudiced eye, he will not find at least as many elements of thankfulness as springs of sorrow and disquiet. The darkest night that falls upon our world has some straggling beams of light; the bitterest cup that is put into human hands to drink has some sweetness in it; in the greatest misery there are redeeming features; and you will find when you can trace no rays of light that there is an ulterior reason still more precious. We are in a world of discipline; let us never forget this is not heaven, it is the place of discipline. It is our school, where the royal priests unto God are prepared and trained for a coming kingdom. And in this world, therefore, there are certain graces that we have to cultivate in order to ripen and prepare us for another. Now there are some flowers that grow best in the dark; there are certainly some graces that blossom only in broken hearts, and when watered by many tears. And if God means that you should bring forth these graces your hearts must be broken, your homes must be laid desolate, your tears must flow fast. And certainly one grace that we all need can exist in suffering only — the grace of patience. You have need of patience. Patience is a beautiful grace. Courage is the mission of the few; patience is the duty of all. We have need of patience under suffering, patience to wait for the fulfilment of God's promise, patience to go through many a struggle that meets us in the world. And if our affliction — affliction of any sort — leads us to patience, that grace nourished in our hearts is more than a compensation for the fiery struggle through which we have passed, in order to reach it.

But let us look at this affliction in another light. Has God in his providential government taken from you the wealth that you had accumulated by the lapse of years, by industry, and amid many toils? Are you obliged to gaze at empty coffers that once were full; and have you found in your own personal experience how truly it was said by him of old, "Riches take to themselves wings and flee away." You ask, am I to be thankful for this? I was thankful when all my wealth was around me and within my reach; but am I now to thank God, when I have not a penny left in the world? There are reasons for thankfulness even here, though you do not yet see them. In the first place, be it remembered, what we call riches in this world are estimated as debts by God; that is to say, what he now gives is future responsibility, though it is to us in this life a present possession; but it will be at the judgment-seat the evidence of obligations that you owe to God for possessing them. No man treads so perilous a path, no man is so laden with responsibility before God, as he who occupies a high position in this world, or has much wealth or great power in it. God never flings down talents at random; he gives them in infinite wisdom; and that man who has the greatest talent and the largest number, has the most weighty responsibility, and most demands to meet at the judgment-seat of Christ. What, therefore, we call riches now will be regarded as debts then; what we regard as power, station, influence, place, will be viewed as responsibilities and obligations then. Many a poor broken-hearted widow, sorrowful and lonely, will thank God at the judgment-seat that he made her thus; and many a rich, and powerful, and influential personage will curse the day that ever he had his own wish gratified, or his own expressed wants filled and satisfied in the providence of God. Depend upon it, we are best just where God has placed us; and often where we are there is more responsibility than we sometimes admit. If, therefore, God takes away our riches, he has lessened our obligations at the judgment-seat; if God has taken away our power, he has simply diluted the weight of our responsibility at the judgment-seat of Christ. It would be wrong to say these things are not blessings. Many people speak of them in a way that is not right. Money is one of the most precious things on earth, if you have only grace to make a right use of it; and those people that depreciate and despise money, will find their words will have no echo in the hearts of the people that hear them. People will say, We know that money is a blessing. Money is not the root of all evils. It is where the apostle enumerates certain evils, that he says, "The love of money is the root of all these evils;" the definite article is used: and he does not say that *money* is the root of all these evils, but the *love of money*. And the love of money is not dependent on the amount we have. Many a man who has two hundred thousand a year, loves money less than many a one who has only two hundred a year. It is not the amount that we have, but the tenacity with which we grasp what we have — that is the root of evil. If God has taken away your money, which is a great blessing, he has not only lessened your responsibility at the judgment-seat, but he has probably given you something else. If he took away Moses, did he not give Joshua? If Jesus departed from the world, did not the Comforter come and occupy his place? And if God has taken away the wealth that you had, he may have given you that contentment which is far greater than that which wealth can bestow. Thus our losses may be our gains, our weaknesses may be our strength, and the departure of what we love may by a gracious God be compensated by the possession of something that is far better for us.

But let us look at another aspect of this truth, and ascertain if in it also we are to give thanks. Are you subject to persecution and trial for your allegiance to Christ, your love for God, and your acceptance of the gospel? I do not think that persecution for conscience' sake is at least a prominent characteristic of the present age. It is true in Tuscany, it is so in Rome; but thank God, it is not and cannot be practised in our native land. But the time may come when persecution will again collect its fagots and kindle them; and martyrs be required where martyrs ever have been found, when called upon to suffer for God's great cause. In such circumstances can we thank God? We answer, yes; for, strange enough, in the New Testament — and the least fanatical book in the world is the Bible; the most common-sense book that was ever written, the book of inspired common sense, is the Bible — we are told, "To you it is given to suffer for Christ's sake." Such suffering is a special honor. Ask our sailors on the Baltic, ask our officers on the Euxine; and they will tell you that it is their best men that lead. Ask our officers in Constantinople; and you will find they will select the guards, or the 93d Highlanders, for the van to face the foe. And so when God has great trials, and his people a great work, he selects his best, his choicest, his most prepared soldiers to occupy the van of the conflict, and thus he makes it an honor — the highest and the greatest honor — to suffer for Christ's sake. And if we are suffering for Christ's sake, what should be our feeling? Thankfulness to God that we are the persecuted, and not the persecutors. Be thankful to God that you are cast to the wild beasts, and that you are not giving the order that Christians should. Very beautifully does the apostle add, "If any man suffer, let him suffer as a Christian; and not be ashamed, but glorify God." And again, he says, "If ye be reproached for the name of Christ, happy are ye, for the Spirit of glory and of God resteth upon you." The best proof of this is, that prison walls have resounded with the sweetest music; that a splendor has irradiated the captive in his cell that never shone upon the occupant of a royal palace; and John Bunyan, the writer of the most magnificent poem — except Shakspeare's dramas, and Milton's Paradise Lost — in the English language, was a happier man as he wrote in his prison than ever he was before. What proof is here, that many thank God in such circumstances! And in the case of the early Christians, "they took joyfully the spoiling of their goods." And in that beautiful passage which I have so often quoted, but so beautiful that it cannot be quoted too often, it is said, "Though the fig-tree shall not blossom, neither shall fruit be in the vines; the labor of the olive shall fail, and the fields shall yield no meat; the flock shall be cut off from the fold, and there shall be no herd in the stalls" — that is, total famine, total desolation; then what is he to do? A Stoic would say, Endure it; and neither laugh, nor weep, nor rejoice. A man of the world, — a mere worlding, — who has no escape beyond his money, would say, Then I will commit suicide. A Christian can say, "Yet I will rejoice in the Lord; I will joy in the God of my salvation." That is Christianity; and if it be so, is there not reason for thanksgiving to God even in the worst of circumstances? But there are other trials that many a Christian will think of very different from these. There are times when the trial is not something external; but that inner sense of desolation, that sorrow of the heart, which Jeremiah likens so expressively to those who have made voyages by sea — "the sorrow of the sea;" that inward sense of something that we need to sustain, to cheer, to comfort — that feeling which is instinctive to humanity — which drives the worldly person to the opera or to the playhouse, and draws the Christian to his Bible and to his God, in order to meet and to remove it. In such feeling, is there any reason for thankfulness to God? I answer, there is no reason in the universe for despair; there is nothing but reason for hope, and, therefore, for thankfulness and praise. Sometimes God takes away from a Christian his comforting presence, but he never takes from a Christian his sustaining presence. You know the difference between sunshine and daylight. We have often daylight, but little sunlight. A Christian has God's daylight in his soul when he may not have sunlight; that is, he has enough to light him, but not enough to cheer and comfort him. Never was Jesus so forsaken by God's comforting presence as when he said, "My God, my God, why hast thou forsaken me?" and yet never was he so strengthened by God's sustaining presence, for angels were at his service to minister to him, and to take care of him if he needed their ministry. And thus in our saddest hours, and in our loneliness of heart, there may be springs of comfort that the world knows not of, and that a Christian will not fail to drink from and be refreshed.

Are we assailed by temptations? And there is not a Christian on earth into whose heart thoughts do not come, that he would not for the world express; through whose mind sentiments do not creep, that he hates as venomous reptiles, and that he would like to crush and to extinguish for ever. And when these temptations come like the birds of night, flapping their foul wings over us, can we then be called on to thank God? I answer, yes; for what is the great solution? It is in these words, "Simon, Simon, Satan hath desired to have you, that he might sift you as wheat" — that is your danger, your bitter temptation, your trial. But what follows? "But I have prayed for you" — my prayer for your safety preceded Satan's attempt upon you — "I have prayed for you, that your faith fail not." And, therefore, when our temptation is the sorest, the great Intercessor — oh! blessed be his name — is the nearest. Besides, in all temptations of which Satan is the author, let us never forget he is a beaten enemy. "I have overcome him."

Therefore, you have to meet, not one flushed with victory and laden with the spoils; but one whose head has been bruised, and against whom, therefore, it will be easy and certain to prevail.

I know no circumstances on earth in which a Christian can be placed, if a Christian, in which he will not find more springs of thankfulness to God than reasons to despair and be sorrowful. We need our blessings to leave us, just to enable us to appreciate them. Very often we never discovered that an angel has been with us, till the splendor of his parting wing tells us he is gone. Very often absence is necessary to the enjoyment of presence; and if God did not sometimes take away the blessings that are choicest, we never should appreciate them as we wish to do with thankful hearts. And when we have not left one tiny taper burning upon earth, we are never without the bright and the morning Star shining down from the sky. When all things below forsake us, there still rings from the midst of the throne that promise, which sanctifieth things that we have, and is more than a substitute for things that are gone, "I will never leave thee; I will never, no, never forsake thee."

Such, then, are some of the circumstances in which believers may be placed, and in which, nevertheless, they are still to be thankful to God. And now, if we thank God in the midst of our trials, when laid low, if we thank him in the midst of our sorrows, he will pour joys into the heart that is broken; if we thank God that he has opened our eyes to see our own hearts, how sinful they are, he will open our eyes to see our Saviour, how precious he is; if we thank him that he has enabled us to see ourselves, he will reveal to us himself, and make all his glory pass before us, and we shall find that the unloading of the full heart in thanksgiving, and the expression of the empty heart in praise, will equally be acceptable to that God, who expects this tribute of thanksgiving for all his mercies and his blessings, and for all his dealings towards us.

Such trials as these we should feel thankful for, because they are necessary for the exercise of our faith. Many persons are continually doubting, Am I a true believer? Have I real faith? Then, if you are thus doubting and anxious to know if you have true faith, why do you quarrel with God, if he puts you in the ordeal that is to test and to try you. If you wish to know whether you are true Christians, you must submit to God's process of letting you know. If you cannot bear the trials, then you do not appreciate the blessings that the apostle speaks of when he says, "Wherein ye greatly rejoice, though now for a season, if need be, ye are in heaviness through manifold temptations; that the trial of your faith, being much more precious than of gold that perisheth, though it be tried with fire, might be found unto praise, and honor, and glory, at the appearing of Jesus Christ."

In the hovels of the poor, which successive waves of sorrow, and poverty, and wants have swept; in the dim chamber of sorrow, which the beloved has left, and a chasm remains that life cannot fill; even in such circumstances as these faith finds nutriment and religion erects its trophies; and at the end the experienced Christian is constrained to say, not in prayer, but rather to sing in joyful praise, "It was good for me that I was afflicted." Look behind you, look before you, look below the level on which you are, look above it, and you will find reason only for praise. Look to yourself in trial, or in bereavement, and you will find only reason for thanks. "All things work for good to them that love God;" "our light affliction, which is but for a moment, worketh out for us a far more exceeding, even an eternal weight of glory." Look at creation, look at nature in its noontide summer, when covered with flowers and giving promise of fruit. Is there no reason to thank God that, though sin has dimmed the light of this world, and the trail of the serpent has stained its countenance once so beautiful, and we deserve that it should be our grave instead of being our footstool, there is left so much to be thankful for, from the green fir to the giant oak; from the minutest insect in the dew-drop on the leaf, to the very largest inhabitant of the deep? In providential dealings is there not much to thank God for? Did you, dear reader, calculate ten, twenty years ago, that you would be where you are now? Is it not obvious from the past chapter of your biography that an unseen hand has led you, that a kind Physician's hand has closed many a wound; that there has been no sick-bed in your home from which you have not gathered lessons of immortality; and that there is no grave, of which you have a freehold in the distant churchyard, that grows not green at least with bright hopes, and that tells you not of a happy meeting with all you love when time shall be no more? Is there any one who can for one moment read his own biography, and not see much to mourn over, much to regret, much to deplore, but oh! infinitely more to thank and to praise God for? And shall I mention the last of all — the gift of a Saviour? How very beautiful and how true is that collect, "We thank thee for our creation, we thank thee for our preservation, and all the blessings of this life; but above all, for thine inestimable love in the redemption of the world by our Lord and Saviour Jesus Christ!" He drank our bitter cup and filled the blessed one; he came to die for us all. The wrath of God let fall an awful shadow upon that bright light. The Son of God trod that sea that had no shore but death, bearing our sins, expiating our guilt. The man that can hear of such a Saviour, and yet not trust, or taste such a salvation, and yet not thank him, is not only destitute of the first glory of the human, but is absolutely destitute of every attribute of the Divine.

# CHAPTER IV.

## QUENCH NOT THE SPIRIT.

"Return, O holy Dove, return,
Sweet messenger of rest;
I hate the sins that made thee mourn,
And drove thee from my breast.

The dearest idol I have known,
Whate'er that idol be,
Help me to tear it from thy throne,
And worship only thee.

So shall my walk be close with God,
Calm and serene my frame;
So purer light shall mark the road,
That leads me to the Lamb."

"Quench not the spirit." — 1 Thess. v. 19.

There is repeatedly announced in Scripture the existence of a Divine Being, or Divine Agent, who takes up his abode in the hearts of God's believing people, as teacher, comforter, and guide. He is called sometimes the Spirit of truth, sometimes the Comforter, and sometimes the Holy Ghost. Repeatedly we are told in Scripture, that the want of this Spirit in the individual heart is the reason of the languor of such graces as are there, or the reason of the absence of such graces as ought to be there. Jude, for instance, describes the strongest brand on the character of the enemies of God, in these words, "Not having the

Spirit." Paul, when he gives the character of the wicked, says, "They are unholy"—that is, not sanctified by the Spirit—and therefore "unthankful." It is the breath of the Holy Spirit, sweeping over the affections of the human heart, that, like the sweet wind upon the harp-strings, brings forth lasting, blessed, and harmonious music. Hence the psalmist says, so happily, "Blessed are they that dwell for ever in thy house;" for what is the consequence? They will be always gloomy? They will be always disquieted? They will be always in distress? and thus prove that religious people are a sort of sepulchral people? No. "Blessed are they that dwell in thy house; they will be still praising thee." In God's house, and in communion with him, is the spring of all that consecrates the character that is wrong, makes joyous the spirit that is heavy; till the very world itself will be constrained to own, they are a happy people whose God is the Lord. We read in other parts of the Scripture of the fruits of the Spirit. Regeneration is ascribed to him. We are told in one place that true Christians are all born of the Spirit. Sanctification is ascribed to him; we are sanctified by him. And the evangelist John is so decided upon this that he says, "Whosoever is born of God"—that is, the truly regenerate person—"doth not commit sin;" an assertion, however, that Christians sometimes interpret very erroneously. They ask, Does this mean that if we be true Christians we shall be absolutely sinless? The right answer is to quote another text of the same writer in the very same book: "If we say that we have no sin we deceive ourselves, and the truth is not in us." Then what is meant by the passage, "Whosoever is born of God doth not commit sin?" It is in the present tense; he does not do it designedly; it is not his wish, his desire, his preference, or his liking. The sin is the incident in his character, not its general tone; the accidental eddy in the current, not the deep and onward stream; it is not his practice to do so. So again, the Spirit is said to transform. "Transformed by the renewing of our minds." All the privileges of Christians are ascribed to him. Are you poor? He places you amid the sons of God, and makes you heirs of God. Are you enslaved? He is the Spirit of freedom. Have you enemies opposed to you, "Greater is he that is in you, than all that can be against you."

But in one sense those who are not truly Christian people, or, as we say, not truly regenerate, are said to oppose the Spirit. This seems very strong language — but there are indications of it, it is barely possible to mistake. For instance, "My Spirit will not strive with them any more" — the withdrawal of the Spirit. We read of resisting the Spirit, "doing despite to the Spirit of grace." The sins of Pharaoh amidst the stupendous miracles of Egypt; the sin of Balaam, a preacher and prophet of the truth, in subsequent times; the sin of Judas, and the sin of Demas, who who began with religion, and ended with the intensest secularism, — were all aggravated, not by the fact that they were sins against the law, but that they were proofs of their resisting, and grieving, and quenching the Holy Spirit of God. So Herod heard John gladly, did many things that John bade him; but when a great festal occasion came, and the daughter of Herodias danced beautifully before the monarch, then he offered her what she should choose; and that was the head of him who had spoken too faithfully to receive the patronage of one whose conscience could not stand it. Such, again, was the sin of Felix. He was convinced that Paul was right; his conscience was touched: but what did he do to get rid of it? His passions said, Now, Felix, Paul tells you that a pure and a holy life is duty; but if you adopt that, then we, like wild beasts, will break loose upon you, because not satisfied and indulged as usual. His conscience said to him, Felix, if you do not comply with what Paul says, then I will scourge you all your life, and in the life hereafter. He did not know what to do; he was drawn between two forces, and he acted morally, as by the laws of dynamics — two forces pulling at right angles find their solution in going along the diagonal. He struck out the intermediate course, and said, I will not reject you, Paul; for my conscience will not let me: I will not accept you, Paul; for my passions will not let me; but I will send for you when I have a convenient season. Well, that seems to be the nearest to the resistance of the Holy Spirit of God.

But the peculiar language, "Quench not the Spirit," arises from the fact that this Divine Being is set forth under a form that makes this imagery natural. For instance, "Ye shall be baptized with the Holy Ghost, as with fire." And again, the disciples journeying to Emmaus under the influence of this Spirit, said, "Did not our hearts *burn* within us, when he talked to us, and reasoned by the way." And by likening this blessed Spirit to fire, which purifies the gold of its dross — which enlightens by its splendor the eyes of the gazer, which raises the temperature of Christian life; resistance to him, or grieving him, as it is otherwise expressed, is likened to quenching, or casting water upon a fire that burns.

But before we show how this Spirit is grieved, or quenched, let us answer a query, Can they that are born again ever cease to be so? In other words, Can one who is a Christian to-day ever be so thrown back, as to cease to be a Christian at all? I do not believe it is possible. The professor of Christianity to-day, whose profession is eloquent and loud, may cease to be to-morrow what he professed to be to-day; but this is not a renunciation of Christianity for the reverse; it is merely the silencing of a profession that had no counterpart in the individual's heart. But the true Christian, if born again, cannot greatly fall, for God is in him. It will not do for any to meet this statement found in the Bible, and say, Then people will live as they like, if they feel that they are always safe. To be made a Christian is followed by living as he likes; but the *likes* that he had before he was a Christian, are superseded by new *likes* that he has inherited since he became a Christian; and to bid a Christian live as he likes — that is, purely — is to bid a stone fall to the earth by the law of gravitation; to bid the wind blow, the flowers blossom, the rivers meander to the main. It is his new nature, to live soberly, righteously, and godly; and while he lives as he likes — notwithstanding drawbacks — notwithstanding deviations and sins which are ever reproved — he lives justly, and loves mercy, and walks humbly with his God. But if any one should say, Because I have reason to believe that I am everlastingly safe, I may therefore grieve the Holy Spirit of God; I may therefore do what will vex and quench that Divine and precious Comforter; to such we answer, Your sense of safety is a delusion; for the moment that a sense of personal safety induces him that feels it to plunge into what his conscience and his Bible prohibit, in this there is the proof, not that a Christian has apostatized, but that your sense of safety was delusion; and now you are to retrace your steps, reanalyze your character, and ascertain what you are as reflected in the mirror of God's holy and perfect word.

But, after this preliminary remark, let us try to ascertain what are proofs of grieving the Holy Spirit. This will be a very practical and very important exposition; and if blessed by that Spirit, whose office we are speaking of, it will be savingly important.

To grieve or to quench the Spirit, is to deny his personality and his Godhead. It is clear, that to deny his personality and his Godhead must greatly grieve him. The atheist says in his heart, "No God," and the man that can say, after reading the Bible, and knowing himself, The Holy Spirit is merely an influence, falls into a similar error. It is parallel to that of a man who says, Satan is simply an influence. Satan loves to hear himself called an influence, because there will thus be no defence against his power and assaults as a malignant person. The Holy Spirit is grieved when he is denied to be a Person, and a Divine one, and you are injured; for then you have no right estimate of what you are, and what is needed to be done within you before you can get to heaven. The Unitarian, who most consistently, and, I have no doubt, — as in the case of the amiable and accomplished Channing, — conscientiously (at least in his earlier days) denies the Deity of the Spirit, consistently denies the ruin, the utter ruin and fall of human nature. But we believe that the superstructure of humanity is so wrecked and ruined, that nothing short of a Divine hand can rebuild and reconsecrate the shattered shrine, and make the heir of wrath the son of God, and the inheritor of everlasting joy. He that sees the depth of his ruin as that ruin lies in the light of God's countenance, will soon cease to deny the Deity of the Holy Spirit; for he will feel that, if it required Omnipotence to create, it requires *a fortiori* Omnipotence to regenerate. When Omnipotence created orbs, he merely fashioned the unreluctant and obedient matter by his plastic touch; but when he recreates fallen humanity, he has to deal with struggling passions, a reluctant will, a ruined nature, and a heart in which nestle a thousand serpent passions ever seeking to crush, and where they cannot crush, delighting still to sting. If this therefore be the condition of humanity, we must see that the Holy Being, to whom the rebuilding, and regenerating, and reconstruction, and reconsecration of it is assigned, in the great purposes of heaven, must be God. To deny this, seems to me, to deny the fall, to deny the depth of our ruin, and to grieve or quench that Blessed Spirit.

Another instance of grieving the Holy Spirit, consists in depreciating the necessity of his presence in the accomplishment of his promises, in the extension of the gospel, in the covering ultimately of the whole earth with the glory of God. When we read the Bible, we find constant allusions to the Spirit, as doing what human energy cannot do. For instance, it is said in one part, and it applies to all: "Not by might, nor by power; but by my Spirit, saith the Lord." Jesus is likened to the sun: let the sun retreat into the depths of space; let his beams be withdrawn for a single hour; and what would be the result? All warmth would be exhausted from the earth; not a tree would bud — not a flower would burst into blossom; the sea itself would become a solid; and all nature, exhausted of its warmth, would fall to pieces. The Holy Spirit is likened in a similar way to the air or the atmosphere. And I know not which would be the greater calamity, the ceasing of the sun to shine, or the exhaustion of the air that we breathe. Take away the atmosphere, and death must be universal. There would be no such thing as fragrance in a rose if there were no atmosphere, because there would be no vehicle to waft the fragrance on its wings. There would be no such thing as music in voices or instruments, because there would be no vibratory medium through and by which that music could be heard. All nature would be wrapped in sackcloth, and the homes of the living would necessarily become the habitations of the dead. What is true of the physical world, is no less applicable to the spiritual. To expect spiritual life without the Holy Spirit to impart it, is to look for an effect without a cause, life without a life-giver.

But we have yet more simple and practical instances of this grieving of the Spirit still. Either to preach or to hear sermons, and think that there is any thing in the preacher's power, or in the hearer's common sense, that will necessitate a saving effect without the Holy Spirit of God, is to grieve him. We cannot feel the truth we are trying to establish too powerfully; nor can we be too careful, lest we depreciate, or forget it. No eloquence can impress, no logic can convince a single soul, with saving energy, unless the Holy Spirit carry home to the heart what is addressed to the outward ear. It is easy to convince the intellect that this book is true; and the evidence is so multiform and powerful, that it is barely possible to escape the conclusion; but none but Deity can convince the heart. We know well how people's logic is conclusive in one direction, and their lives just the contradiction of it on the opposite. All this indicates the necessity of some higher power. In mere eloquence, the ear may be regaled, but the heart will be impenetrable still; the imagination may be charmed, but the affections will continue rebellious still. It is the Holy Spirit alone that lifts the orator of nature into the ambassador of Christ; that turns the crowd into a congregation, and the meeting place into a church of the Lord Jesus Christ; it is he alone that makes what would be a speech, falling on the ear like the tinkling cymbal and the sounding brass, a sermon fraught with demonstration and with power, that by his blessing will empty the earth of its hoarded spoils, and people heaven with trophies gathered from the four quarters of the globe. Let me ask you, then, my dear reader, if, when you go into the house of God, you ever think that prayer is not the word spoken, so much as the feeling cherished and defined in the depths of the heart? When you seat yourself in your Sunday pew, do you ever feel, this day we are going to hear what in the worst case will be ruinous; in the best case must be a blessing, but in no case can have a neutral effect? What a solemn thought, that no human being ever enters his church and hears truths, few as they may be, but faithfully spoken, who shall go home with the same responsibility with which he came. We are told by an apostle, that the gospel preached, is either the savor of life or the savor of death. Nobody leaves the sanctuary just as he came, but vastly more responsible; men had better not come, than come and leave despising; or rather, not despising only, for it is written, "How shall we escape," not if we *reject;* that is very obvious; but "how shall we escape if we *neglect* so great salvation!" It must be a very solemn thought to every minister who preaches to a mass of human beings, that the truths spoken will awaken echoes that will startle the silence and solemnity of a judgment morn. In such cases, preacher and people become associated together by links that will rise from the grave at the resurrection day; one to answer for the use they have made of what they have heard, and the other to answer for the honesty, not for the ability, but for the honesty with which he has proclaimed the things that belong to their eternal peace. When we enter the sanctuary and seat ourselves, Sunday after Sunday, do we pray, or, if we do not formally pray, do we earnestly desire that the Holy Spirit of God would enable the speaker so to speak that some one shall get good, and the people so to hear that they shall receive a blessing? When men sit down to their daily meals, none, surely, are so sunk below the brutes that perish, that they do not ask a blessing upon the bread they are to break. If this be necessary in daily meals, how much more necessary that we should ask a blessing when the bread of life is to be broken in the midst of us! To do so is common sense: the truest and the noblest Christianity is most in harmony with good and universal sense.

Another way in which we may grieve and quench the Holy Spirit, is when we pray without special reference to him, in the same manner as we might pray without special reference to the Lord Jesus Christ as the only Mediator. We must never forget that we believe in a Trinity; in the Father's electing love, in the Son's redeeming love, and in the Spirit's effective love; and that when a Christian prays, all his prayer must have underlying it, and running through it, the Divine chord of a Triune God — the Father we pray to; the Son in whose name we pray; and the Holy Spirit who inspires and teaches us to pray. I not only must pray to the Father, in opposition to all saints, and angels, and images; I must not only pray in the name of the Son, in opposition to the name of the Virgin Mary, or of any other; but I must also pray depending on, and seeking to realize the presence of God's Holy Spirit. We read in the Levitical economy, so instructive in all respects, that the nineteenth century might steal a page from the days of Moses and Levi, and of the pilgrims in the desert, that there was not only to be no strange altar, which was the type of Christ, but there was not to be burnt upon the true altar a strange fire. And so there must not only be no prayer that is not offered in the name of Christ, but there must be no prayer that is not illuminated, inspired, dictated, by the Holy Spirit. And, therefore, it must grieve that blessed Comforter, that Spirit of truth, when he sees any giving honor to Christ, which is right, but withholding honor due to him, which is no less dutiful.

The Holy Spirit is grieved, in the next place, when his presence is shrouded, the necessity of his power not recognized as more than incidental, or as supreme, in the ordination of Christian ministers. There is one clause in the Ordination Form of the English Church which, to my mind, is most admirable. When a man comes to the bishop in that church to be ordained, he must profess that he is moved by the Holy Ghost. Now that is most precious; it makes the man an awful liar, or it secures a true Christian. So far, this is to honor the Holy Spirit. To omit this thought (and it is easy to keep it in a rubric, it is so difficult to keep in the heart) in our feelings is to grieve the Holy Spirit. A stated ministry ever has been, and in these days, a highly educated ministry, is more than ever, necessary; and, unless it be so, the parliament, the platform, and the press will take the lead, and the pulpit will linger far behind. But while, granting all this, to believe that the imposition of the two hands of a bishop, or of the hundred hands of a presbytery, on the head of a candidate for orders, is the great essential, constituent element of a true minister, is to fly in the face of fact; and worse still it is to grieve and vex the Holy Spirit of God by excluding him from the place of his special presence. Nay, more, were the Apostles Peter and Paul to rise from the dead and lay their hands upon the head of an unconverted man in order to ordain him as a minister, he would be no more a minister of Christ after the imposition of hands than he was before. Two things are necessary. First, the inner call, which the Spirit alone can give; secondly, the outer ordination, which is dutiful because enjoined and commanded in God's holy word. But while this is true, let us never forget, that many a man is a true minister who never had hands of presbytery or bishop on his head; and many a man is no minister at all who has been ordained by both in rapid succession. It is the inner thing that is the great thing; and to suppose that the apostolical succession, in the Tractarian sense of that word, is a guaranty that every man ordained under its supposed influence is a Christian, is historically untruth, is theologically nonsense, and is contradicted by every-day fact; and it must grieve the Holy Spirit of God. The idea of the Tractarian is that the first link was an apostolic one, that then an influence was imparted to it which was transmitted through all the links of the chain, till the last link created yesterday becomes the recipient of the virtue transmitted horizontally, like the electric fluid, along the eighteen centuries of the Christian era: while the Protestant idea is, that each link of the chain receives no virtue from the one before it, but a direct descent of Divine virtue from the Holy Spirit of God above it. The Tractarian notion is a horizontal transmission parallel with the plane of the earth; the Protestant idea is a vertical transmission; on each minister chosen of God, and called directly by the Holy Spirit of God, this influence must fall, or he cannot be a true minister. The apostolical succession is a dogma that must grieve the Holy Spirit of God; the Protestant idea is the recognition of his sovereignty, of our dependence on his blessing, and the proof of giving glory to his great name.

Another way in which the Holy Spirit is grieved, is when we read the Scriptures without seeking his direction and teaching. In order for me to find my way to heaven two things become necessary. I must have an inspired chart external to me, which is the Bible; I must have, secondly, an inspired heart, which is internal to me, in order to enable me to read profitably that book. Now of all charts, or, to use the more common phrase, of all books, the Bible is the plainest. Comments, commentaries, sermons, explanations, are most precious; but still the Bible itself, in things that are vital, is so plain, that the humblest peasant can understand it; while, in things that are mysterious, it is so difficult that we shall spend heaven, and still not exhaust them. The Holy Spirit is needful, not to enable me to understand the Bible; for I can understand it by study just as well as Homer, or Shakspeare, or Milton, or any other writer; but so to understand it that, instead of being a mere outer truth, it may exercise an influence within, overcoming the hostility of my heart, sanctifying its governing principles, and giving new life and energy within. Hence it is the Spirit that fills every symbol in it with celestial glory, that inspires every truth in the Bible with life, gives to its every promise sweet music, and communicates to the heart that studies it receptive power, and makes this book the guide unto life everlasting. The Romanist looks to the pope to interpret the Bible; the Tractarian looks to the church to interpret it; the Socinian looks to reason to interpret it; the Christian looks to the Holy Ghost to explain and interpret the Bible to him. To show you the necessity of the Spirit, let us take the very simple illustration of a sundial. If you go to a sundial at midnight and study it with a brilliant lamp, you will be able to trace every figure, and to understand it as thoroughly as any human being ever understood it. But while the lamp or moonlight applied to the sundial, will enable you to understand its structure most accurately, neither will enable you to reach its practical use. If you want to do that, you must go out when the sun has risen, or shines from his meridian, and then you will not only be able to see the structure of the dial, but to discover from it the hour of the day. So in reading this blessed book, you can by the lamplight of human reason, or by the moonlight of tradition, or by a light which is a mixture of the darkness of both — the pope, understand this book in its outward facts; but in its inner, its practical, and saving meaning, you must ask the Author of the book to explain it to you. Suppose that you have heard that a person has written a book, and on reading that book you find a passage in it which you can make nothing of; and you appeal to this divine or to that divine to ask them to explain its meaning, but in vain. Suppose you heard that the author of the book would be in the vestry at a certain hour ready to explain the passage, you would say,

What is the use of going to others, when the author of the book is accessible and ready to explain his meaning? He will be the best able to make it plain.

The Author of this book, the Bible, waits, wherever there is a heart that can pray, or lips that can move, to explain the meaning or the mystery of the passage that the reader himself cannot understand.

Another way in which the Spirit is grieved, is by slighting the ordinances that he himself has appointed. There are two extremes in this. If we neglect the ordinances that he has appointed, we grieve him; if we make more of the ordinances than he meant, we grieve him. We must neither repudiate baptism and the Lord's supper, as useless ceremonies, nor must we idolize them as substitutes for Christ, or superseding God. We must not, with the Romanist, regard baptism as an exorcism, and the Lord's supper as an idol to be adored; and we must not, with some extreme persons, view the Lord's supper as useless, and baptism as unnecessary. We are to use the ordinance, but to look above the ordinance to the Lord of it; we are to employ the means, as if all depended on the means — but we are to look above the means for him that can make them efficacious. Those who say, We need not come to the Lord's supper, to say the least of it, grieve the Holy Spirit of God, who does not endure that his own ordinances shall be slighted; and those persons who come to the Lord's supper, and make a god of it to adore, must equally grieve that blessed Spirit; for they transfer from the Lord a ray of his glory, to the ordinance that he himself has ordained.

We grieve this Holy Spirit by excessive conformity to this present world. Let us understand what this means. Conformity to the world in things that are indifferent is the very best way to escape the censure of the world, and to do the world good. But non-conformity to the world does not mean that we are to wear a Quaker's garb, or a monk's cowl, or express ourselves in a whining and peculiar tone, as if that were religion. This is a resemblance to the Pharisees; these are not Scripture elements of non-conformity to this world. In those things that are in themselves indifferent, let us dress like the world, and walk like the world, and act outwardly like the world. To do otherwise is to do violence to common sense. Fastidiousness here is fanaticism, or folly, or superstition, or, what is as bad as any of them, monkery itself. Such is not real non-conformity to the world. But, on the other hand, there is a conformity to the world, which not only verges on the borders of evil, but quenches divine influences within us, grieves that blessed Spirit, and tempts him to depart from us. It cannot be, surely, altogether without a meaning and an end, that our blessed Master says, "I pray not for the world. I am no more in the world, but these are in it. Holy Father, keep them from the evil of the world. The world hath hated them, because they are not of the world. I pray not that thou wouldest take them out of the world, but that thou wouldest keep them from the evil of the world." And it cannot be without a meaning and an end, that the apostle says, "Be ye not unequally yoked together with unbelievers; for what fellowship hath righteousness with unrighteousness? and what communion hath light with darkness? and what concord hath Christ with Belial? or what part hath he that believeth with an infidel?" All this must mean something. No doubt there are places in the world you must occupy in the discharge of duty; and there are companies in the world of all kinds and classes you must mingle with, in order to fulfil what becomes your place in the world. All this you are compelled to do in the discharge of duties that you cannot easily shake off. But, on the other hand, when you voluntarily choose the frivolity of the dissipated, when you deliberately select the company of the irreligious, and court the society of the ungodly, because it is great, or fashionable, or noble, and shrink from the society of the holy, the godly, and the spiritually minded, because poor and lowly; not to pronounce where man should pray, we may yet express a fear that such a spirit walks on the verge of the line that separates a world that is passing to ruin, from the company of Christ's true and faithful people, and hovers on the very verge of quenching the Holy Spirit. Or, on the other hand, when you allow your affections to root themselves in the earth, when you make money, or ambition, or fashion, the governing instead of the subordinate forces; if you are silent when a truthful word would be in season, or if you bring your business into the church, or outside the church prosecute your business with absorbing intensity; if you would rather marry a rich fool than a poor wise man; if you would rather marry an ungodly noble than a godly commoner; if things which in their place are good, become dominant, and in a great question, not fashion, not wealth, but religion must go to the wall — then there is something wrong, radically wrong; if you have not yet quenched, you are certainly grieving the Holy Spirit of God; or at least you lower the temperature of the Christian life, you damp its first fervor; it may be, you quench the Spirit. The spirit of the world and the Spirit of Christ are ever stated as correlatives; both will not live in the same bosom, both will not inhabit the same place. You must take your choice. We do not ask you to cease to dress or to live according to the sphere in which God has placed you. For the higher class to dress and to live as the humblest class, would be turning the pyramid topsy-turvy; or trying to rest it on its apex, instead of upon its base; it would be ruin, it would be chaos: all attempts to macadamize society have always ended in the macadamizing of all that are above, and the evoking of reckless spirits from below, who having neither the *prestige*, nor the power, nor the delicacy, nor the generosity of truly great ones, have lorded it with an iron rod over those that listened to their democratic pretensions, or yielded to their fierce and unsanctified power. There is, nevertheless, a line of demarcation between what is called the world, and what is called the church. It is not dress, but principle, that determines it. If religion be the regulating power, your first inquiry in any course will be, Is this compatible with God's word? Your second, and always the second, is optional, whether it will lead to wealth or to progress. You do not do wrong in trying to advance yourself. The young apprentice who does not try to be a master, is not doing his duty; and that man who does not try to better his position by every lawful means, is not acting rightly. But what we require in Christian men is, that the first and the governing thought shall be the demands of religion, the will of God, the duty that they owe to their Saviour, and the homage they feel towards his Holy and blessed Spirit.

Another way in which we quench the Spirit is, what in this day it is so necessary and important to remember, the tendency that prevails among many to apologize for great errors, to speak gently of our sister's fall, as it has been said at Oxford in reference to a dear sister at Rome. The tendency to speak gently and apologetically of great and grievous errors seems to me one of the ways of grieving and vexing God's Holy Spirit. He thus leaves the heart. And the worst errors have had their roots in the marshes of a heart that has become corrupt. The heart has had more to do with recent perversions to Rome, than ever the head had; and it may be that the first deviation began in tampering with evil, and the final conclusion was absolute proselytism. We are very apt to give ear to a convenient system, or doctrine, or proposition, that will sustain what we like; and when we have given ear some time to plausible thoughts, and tried to prove that to be true which suits our own evil desires, by a strange law, what one is in the habit of laboring to prove comes, by a sort of self-imposture, to be accepted in the end as if it were actually and absolutely true. The explanation of many a recent perversion is this, "Wherefore God gave them up to strong delusion, that they should believe a lie." Why? "Because they believed not the truth, but had pleasure in unrighteousness." What an awful statement is here! that, after men have tampered with the claims of truth, God gives them up to strong delusion in righteous retribution, that they should believe a lie; not because he delights in their ruin, but because they believed not the truth, but had pleasure in unrighteousness. When human nature, corrupt human nature, is induced to hear reasons in favor of going over to Rome, it listens to arguments to it irresistible. Human nature prefers the penance that the foot can traverse, or the hands can pay, to the repentance that the heart must feel. Human nature prefers the mortification of the flesh, which is not a very difficult thing, as the practice of thousands of Hindoos will tell us, to the mortification of the lusts of the heart, which is a very different thing. Human nature prefers confession to a sympathizing priest, who sympathizes, not in hatred to the sin, but with the indulgence that is confessed. It prefers to confess to a sympathizing priest today, to get absolution at its close, to commence a fresh score at the other end of the street, and return to the dear Father, and get absolution after confession again. All this is so much more delightful to human nature, than to lay bare the heart to the Searcher of hearts, and to disclose its hidden griefs and evils, and to get safety, not from the danger of the sin without absolution from the love of that sin, but absolution from the penalty that embosoms in its very nature deliverance from the love of the sin that is forgiven. Hence Tractarianism and Romanism — the one the child, the other the full-grown parent — all spring from human nature in its unconverted state, seeking indulgence for its peculiar idiosyncrasy, and trying to work God's book into its service, instead of subordinating the thoughts into obedience to God's word. For what, after all, is the Tractarian system, as it is called, in its full power? Just a compromise between passion, conscience, and deep and ineradicable conviction; a compromise between all three. It is the transference of the world to the church; such an admixture of the world with Christianity as will make Christianity palatable to worldly and unconverted people. Hence the worship of Tractarianism is a sacred opera, a Christian pantomime, a religious drama — a composite of St. Barnabas and Covent Garden; where it is difficult to know whether it is the one or the other; except that the one is licensed by a bishop, and the other is supported by the free contributions of the people. What is Romanism? A provision, not, like Christianity, for the sacrifice of the evil that we hate, but a provision for a canonization of the evil that we love. Are you poor? Romanism provides for you a nook in which you may glory in your rags. Are you rich? It provides a side chapel for you, where you may not bless God for your wealth, but glory in your riches. Are you of an ascetic and severe turn of temper? It fits up for you a monk's cell. Are you very sour and morose? It will consecrate a whip, and put it in your hand, and teach you how to use it. Do you love sin, yet fear the consequences of sin? It is not without indulgences and penances for you. In short, it is such an adjustment of passion and conscience, and such a compromise of both with God's holy word, that we cannot but believe that the Holy Spirit, grieved, and quenched, and resisted, has abandoned it long ago, and left it to experience, as its doom pronounced in the Bible, that terrible destruction from the presence of the Lord, which is accompanied by the previous warning, "Come out of her, my people, that ye partake not of her sins, and that ye receive not of her plagues." Do not tamper with that system. Do not go to hear Dr. Wiseman because of the fine music; do not visit a Romish church because there are splendid ceremonies; do not listen to a priest's apology, because you are thorough Protestants, and suppose you cannot be injured. You are invincible within the boards of the Bible, invincible on the deck, or on the Baltic, or the Black Sea; but you are unstable as water, and helpless as babes, if you go where you have no business, and where God has not sent you.

We grieve the Holy Spirit of God in another respect, by awakening quarrels among Christian brethren, where there is harmony and unity in all that is true, and difference only about forms. We shall differ to the end about ceremonies; I see no chance of absolute unity till the Lord of unity arrive. But though we cannot agree with each other about all things, yet we have so much in common, vitally precious, that we may well afford to differ in circumstantial and ceremonial details. What is the real difference between the Scotch church and the English church — I mean as represented in their articles? I cannot see any. I can see nothing to prevent me signing the Thirty-nine Articles; and, I venture to say, the present excellent and truly Christian archbishop of Canterbury would subscribe the Confession of Faith just as freely. The only difference lies in the form, not in the substance; the white gown is different from the black gown, but there is as much a preacher in the one as in the other. A Liturgy may have, and I think it has, immense advantages; extemporaneous prayer is not without great advantages also. But in all the substantial essentials of truth the difference is nothing at all. Whenever two Christians, either of this church or that, begin to quarrel about matters of ceremonial detail, what is the natural result? The still small voice of truth is lost in the clamor of controversy; love decays, life dies, and the world exclaims, not as of old, "Behold, how these Christians love one another;" but, "See how they hate and assail one another." Where we must differ from a Christian brother in many things that he thinks right, let us do so without calling him by a single bad name; use the softest words, the strongest reasons; and, depend upon it, strong reason, couched in courteous language, will gain the day, when violent declamation, ensoured by a bitter spirit, will do evil, and gain no laurels. And instead of spending our aggressive energy upon internal disputes, let us expend it upon the masses of London, that hear no chimes of sabbath bells, see no sabbath sun, and are ignorant of those precious things that we know. Oh! while patients are dying in the wards, let not the physicians quarrel by the bedside about who has the best diploma. While souls are passing to the judgment-seat, we should have no time to dispute about mere mechanical and paltry differences.

Another means of quenching the Spirit, is the unsanctified use of past afflictions. If you have lost the near and the dear; if you have lost your property; if you have been solemnized and saddened by the gap that was left here, and the chasm that could never be filled there; if your soul still retains the images of the lost, while the heart has ceased to feel the sadness that once saturated it; if you have at length so far forgotten the vows that you made, the impressions that you felt, that you are more worldly, more gay, more dissipated than ever; you will learn that, of all the evils that overtake the Christian, unsanctified affliction is not the least; the heart becomes hardened by the very fact of resistance, and, like the sands of the desert, amidst the sunshine and the showers it brings forth no fruit; it is only fit for being rejected.

Let our first and most fervent prayer be, "O Lord, teach us to pray." Let our second be, "Holy Spirit, take possession of my heart, and give me the spirit of prayer." Or, as it is expressed in a very sweet and a very beautiful hymn,

"'Return, O Holy Dove, return,
Sweet messenger of rest;
I hate the sin that made thee mourn,
And drove thee from my breast."

8*

## CHAPTER V.

### DESPISE NOT PROPHESYINGS.

> " Sail on, it says, sail on, ye stately ships,
> And with your floating bridge the ocean span.
> Be mine to guard this light from all eclipse;
> Be yours to bring man nearer unto man."

> "Despise not prophesyings." — 1 THESS. v. 20.

"DESPISE not prophesyings;" that is, despise not the record in which you find all that you need to regulate your life in this world, and all that heart can desire to ripen and prepare it for the world that is to be.

It will scarcely be necessary that I should here explain what is meant by prophecy. It does not mean the prediction of events that are future, but the proclamation of duty that is instant. Certainly it is used in Scripture occasionally in the sense of foretelling future events, but not exclusively so. The prophets in the Old Testament were not simply men predicting the future; but proclaiming the responsibilities and duties of the present. The two prophets in the camp of Israel were not engaged in predicting futurity, but in proclaiming present obligations. So the apostle, in the Epistle to the Corinthians, uses it; he says, "Follow after charity, and desire spiritual gifts, but rather that ye may prophesy." This is spoken to Christian laymen.

"For he that speaketh in an unknown tongue speaketh not unto men, but unto God; for no man understandeth him: howbeit in the spirit he speaketh mysteries. But he that prophesieth speaketh unto men to edification, and exhortation, and comfort. I would that ye all spake with tongues, but rather that ye prophesied; for greater is he that prophesieth" — that is, preacheth — "than he that speaketh with tongues" — as at Pentecost — "except he interpret, that the church may receive edifying." Well then, the prophesyings that we are called upon here not to despise, are simply the declarations of God's truth, and the varied *formulas* in which that truth is conveyed, whether in Scripture or in sermons. If in the written word, that is one way, and the best way; if in the preaching of the gospel, that is another way; if in tracts and sermons, this is a third way. But in whatever shape God's good word is conveyed, the command is, "Despise it not." If man be asked, what is meant by the prohibitory language — "Despise not?" Like many a negative in the Bible, it means a very decided positive in the opposite direction. For instance, we read, "Forget not to entertain strangers:" that really means, "Be sure to recollect to do so." Again we read, in another passage, "Despise not thou the chastening of the Lord:" that means, "Highly value, deeply appreciate the chastening of the Lord." So here the command, "Despise not prophesying," means, highly value it, deeply appreciate it. Never say, or think, or do, what is fitted to disparage this book, or to degrade it, or in any way to dislodge it from that central supremacy that it ought to wield over every thought and affection of the inmost soul. The simple meaning of the prescription is, Receive the Bible; love it, read it, study it, reverence it, cherish it as a precious possession, entertain it as a life in the heart, and not as a mere direction outside. This idea has suggested here what may be practically useful, some of the reasons why many persons object to Christianity and the Bible, and religion altogether; and the reasons why others do not give it that directive supremacy which is its just and legitimate due. We are not speaking here so much of that sober and awful conclusion to which it is barely possible for a man to come, after having examined the various evidences of this book, when he concludes it to be a falsehood. If any one has arrived at that conclusion, and I can conceive a person coming sincerely to it, he is much to be pitied; he is deeply mistaken, I would almost add fatally mistaken; but still I can believe it to be his deliberate conviction. It is, however, such a terrible conclusion, so awful, so undesirable, that when one is constrained to confess it, it must be with tears, and grief, and deep distress. When I meet a sceptic parading his scepticism, glorying in it, anxious to make proselytes, I always suspect, and I hope it is not uncharitable to do so, that there is a conscience inside, and a life outside, not as either should be; and therefore there is this shuffling, this display of bravery, this obtrusive bravado, to conceal if possible from himself — for such is man's self-deception — the state in which he is living in the sight of God. But a really sober conviction that this book is a falsehood, must be to a right mind a very awful thing. Can any thing be more distressing than to quench the lamp that thousands are walking by, as they believe, to heaven? How painful must it be to a right-minded man, to strike down from its pedestal that book which, its worst enemy will admit, has given freedom to the slave, dignity to the poor, a sense of duty to the rich and the great! What result can be more awful and painful, than to have come to the dread conviction that man does not know of a God, a home, an eternity; and that he goes down into the deep shadow of the grave without a ray of hope to penetrate it, and reveal to him immortality and glory? It is so dreadful a conviction, that surely one must hesitate before accepting it; and if any one come to entertain it sincerely, surely it must be with pain and sorrow that he feels constrained to admit or pronounce it. But the sceptics that we have here to deal with, are rather those that love infidelity for its license, and prefer to give evasive reasons for not manfully rejecting the Bible as an imposture, and burning it. They prefer treating it with affected contempt, giving it an incidental compliment to-day, and a heavy blow to-morrow, always and everywhere professing to despise it on the whole. Now what may be some of the reasons, as far as we can discover, why men act so wicked and yet inconsistent a part? One reason lies at the root of nearly all others, and explains much of that despising of the word of God which is here condemned. It is man's deep sense of his sinfulness, his alienation from, and, it may be added, his antagonism to, God. Man loves sin; he knows that God condemns it; but notwithstanding he will not renounce it. He can neither justify his conduct, nor will he give up his conduct. He prefers, therefore, to forget the Bible, to cease to think of the Bible, and to get rid from memory and conscience of its remonstrances the best and quickest way he can. But, in spite of all, he cannot help hearing chimes of bells on Sundays, meeting even preachers in the streets, stumbling on a Christian conversation, reading an incidental allusion to, or illustration of, the Bible. And some way or another this book has so struck itself into the very texture of all society, and the earliest recollections of mankind, that, run as man likes a refugee from its presence, he will incidentally hear it ringing in his ears, or the echoes of it lingering in his heart, reasoning of righteousness, and temperance, and judgment. He cannot answer it; he will not obey it; he dares not therefore manfully meet it. He flees from it, and attempts not, even to his own satisfaction, to treat with supercilious contempt the prophet that prophecies only evil continually about him. This is one deep-rooted reason why man learns to despise the Bible. Another reason is, confounding such feelings with want of evidence; making the conscience and the intellect exchange places, and constraining the one, notwithstanding its objections, to do duty for the other. Hence man gives utterance to the conclusion, We are not convinced that the Bible is true; whereas the real translation of his words is, We do not wish to be convinced that the Bible is true — such a conviction would be very inconvenient. The conscience does not want light to touch it. The passions wish the conscience to be quiet, and the passions know that the avenue by which light gets to the conscience is the intellect; and if it can put on the shutter there, and exclude the light from admission, they hope they may prevent the light touching the conscience, and so disturbing, if not curbing, them. This, however, is discontented feeling, not insufficient evidence: and it is not fair to confound insufficient evidence, which may be, with discontented feeling, which is actually the fact. You will not meet with a dishonest person in London, who does not complain of the hardship of the law that consigns to the police and to Bridewell the man that picks his neighbor's pockets. We rarely meet with a disloyal man who likes a monarchy, or a throne, or its laws and government. Few can conceive what a serf and drudge the intellect becomes when passions, that want to be indulged, and conscience, that desires to exclude light, muster behind it, and urge it on to subserve their purposes. Only let it be clearly before us that insufficient evidence is one thing, and in its place a thing that ought to be dealt with, but discontent or dissatisfaction with the purity of the truth, and therefore anxiety to escape from the presence of the truth, is quite a distinct, indeed a totally different thing.

Another cause, however, far less offensive in its nature,

but yet leading persons to treat the Bible with incredulity or neglect, as if it were a questionable or equivocal thing, not a book yet clearly settled to be from God, is the requiring a sort of evidence for the truth of Christianity, and for the genuineness and inspiration of the Bible, which is not possible in moral subjects. All who have attained the ordinary level of education well know, that there is a vast difference between what is called mathematical, and what is called moral evidence; the difference consists not so much in the fact that mathematical proofs deal with subjects that come under the cognizance of the senses, but that mathematical evidence has no room for prejudice, or passion, or self-will, or an evil heart of unbelief, or an unholy appetite or sinful desire of any kind. If I am proving that any two sides of a triangle are greater than the third side; or that the square of the hypothenuse of a right-angled triangle is equal to the sum of the squares of the two sides, I am engaged in proving a proposition, that no prejudice, no passion, no unholy appetite or desire, ever can or does interfere with. This process does not touch the heart, the affections, and the passions, and they never think of touching it. It is a sort of transcendental process, in this respect altogether out of the reach of prejudice, passion, unholy appetite and desire. But when I am trying to prove to men the propositions that speak of what they are, and what they should be, and whither they will go if they do not turn round and come back, or if they persist in their present palatable but sinful course, then I have to deal, not only with an intellect that needs to be convinced, but with prejudices and passions innumerable. Inveterate prejudice says, I do not consent to be put down; and violent passion, flushed with indulgence, says, I will not consent to be no more indulged; this is all very well, but it does not suit my taste; I do not like it. The instant that we deal with moral reasoning, all the appetites, and passions, and desires of the human heart thrust themselves forward, and try to prevent the clear, and logical, and triumphant conclusion, to which we should otherwise arrive. Such is the important distinction between the two. If men therefore ask for mathematical evidence upon this book, and upon religion, they demand what is impossible. It belongs to another province. But if you ask for and accept moral evidence, it will be found in itself triumphant. It is not a precarious or equivocal process. When a man is tried for his life, and when twelve respectable men hear the trial and the proof, they come to the conclusion, he is or is not guilty! How rarely do we find a jury in error! almost never. Why? Because moral evidence has power — it does satisfy. And yet those twelve jurymen are not without feelings, sympathies, passions, pity, compassion, constantly thrusting themselves up, trying to arrest their honest verdict; but they are able, notwithstanding, to keep all down, and come to an impartial conclusion; their reason overcomes every resistance. Men's lives are taken away by the force of moral evidence, and all are satisfied it is right. If a physician come to me when I am ill, he cannot mathematically demonstrate my illness, he cannot mathematically convince me of it; but we do not ask mathematical evidence on such subjects; we are satisfied with moral. Take care, then, lest in the matters of Cæsar you daily accept moral evidence, as all that is requisite; but in the matters of God and eternity, where the moral evidence is so magnificent, varied, and vast, you criminally reject it as incomplete, and unable to prove its end and its object.

Another cause of despising prophecy, or disregarding God's word, arises from having erroneous views of the province and the power of reason. Some deify reason, and dignify it with a sort of intuition. Others, again, seem to defer to the very first suggestion of reason, as if conclusive on a subject beset with great difficulties, and reaching far above its highest level. This is not right; reason is not an authority propounding truth; but a servant, or agent, trying to discover honestly where and what is truth. The moment you take reason out of its place as an examiner of the document, and put it in the place of the document itself, you do violence to both the reason of man and the revelation of God. Others understand by reasonable, what accords with preconceived opinions and views, or peculiar prejudices. Hence you go to the Bible not to say, Whatever is here, I accept, because God has said it; but to argue, My reason is now to be exercised; what my reason rejects, I reject; what my reason receives, I receive: and therefore your Rule of Faith is not an open Bible, but it is reason, or your own mind, in some degree upheld and aided by the Bible. This persisted in, leads of course to disparaging the Bible: we make it a piece of wax, shaping it as we please, adding or subtracting, or making it answer and subserve any purpose we prefer.

Another ground on which men come to despise God's word, and to disregard or reject Christianity, is confounding with and in the exercise of this reason, God's physical and moral omnipotence. It appears at first, perhaps, that there is no difference; but there is really a great one. They are notwithstanding often confounded. If God be omnipotent, why did not he prevent man falling? If God be omnipotent, and wish everybody to be saved, why does not he save everybody at once? If God have all power, why does he allow any to perish? The right answer to all this is, God's omnipotence governs the solar system, but he does not keep planets in their orbits by the Ten Commandments. The two things have no connection with each other. So God's moral omnipotence governs the intellect of man, but he does not govern it by the law of gravitation. The law of gravitation is that by which he governs the orbs and the planets; moral law, moral government, moral truth, is that by which he governs his responsible and intelligent children. If you confound the two, you land in mischief and confusion; if you distinguish, you will see that if man is to be what he is — an intelligent, responsible being — he is not to be conducted from earth to heaven as a locomotive engine is driven from London to Edinburgh, placed upon its groove, and propelled mechanically along; he is to be moved by motives, by hopes, by fears, by reasoning, by fact; and if he resist all, it is not want of light, but something that has gone wrong within him, and that must be put right before he can be governed or righted himself.

Another cause why persons despise, and depreciate, and undervalue this blessed book, is a very common one; a sort of dissipation of mind. We are very prone to think those young men only are dissipated who fall into coarse and vulgar wickedness. So indeed they are. But there may be a great deal of dissipation of mind, without any immorality in the conduct. We have all met with persons in passing through life, who are excessively fond of all sorts of discussion. They are endowed with a kind of intellectual pugnacity, that courts and provokes a battle wherever it can have a chance or a possibility of doing so. They are so fond of such discussions, that they will take the wrong side or the right side, just as their fancy, or whim, or caprice, may guide them; they display the most extraordinary attachment to paradoxes and odd opinions. Such a habit of mind is most mischievous. I pity a barrister, I excessively pity him; for he must be often tempted to advocate the wrong side. Not that he does wrong in setting forth all the claims of his client, the law of the land, and indeed all that can fairly be said; but the temptation to identify himself with a person in peril, sympathy growing with suffering, and to make the criminal's cause his own, is very great. And instead of saying very smart and bitter things against barristers, that have done so, one should weigh more their temptations, and be slow to censure, even if we dare not justify. One may sympathize with great infirmity, though bound to rebuke sin. But the habit of those who have no professional peril of this kind, who argue upon all questions, who court discussion upon every subject, and the more extraordinary the more welcome; always arguing without concluding; ever discussing, not for the sake of truth, but for the sake of discussion; like a people at war for the sake of war, and not at war for the sake of peace; such a habit is most destructive to that balance, that quiet, that calmness of mind, which are always needful for arriving at truth, and always and everywhere dutiful in all.

Next to this habit is the dissipation engendered by the practice of reading novels and romances. Of all mischievous habits, this is the worst. Many minds cannot do it. If I may refer to personal experience, I may add, I tried long ago to read a novel, but could not finish it, for the simple reason, that in the most unexceptionable of all — I mean Scott's — I felt at every step haunted with a sense of unreality: "This is not real; it is not truth." Romance is very different from poetry. I can read true poetry, because it glories in bringing up hidden thoughts; in laying bare delicate links and affinities that lie in the silent depths of nature, waiting for the master-mind to bring, what are to us airy nothings, into a body and a shape. But the mere novel, which is a tale worked up into the appearance of a reality, and full of vapid and spurious excitement, is not natural or wholesome food. The habit of novel reading is most injurious to real religion. It is exactly to the mind what drinking alcohol all day is to the body. And the consequence of a long indulgence in novel, or romance reading is, that mental and moral *delirium tremens* which, in its despair, and its agony, flees either to the atheism of Voltaire, or sends for the advice of Cardinal Wiseman. Unquestionably, of all habits, that of novel and romance reading tends most to shake the mind, to dispossess it of its equilibrium, and to make it ready for the reception of the next new crotchet, or the wildest Pantheism and Infidelity.

Another cause of despising prophecy, or disregard or depreciation of God's word, is dissolute, immoral, and dishonest habits and conduct. It is impossible to overstate the intimate connection between pure moral character and true mental conclusions. A great deal more infidelity than most people imagine has its roots in the marshes of a corrupt and a debased heart. Whenever man's heart and habits become tainted, he longs not only to get rid of truth, but if he has been taught its holy lessons when young, and now wishes to do what it forbids, his first attempt will be to bend the words of the Bible, if peradventure they will sanction his course. But he finds the instant he withdraws the constraining force, the truth, like the bow that has been bent, recoils to its original position. When this fails, he endeavors to find reasons for rejecting the Bible, and begins to send to the nearest lending library for a copy of Voltaire, or of Paine, or of David Hume, in order to see what they have got to urge in favor of what he has already labored to believe, that the Bible is false; but very often he cannot prevail on his intellect to adopt the conclusion he wishes; and, finally, in his desperation he rushes at it as a passionate man at his enemy, and tries to strike it down and utterly destroy it, that he may not hear it speak to him any more. Such is human nature; anxious to get rid of that book that prophesies only evil about it, while it continues evil itself. Many a young man comes to London from a pure home, from affectionate parents, from a warm and bright roof-tree. He has none to take him by the hand; he falls into the company of courteous, polite, accomplished, but irreligious men. They begin to talk of his old-fashioned habits, and of his antiquated notions on the subject of religion. They appeal to what they call his sense of manliness to throw off these old woman notions; they tell him that he will soon get wiser as he grows older and becomes more acquainted with London life. He is at first shocked; but by and by his conscience is lulled, resistance grows feebler, and eventually he must find out reasons for being a sceptic. And having finally got rid of the sense of moral law, of the restraints and the influences of God's word, he plunges into every criminal excess; till, in a few years, amid the wreck of health, and mind, and heart, and soul, and all besides, he learns what a bitter thing it is to labor to depart from the living God.

Another cause of despising God's word, is the fact that we identify true religion with the weaknesses, the oddities, and the eccentric notions of good but ignorant men. It is very wrong to do so. Christianity is for every class; men of rude and uncultivated tastes must be among Christians, as well as among other sections of society. Not unfrequently we find Christian men, who cannot speak good, plain, simple language on any subject without interlarding it with religious phrases, not always in very good taste, certainly often unnecessary, and extremely liable to misconstruction. And you will find other men, again, who display oddities in their conduct, give utterance to strange notions, use a sort of whine in their speech, and assume an appearance of seriousness, as they call it, on their face; they cannot think it possible that religion can exist without these and similar grotesque extravagances and oddities. People of cultivated taste, anxious to learn what real religion is, see such things; and they most unjustly attribute to Christianity their growth and guilt, instead of recollecting that these were characteristic traits before; and that if they are to measure at all, they ought to ascertain how much good Christianity has done, not how much of peculiar or corrupt human nature it has left. Fanaticism is not piety; violence is not religion. Many of those "revivals," as they are called, that we have heard of as having taken place in other countries, had in them much that was not religion, as well as much real and true. Nervous excitement is not religion; rudeness is not faithfulness; vulgarity is not true piety. We must learn in all fairness to distinguish and eliminate the precious from the vile; and to recognize a Christian in spite of these things, and not to give Christianity the discredit which is due to man as an imperfect being. Christianity will elevate the taste as it will purify the morals; but, at the same time, there is an esthetic as well as moral *residuum* of the old man in every one of us; and we should not disparage the religion which rejects what is extravagant and absurd, on the ground that those that profess it have occasionally displayed sad defects of taste, temper, and character.

Another cause why people become sceptical, and despise or regard not prophesyings, is their seeing many learned men who never were Christians at all, or positively reject Christianity. Learning hostile to Christianity, is of no weight, if its possessor has never brought that learning and talent to bear upon the investigation of the claims of this book. Learning that never weighed the Christian evidence, proves nothing against Christianity. There are learned men among the Hindoos; there are learned men among the Brahmins; there have been learned men among the heathen; but the fact that a man is clever, talented, able, learned, is worth nothing as an argument, unless he has brought his talent, his learning, his intellect to bear upon the examination of these evidences. To say that such a learned man never was a Christian, is therefore no argument at all. It would be so, if you were able to say, Such a learned man brought his intellect and his learning to bear upon the character of this book, and came to a hostile conclusion. But I venture to assert, that the most accomplished intellects that have thoroughly examined the claims of Christianity, have come unanimously to one conclusion. Voltaire, who wrote his Dictionary full of satire against Christianity, I believe never read the Bible in his life. And Paine, the coarse and vulgar infidel, it is admitted, never searched the Bible except to gather texts against it. And David Hume allowed that he had not read it from beginning to end. Now here is a striking fact; that the very greatest and most powerful intellects that have attacked the Bible and repudiated Christianity, have been least acquainted with it. But Sir Isaac Newton, who came down from measuring the size, the weight, the distance of the stars; who detected the laws that regulate the balance of the worlds, who unbraided the beautiful sunbeam, and separated it into its constituent films, sat down and diligently read this book; and he not only believed and concluded in the exercise of his mighty intellect that it was God's; but he has written a Commentary upon the Book of Daniel, that, at this day, is read by every student, and is one of the most able and learned that ever was published upon the subject. I need not mention very many other master intellects, who have studied this book and accepted it. Therefore when you quote learned men as not being Christians, you must adduce learned men that have examined and concluded it is not true. It will not do to quote learned men who have studied mathematics, or astronomy, or some other science, and excelled therein, but who have studied and read nothing else. Let a just comparison be made, and it will be found that genius, and learning, and science, and mighty intellect, and soaring fancy, have all recognized this blessed book to be God's, and this religion to be Divine.

Another cause why some persons are led to disparage and disregard this book and its contents, is what they call the variety of opinions that prevail on the subject. You cannot meet a person of this temper in ordinary society without hearing, Oh, who knows what you are to believe? There are so many different opinions. Everybody has an opinion of his own. I answer, that, suppose there be many opinions upon this book, they lie upon its surface. I venture to assert, that if you will take all the Christian denominations of Europe at this moment, — the two ultra extremes, the Romanist and the Socinian excepted, — you will find they differ only in ceremonial or external details, not in the great essential truths of Christianity. But, you say, why except the Romanist and the Socinian? For a very simple reason. The Socinian detracts from the Bible much that is Divine, to suit his own reason; and the Roman Catholic adds to the Bible much that is corrupt, to subserve his own superstition. Now all churches that take the whole Bible — nothing less, nothing more — as the rule of faith, are my witnesses; these churches make up the catholic and universal church of Christendom. If we compare them, we shall find that their differences lie all upon the surface, and that their depths below are one. But suppose there were many opinions deeper than the surface, it is very pusillanimous of any to refuse to come to examine because there are many opinions. It would be like a soldier, or a battalion, refusing to obey orders, because the walls of the fortress were strong, or the defenders of the besieged town very brave. The more formidable the dangers are, the more the brave heart braces itself to meet them. So, if there were more differences than there are, it is a most cowardly thing in you to say, I will not examine because there are many opinions. Your duty is to search and carefully examine, and find out which is the right and the true opinion. But our duty is not to collect and study opinions. If I want to find out the way to heaven, I should never dream of collecting together all the opinions of all men, and weighing, estimating, and examining them, till I find the way. Our rule of faith is not what the most men say, nor is it what the best men say; but it is what God has said, in his own holy and infallible word. And my duty therefore is not to tease myself and lose my time by examining people's opinions; but to go to the original document itself, to rise to the fountain itself; to ascertain what is there: and what is there is true, if all men should contradict it; and what is not there is not necessary, if all men should shout and assert it.

Another reason of many for rejecting Christianity, is the habit of attributing to it in its past history what really does not belong to it. Many a man — alas! it is too true — can quote the long midnight of Europe, in which the human mind seemed to have slept, except from wickedness, and every thing like religion seemed to have died away; in which power was an iron sceptre; and the more terrible, because it was priestly and ecclesiastical; an era when liberty lay in chains, and virtue was branded as a felon, and the Bible was banished as a criminal from the professing church of Christ: and the fraud, and folly, and cruelty, and crime of those ages have left, alas! their stains upon religion that will not be washed out till the days of the millennial state. But Christianity is not answerable for these things; corrupt human nature mainly is. Man takes the very best gifts that we have, and debases and destroys them; and to quote priestly abuses of Christianity as a reason for rejecting and despising it, is to misquote and misinterpret things most absurdly and most wickedly. The apple-tree is not to be cut down because the spider weaves its web amid its leaves, or the caterpillar gnaws them. This beautiful tree, under which nations have found a shadow, and humanity a shelter, and weary and hungry souls the choicest fruit, is not to be hewn down because the priest, and the pope, and superstition, and cruelty, and murder, and crime, have all nestled wickedly in it, or chosen it as their rallying place and their shelter. It is not religion that is here to blame. Rebuke the priestcraft, and the perversions of truth — protest against them; expose Popery, and denounce it. It is due, not to the Papist, that you would emancipate, but to the sceptic, that you deprive of his reasons for refusing our faith. But despise not the gospel.

These reasons — and probably more, but surely such as these — I ask all honestly and fairly to examine. Examine the thing itself, study religion itself; and I shall have more to say upon this in another chapter, "Prove all things." Here is the original; read this book, the Bible; does it not give a picture of God so magnificent, that nations have stood in awe before it, as they have gazed upon it? Here is a book that assigns an assemblage of attributes to God so grand, so sublime, yet *a priori* so just, that no picture ever approached it, and the brightest definitions of heathendom were mere plagiarisms from the word of God; and the creeds of Plato, and Socrates, and Zoroaster, and Confucius, were only incidental, distorted rays, seen dimly as they came from Christianity. In what book, in what document, will you find such a picture as this? "The God that measured the waters in the hollow of his hand, meted out the heavens with a span, comprehends the dust of the earth in a measure, weighs the mountains in scales, and the hills in a balance." What a magnificent thought! "Behold, the nations are as a drop of the bucket, and are counted as the small dust of the balance: behold, he taketh up the isles as a very little thing. It is he that sitteth upon the circle of the earth, and the inhabitants thereof are as grasshoppers; that stretcheth out the heavens as a curtain, and spreadeth them out as a tent to dwell in." Is it meet to despise a book that is full of such portraits as these? Is it rational to treat with contempt such an apocalypse as this? Is that man the fool that despises it, or he that accepts it as the portrait of the Almighty, studies it, and is thankful for it?

Study the character of Jesus as drawn by the evangelists. One of the most triumphant and conclusive proofs that this book is from God, is the portrait it contains of the Lord Jesus Christ. All antiquity, it is needless to tell the scholar, labored and studied to find Plato's just man, or to delineate a perfect character; and all antiquity failed. Sin had blotted out Eden; the ideal of a perfect man had disappeared from actual life, and had ceased to be recollected in the memories of mankind; all heathendom had failed to delineate it, and was silenced. The illiterate fishermen, peasants, and tax-gatherers of Galilee, took up and accomplished what all philosophy and science had given up in despair. And these peasants, these fishermen, had to sketch not merely a perfect man, but a Being that they themselves said was God manifest in the flesh. Now suppose the fishermen and publicans of Galilee had to sketch this character unaided, if they had no original, the difficulty and the delicacy of depicting God manifest in the flesh, is incalculable; and no one can conceive how it is possible for human nature to do it. They must show in all his life the power, the beneficence, the greatness, the grandeur of a God; they must also show in his acts the tenderness, the sympathy, the sorrow, the joy, the suffering of a man. To sketch this complex character is a problem too difficult ever to be placed to human account. And yet these rude fishermen, these humble peasants, followed this complex character into the manger, into the cradle, into boyhood, into his home, into the temple, into the publican's house, to the sea-shore, to the garden of Gethsemane, to the cross, to the grave; and they sketch him in each of these places, they portray him in every light, at every angle, in every affliction, in every duty, in every place; and the portrait that these rude fishermen of Galilee have drawn, has been hung in the skies for 1800 years; the eyes of all nations have gazed at it; the Argus eyes of all critics have examined it; and what is the result? That the impression is deepening every day in the minds of the greatest, the wisest, and the best, till it promises to be the unanimous verdict of all the wise, the great, the good, that this man was not the creation of his age, for he was the very opposite: this man was not sketched as a fanciful being by these rude fishermen; for that would be to suppose a miracle more stupendous, if possible, than any. But this Being is an original; he must not only have sat for the portrait that the rough fishermen sketched, but he must have directed the pencils that sketched him. The evidence is irresistible here that Jesus is no imaginary person, but that he was an original Being; and human nature, unsophisticated by priest, and scribe, and Pharisee — for human nature in itself is far nobler than when corrupted by a false religion — human nature, I say, gazing on the Original, declared with irrepressible eloquence, its deepest and innermost conviction, "Truly this was the Son of God."

The most eloquent, the most just, the most beautiful sketch of Jesus that ever was given by uninspired man, is a callotype from St. Matthew. "I will confess to you that the majesty of the Scriptures strikes me with admiration, as the purity of the gospel hath its influence on my heart. Peruse the works of our philosophers with all their pomp of diction; how mean, how contemptible are they, compared with the Scriptures! Is it possible that a book, at once so simple and sublime, should be merely the work of man? Is it possible that the sacred personage, whose history it contains, should be himself a mere man? Do we find tha the assumed the tone of an enthusiast or ambitious sectary? What sweetness; what purity in his manner! What an affecting gracefulness in his delivery! What sublimity in his maxims! What profound wisdom in his discourses! What presence of mind, what subtlety, what truth in his replies! How great the command over his passions! Where is the man, where the philosopher, who could so live, and so die, without weakness and without ostentation? When Plato describes his imaginary good man, loaded with all the punishments of guilt, yet meriting the highest rewards of virtue, he describes exactly the character of Jesus Christ; the resemblance was so striking, that all the fathers perceived it. What prepossession, what blindness must it be, to compare the son of Sophroniscus" — that is, Socrates — "to the Son of Mary! What an infinite disproportion there is between them! Socrates, dying without pain or ignominy, easily supported his character to the last; and if his death, however easy, had not crowned his life, it might have been doubted whether Socrates, with all his wisdom, was any thing more than a mere sophist. He invented, it is said, the theory of morals. Others, however, had before put them in practice; he had only to say, therefore, what they had done, and to reduce their examples to precepts. Aristides had been just, before Socrates defined justice; Leonidas had given up his life for his country, before Socrates declared patriotism to be a duty; the Spartans were a sober people before Socrates recommended sobriety; before he had even defined virtue, Greece abounded in virtuous men. But where could Jesus learn among his contemporaries, that pure and sublime morality, of which he only

10

hath given us both precept and example? The greatest wisdom was made known amongst the most bigoted fanaticism, and the simplicity of the most heroic virtues did honor to the vilest people on earth. The death of Socrates, peaceably philosophizing with his friends, appears the most agreeable that could be wished for; that of Jesus, expiring in the midst of agonizing pains, abused, insulted, and accused by a whole nation, is the most horrible that could be feared. Socrates, in receiving the cup of poison, blessed indeed the weeping executioner who administered it; but Jesus, in the midst of excruciating tortures, prayed for his merciless tormentors. Yes, if the life and death of Socrates were those of a sage, the life and death of Jesus are those of a God. Shall we suppose the evangelical history a mere fiction? Indeed, my friend, it bears not the marks of fiction: on the contrary, the history of Socrates, which nobody presumes to doubt, is not so well attested as that of Jesus Christ. Such a supposition, in fact, only shifts the difficulty without obviating it: it is more inconceivable that a number of persons should agree to write such a history, than that one should furnish the subject of it. The Jewish authors were incapable of the diction, and strangers to the morality, contained in the gospel; the marks of whose truth are so striking and inimitable, that the inventor would be a more astonishing character than the hero."

Who do you think, dear reader, wrote this beautiful, this true portrait? The wretched Rousseau, who lived an infidel, and died an infidel, blaspheming God. And yet, here is one who gazes upon the picture, not upon the original; and his genius is provoked to give this eloquent testimony. We want nothing more just; we want nothing to be put before Hume, and Paine, and Voltaire, and every infidel, beside the Bible, but the picture that Rousseau the sceptic drew.

Refer to the lessons that Jesus taught; what illustrations of beauty, charity, and love, did he give! Read the parable of the prodigal son; read the fifteenth chapter of St. Luke's Gospel at your leisure. Read the following touching account in the Gospel according to St. John. They bring unto him a woman caught in sin. "Now, Moses in the law commanded us, that such should be stoned; but what sayest thou? This they said, tempting him, that they bright have to accuse him, But Jesus stooped down, and with his finger wrote on the ground, as though he heard them not. So when they continued asking him, he lifted up himself, and said unto them, He that is without sin among you, let him first cast a stone at her. And again he stooped down, and wrote on the ground. And they which heard it, being convicted by their own conscience, went out one by one, beginning at the eldest, even unto the last; and Jesus was left alone, and the woman standing in the midst. When Jesus had lifted up himself and saw none but the woman, he said unto her, Woman, where are those thine accusers? hath no man condemned thee? She said, No man, Lord. And Jesus said unto her, Neither do I condemn thee; go, and sin no more." Now, where have any read a lesson like this? It would take many days justly to unfold and expound it; such purity, yet such beneficence; such tender, and yet such faithful rebuke. No conniving at sin, no courting popularity, no desire after human *éclat*.

All this and more, is in this book. How could corrupt man teach such lessons of purity? How, we ask, could impure man inculcate such lessons of holiness? Good men would not have written the Bible unless they had sketched from an original, and were inspired to do it; and bad men would not have written a book that condemns the very sins in which they themselves indulged.

We ask now, in conclusion, who is the man that is credulous? Who is unworthy of respect? The man that can afford to despise such a book, or treat such a book with contempt. It requires prodigious credulity to be an infidel; it requires prodigious baseness of heart to say so. It requires but common sense, honest and impartial inquiry, to believe that this book is true; it requires the Holy Spirit to apply it to the heart, and to make it the savor of life to all that read it.

# CHAPTER VI.

## PROVE ALL THINGS.

"Seize upon truth where'er 't is found,
Among her friends, among her foes,
On Christian or on heathen ground;
The flower 's divine where'er it grows:
Refuse the prickles and assume the rose."

"Prove all things; hold fast that which is good." — 1 THESS. v. 21.

I NEED not reiterate the proof of the connection existing between the different prescriptions in this beautiful passage. First, "Rejoice evermore." A Christian's air and life is joy. In order to do so, "Pray without ceasing." And in order to pray without ceasing, "In every thing give thanks;" thanking God for the mercies that he gives in answer to prayer, and thus encouraged to pray again and seek what God again will give. And for this purpose, grieve not, quench not that Holy Spirit who is the Spirit of prayer, and inspires true gratitude to God. And, in order not to grieve the Spirit, despise not the word that he has inspired. In this chapter I will adduce some of the proofs — or rather specimens only of the proofs — on the strength of which we come to the conclusion that the book called the Bible is from God. In our next, I will show the doctrines contained in this book, as proved from it alone, and as contradistinguished from the perversions and corruptions of them more or less widely introduced. In our present chapter, we will try to prove, or rather to give specimens of proofs of the evidence that the book that we hold in our hand, is what it pretends to be, — the reflection of the mind, the record of the acts, the oracle of the truths of God. The reception of the truth without inquiry is the surest precursor to, and precedent for the reception of, error. A man who receives the truth without reason is liable, when error is presented with more plausible attractions, to receive it without reason also. But, besides, when teachers of the truth refuse to give reasons for the maintenance of that truth, or discourage the investigation of its claims and pretensions, they convey, intentionally or unintentionally, the impression that they hold a creed that is incapable of proof. And infidels are prone, very prone, to encourage the notion that the Christian religion is always to be received without reason; that it is believing, and not reasoning; that implicit credence, not rational investigation, is the ground and basis of the claims and the acceptance of Christianity. But the inspired writers do not shrink from discussion. They court it; nay, they demand it. They substantially assert that the man that cannot give an answer for the faith that is in him, either has believed the truth on insufficient grounds, or has accepted error in its stead, which is incapable of support by right reason, or of evidence that will stand. If we refer to any part of the Epistles, or to any chapter of the Acts, we shall see it constantly urged against the Jews, that they received by tradition from the fathers, not as the result of personal inquiry, what they believed, and therefore they were wrong, or received truth on wrong grounds. But, on the other hand, we find the apostles asserting, "these things are written that ye might believe" — facts are stated, reasons are assigned, the ground is given on which you are to believe — "that Jesus is the Christ, the Son of God; and that believing ye might have life through his name." In the Acts of the Apostles the Bereans were praised, because when an apostle preached — and *à fortiori*, if an apostle's successor, real or pretended, preaches — they did not implicitly accept, but carefully test; and these Bereans were therefore more noble than the rest, because they searched the Scriptures, whether these things were so. Now, they did so when an apostle preached; they acted on the prescription, "Prove all things.' Test them, bring them to the ordeal; and do it, not for the sake of gladiatorial display, but for the sake of coming to a just and saving conclusion. "Hold fast that which is good." In all discussion, it is not the arena that we love, but the prize that lies on it. It is not the battle that we court, nor the victory so much that we desire; but the peace to which one and the other permanently and surely lead. And, therefore, when we prove things, we are not to do so in order to show how clever we are, how talented our logic is, but for the purpose of establishing, vindicating, and eventually of holding fast that which is good. I am not at all surprised that the church of Rome should not agree with us in this matter. Her maxim is substantially, "Prove nothing — do not venture to do so; but believe all that the church teaches, and hold fast that which she lays down." In fact, she reminds one in this matter very much of Nahash the Ammonite, when he answered the request of the people, "Make a covenant with us, and we will serve thee." Nahash the Ammonite received the proposal very much after the manner of the modern pope. He answered, "On this condition will I make a covenant with you; that I may thrust out all your right eyes, and lay it for a reproach upon Israel." Now, in the church of Rome, they will insist on a similar condition, that you put out your eyes, or let them do it for you, that is, that you surrender the authority of your senses, give up the employment of your reason, investigate nothing, abjure argument, shut up the senses, and receive implicitly truth or error, as the church may be pleased or feel it convenient to give. And yet it is very singular, not to say inconsistent, that this very church, that disparages reason, and labors to quench it in her people, yet gives us reasons for so doing; and, at the very moment she asks you to destroy your reason, she is working by your reason to guide you to do so! So inconsistently do men act when they deviate from simple truth and plain common sense. On the other hand, there is something in human nature favorable to Rome; it likes to be spared the trouble, the fatigue, the painful drudgery of investigation. We are all instinctively anxious to make everybody think as we think, and cast all society as a stereotype each of himself. But, singular enough, society is as willing to be deceived as the priest is to deceive. It wants to get rid of trouble, to be spared all investigation; and to have a religion prescribed by the religious physician in whom it has confidence, which it can receive without incurring the trouble of investigating the prescription, and above all, one whom it can intrust with its responsibility, and appearance, and issue at the judgment-seat of Christ. But all this is incompatible with the plainest parts of the Bible, and surely inconsistent with Protestant Christianity. If the Bible has nothing to say for itself, and its advocates have nothing to say for it, it is not worth holding. But, in reality, there is much, very much, to be said for it; we believe that all that is conclusive can be said for the Bible, and therefore we proceed to pass some remarks on the force, and weight, and number of the claims of this book to be the book of God.

But persons often want to learn what evidence exists about the Bible external to itself, and therefore the question is often asked in seeking to prove and hold fast this blessed book, Is there evidence beyond the Bible, and external to itself, that it was written at the time it says and alleges it was written; and that the apostles and persons whose names are contained in it, did actually write this book, and that they wrote and recorded facts and phenomena which actually took place? Now, in order to answer these questions, it will not do in reasoning with scepticism to open the Bible, and say, Paul says so, and Peter says so, and John says so; though I cannot see why such honest men as Matthew, and Paul, and John should not be regarded as being as worthy of credit as any sceptic or infidel that ever wrote. But still, for the satisfaction of those who would take an opinion from Celsus, but would reject it from John; who would accept the testimony of Porphyry, but would not that of St. Paul; I will here adduce some extracts faithfully and carefully made, which will show that the truths and facts recorded in this book did exist, and were known at the time when the book was written; and that therefore Christianity can be traced up to the cross, independent altogether of testimonies contained in the word of God. This is most important.

The first evidence I will adduce is that of a celebrated historian, known to every scholar, Tacitus, a most elegant and accomplished writer, who so hated the Christians and Christianity, that he never was at the trouble to investigate it; who was nevertheless a faithful annalist of facts that actually occurred. The statement of Tacitus, as translated by Gibbon, a fair and impartial translator, is, — "With this view he," that is, Nero, "inflicted the most exquisite torments on these men, who, under the vulgar appellation of Christians, were already branded with deserved infamy." Now this relates to about thirty years after the crucifixion; and Tacitus, forty years afterwards, records these facts.

"They derived their name and origin from Christ, who, in the reign of Tiberius, had suffered death by the sentence of the procurator, Pontius Pilate. For a while this dire superstition was checked, but it again burst forth, and not only spread itself over Judea, the first seat of this mischievous sect, but was even introduced into Rome, the common asylum which receives and protects whatever is impure, whatever atrocious. The confessions of those who were seized discovered a vast multitude of their accomplices; and they were all convicted, not so much for the crime of setting fire to the city, as for their hatred of human kind." We must take his prejudices and his antipathies as peculiar to himself; and value his testimony for the facts that are embosomed in it. "They died in torments, and their torments were embittered by insult and derision. Some were nailed on crosses; others sewn up in the skins of wild beasts, and exposed to the fury of dogs; others, again, smeared over with combustible materials, were used as torches to illuminate the darkness of the night." Let us recollect, these facts happened within thirty years after the crucifixion; and they were recorded by Tacitus forty years after the time they actually occurred. "The gardens of Nero were destined for a melancholy spectacle, which was accompanied with a horse-race, and honored with the presence of the emperor, who mingled with the populace, in the dress and attitude of a charioteer. The guilt of the Christians deserved, indeed, the most exemplary punishment; but the public abhorrence was changed into commiseration, from the opinion that these unhappy wretches were sacrificed, not so much to the public welfare, as to the cruelty of a jealous tyrant."

We can here gather enough, from the testimony of this dispassionate and eloquent heathen historian, to prove the existence of the facts that are recorded in the Gospels, at the time asserted by evangelists, though mixed up with an amount of prejudice, passionate prejudice, against the Christians, which resulted from his ignorance, and the circumstance that he had never investigated, or paid any attention to, the claims of Christianity.

Gibbon makes the following remarks upon this passage of Tacitus. "The most sceptical criticism is obliged to respect the truth of this extraordinary fact, and the integrity of this celebrated passage of Tacitus. The former is confirmed by the diligent and accurate Suetonius, who mentions the punishment which Nero inflicted on the Christians, a sect of men who had embraced a new and criminal superstition. The latter may be proved by the consent of the most ancient manuscripts; by the inimitable character of the style of Tacitus; by his reputation, which guarded his text from the interpolations of pious fraud; and by the purport of his narration, which accused the Christians of the most atrocious crimes, without insinuating that they possessed any miraculous or even magical powers above the rest of mankind."

These facts will leave in our minds clear and satisfactory proofs, external to the inspired records, of the existence, the spread, and the recognition of Christianity after, and immediately succeeding, the days of the crucifixion of Christ. It appears that, during the year 106 or 107 of the Christian era, — that is, not above ten years after the death of the last of the apostles, — Pliny was intrusted, by the emperor Trajan, with the government of Bithynia and Pontus, provinces upon the Euxine Sea. According to the customs of every governor of a province, he writes home to his royal or imperial master accounts of all that occurs, and on one occasion in these words.

Pliny writes to Trajan. "Health. It is my usual custom, Sir, to refer all things of which I harbor any doubts to you. For who can better direct my judgment in its hesitation, or instruct my understanding in its ignorance? I never had the fortune to be present at any examination of Christians before I came into this province. I am, therefore, at a loss to determine what is the usual object of inquiry or of punishment, and to what length either of them is to be carried. It has also been with me a question very problematical, whether any distinction should be made between the young and the old, the tender and the robust; whether any room should be given for repentance, or whether the guilt of Christianity, once incurred, is incapable of being expiated by the most unequivocal retraction; whether the name itself, abstracted from any flagitiousness of conduct, or the crimes connected with the name, be the object of punishment. In the mean time, this has been my method with respect to those who were brought before me as Christians. I asked them whether they were Christians; if they pleaded guilty, I interrogated them twice afresh, with a menace of capital punishment. In case of obstinate perseverance, I ordered them to be executed. For of this I had no doubt, whatever was the nature of their religion, that a sullen and obstinate inflexibility called for the vengeance of the magistrate. Some were infected with the same madness, whom, on account of their privilege of citizenship, I reserved to be sent to Rome, to be referred to your tribunal. In the course of this business, informations pouring in, as is usual when they are encouraged, more cases occurred. An anonymous libel was exhibited, with a catalogue of names of persons who yet declared that they were not Christians then, or ever had been; and they repeated after me an invocation of the gods and of your image, which for this purpose I had ordered to be brought with the images of the deities. They performed sacred rites with wine and frankincense, and execrated Christ, none of which things, I am told, a real

Christian can ever be compelled to do. On this account I dismissed them. Others, named by an informer, first affirmed and then denied the charge of Christianity, declaring that they had been Christians, but had ceased to be so, some three years ago, others still longer, some even twenty years ago. All of them worshipped your image, and the statues of the gods, and also execrated Christ; and this was the account which they gave of the nature of the religion they once had professed, whether it deserves the name of crime or error; namely, that they were accustomed on a stated day to meet before daylight" — owing to the persecution of the times — "and to repeat among themselves a hymn to Christ as to a god" — the recognition, you observe, from the lips of a heathen of the admitted Deity of Christ, and the fact that the early Christians worshipped him as God. These Christians also, says Pliny, "were accustomed to bind themselves by an oath with an obligation of not committing any wickedness, but, on the contrary, of abstaining from thefts, robberies, and adulteries." The expression, "bind themselves by an oath," a word which is explained in this way. The Latin word for an oath is *sacramentum;* and that word came very early to be applied to the Lord's supper; when, therefore, he says here, "They bound themselves by an oath" — *sacramentum* — there is no doubt that they pledged themselves at the communion table not to commit wickedness, but to abstain from it. And mark, incidentally, here, what a precious testimony there is not only to the Deity of Christ, but also to the purity of the lives of those men who were made martyrs, not for crimes, but simply for professing Christianity. He continues; "also, of not violating their promise, or denying a pledge; after which it was their custom to separate and meet again at a promiscuous, harmless meal; from which last practice they, however, desisted after the publication of my edict, in which, agreeably to your orders, I forbade any societies of that sort. On which account I judged it the more necessary to inquire, by torture, from two females, who were said to be deaconesses, what is the real truth, but nothing could I collect, except a depraved and excessive superstition." Here is a testimony to the early existence of deaconesses in the Christian church. No doubt they existed in the days of the apostles. The institution of nuns is a perversion of it. The institution of district visitors, or females in any way engaged in the promotion of Christianity, is the spirit of it, if it be not the literal transcript of the original. Then Pliny says, "Deferring, therefore, any further investigation, I determined to consult you. For the number of culprits" — testifying, you observe, to the rapid spread of Christianity — "is so great as to call for serious consultation. Many persons are informed against of every age, and of both sexes, and more still will be in the same situation. The contagion of the superstition hath spread, not only through cities, but even villages and the country. Not that I think it impossible to check and to correct it. The success of my endeavours hitherto forbids such desponding thoughts; for the temples, once almost desolate, begin to be frequented; and the sacred solemnities, which had long been intermitted, are now attended afresh; and the sacrificial victims are now sold everywhere, which could once scarce find a purchaser. Whence I conclude that many might be reclaimed, were the hope of impunity on repentance absolutely confirmed." From this letter of Pliny we learn that in ten years after the death of John, the last of the apostles, this religion had spread through cities, villages, and countries; till this Roman governor, an accomplished *litterateur*, confesses that it is absolutely impossible — they were so numerous — to dispose of them. The emperor Trajan writes a reply to this document; in which he says, "You have done perfectly right, my dear

Pliny, in the inquiry which you have made concerning Christians. For truly no general rule can be laid down, which will apply itself to all cases. These people must not be sought after. If they are brought before you and convicted, let them be capitally punished; yet with this restriction, that if any renounce Christianity, and evidence his sincerity by supplicating our gods, however suspected he may be for the past, he shall obtain pardon for the future on his repentance. But anonymous libels in no case ought to be attended to; for the precedent would be of the worst sort, and perfectly incongruous to the maxims of my government." We have in these three ancient documents the clearest proof of the existence of Christianity up to the very moment that the apostles say it commenced; and this on testimony independent of the sacred writers; and the more likely not to be partial to Christianity, because the parties giving it were opposed to Christianity in every respect. Not only did every governor of a province, like Pliny, write to his imperial master from those districts on the borders of the Euxine; but also wherever there was a Roman procurator, he wrote an account of every thing of moment that took place. We find accordingly, by referring to certain Christian writers of early date, that they all reiterate the fact that Pontius Pilate wrote to Rome an account of every thing that took place at the crucifixion. Justin Martyr, writing in the year 140, says, "And that these things were so done, you may know from the acts written in the time of Pontius Pilate." He was appealing to accounts in their archives at the very time at which he wrote. Tertullian also, writing in the year 198, says, "Of all these things relating to Christ, Pilate, himself in conscience already a Christian, sent an account to Tiberius, then emperor. The allusion to Pilate's conviction is remarkable. Pilate was opposed to the crucifixion, washed his hands, as he thought, of the guilt of it; and only by the fear of losing his procuratorial government did he yield to the fury of the priests and Pharisees. And what signally confirms the impression we gather from Scripture is the patristic observation, that Pilate was "in conscience already a Christian." And yet we are prone very much to abuse Pilate. Pilate did every thing that man could do to rescue the Son of man, except what he ought to have done, — to fling his power, and rank, and authority to the winds, rather than imbrue his hands in innocent blood.

Eusebius, the celebrated historian, also writes, somewhere about the year 315, "When the wonderful resurrection of our Saviour and his ascension to heaven were in the mouths of all men, it being an ancient custom for governors of provinces to write to the emperor and give him an account of new and remarkable occurrences, that he might not be ignorant of any thing, Pilate informed the emperor of the resurrection of Christ, and likewise of his reputed miracles, and that, being raised up after he had been put to death, he was already believed by many to be a God."

I have given you the testimony first of those who were neither opposed to Christianity on its merits, nor accepters of it. Let me give now some evidence of the facts of Christianity, not from the lips of mere heathens, but from the lips of the most inveterate, powerful, and violent opponents of Christianity in heathen times. The first I will give is an extract from Celsus. He was a very violent opponent of Christianity; and in all respects did every thing that man could do to oppose and to resist it. He is giving his own account of what the Christians believed, and what reasons he had for opposing Christianity. You must not mind his objections and silly remarks, which can all easily be replied to. I give them merely for the facts that they contain. He wrote in the year 175. "I could say," writes Celsus, "many things concerning the affairs of Jesus, and those, too, true, different from those written by the disciples of Jesus." "It is a fiction of theirs that Jesus knew and foretold all things which befell him." "Some of the believers, as if they were drunk, take a liberty to alter the gospel from its first writing, three or four ways, or oftener, that when they are pressed hard and one reading has been confuted, they may disown that and flee to another. These things then, we have alleged to you out of your own writings, not needing any other witnesses. Thus you are beaten with your own weapons." "He" (Jesus) "threatens and feebly reproaches, when he says, 'Woe unto you,' and 'I foretell unto you;' for thereby he plainly confesseth his disability to persuade; which is so far below a God, that it is even unworthy a wise man." One can easily understand the reason of all this blundering; but I quote it to let be seen the facts in it, and the very texts in the Bible quoted by Celsus as existing in the Bible in the year 175, when he wrote this. Then he says, "Jesus with his own mouth expressly declares these things as you have recorded it, that there will come unto you other men, with like wonders, wicked men and impostors." "Moses encourageth the people to get riches and destroy their enemies. But his" (God's) "Son, the Nazarean man, delivers quite contrary laws. Nor will he admit a rich man, or one that affects dominion, to have access to his Father. Nor will he allow men to take more care for food or treasure than the ravens; nor to provide for clothing so much as the lilies; and to him that has smitten once, he directs to offer that he may smite again." "To the sepulchre there came two angels, as is said by some, or, as by others, one only." "It is but a few years since he delivered this doctrine, who is now reckoned by the Christians to be the Son of God." "Having been turned out of doors by her husband, she" (the mother of our Lord) "wandered about in a shameful manner till she had brought forth Jesus in an obscure place; and he being in want, served in Egypt for a livelihood; and having there learned some charms, such as the Egyptians were fond of, he returned home, and then valuing himself upon these charms, he set up himself for a God." "It was given out by Jesus, that Chaldeans were moved at the time of his birth to come and worship him as a God, when he was but a little child; and that this was told to Herod the tetrarch, who issued out an order to have all killed who had been born at that time, intending to kill him with the rest, lest, if he should live to mature age, he should take the government." "What occasion had you," (Jesus,) "when an infant, to be carried into Egypt, lest you should be killed? A God has no reason to be afraid of death. And now an angel comes from heaven to direct you and your relations to flee into Egypt, lest you should be taken up and put to death; as if the great God, who had already sent two angels upon your account, could not have preserved you, his own Son, at home." "But if he" (Herod) "was afraid that when you was come of age, you should reign in his stead, why did you not reign when you was of age? But so far from that, the Son of God wanders about, cringing like a necessitous beggar." "You say that when you was washed by John, there lighted upon you the appearance of a bird. What credible witness has said that he saw this? Or who heard the voice from heaven declaring you to be the Son of God, excepting yourself, and, if you are to be credited, one other of those who have been punished like yourself?" "Jesus taking to himself ten or eleven objects, vile publicans and sailors, went about with them getting his subsistence in a base and shameful manner." "How should we take him for a God who, as we understood, performed none of those things which were promised? But when we have judged him guilty, and would bring him to punishment, though he shamefully hid himself and fled away, yet was taken, being betrayed by those whom he called his disciples. But it became not a God to flee nor to be taken and executed, least of all did it become him to be deserted and betrayed by his companions, who knew all his secrets, who followed him as their master, who esteemed him a Saviour and the Son and messenger of the most high God." "If he foretold who should betray him and who should deny him," — you observe, evidently recognizing the reference to the gospels, — "how came it to pass that they did not fear him as a God, so that the one should not dare to betray him nor the other to deny him? But they betrayed him and denied him, so little did they regard him." "It was God who foretold these things; therefore there was a necessity that they should come to pass. God therefore compelled his own disciples and prophets, with whom he ate and drank, to be wicked and abominable, for whose welfare above all others he ought to have been concerned. Never did man betray another with whom he sat at table. Here he who sits at table with God betrays him, and, which is still worse, God himself lays snares for those who sit at table with him, making them impious traitors." "If he thought fit to undergo such things, and if in obedience to the Father, he suffered death, it is apparent that they could not be painful and grievous to him, he being a God and consenting to them. Why then does he lament and bewail, and pray that the fear of destruction may be removed, saying to this purpose, 'O Father, if it be possible, let this cup pass away?' Why did he not now, at last, if not before, deliver himself from this ignominy, and do justice upon them who reviled both him and his Father?" "They who conversed with him when alive, and heard his voice, and followed him as their master, when they saw him under punishment and dying, were so far from dying with him, or for him, or being induced to despise sufferings, that they denied they were his disciples; but now-a-days you die with him." "But let us consider whether any one that has really died ever rose again in the same body, unless you think that the stories of others are indeed, as well as seem to be, fables, while your fable is probable and credible because of his voice on the cross when he expired, and the earthquake and the darkness, and because that when he was living, he could not defend himself, but after he was dead, he arose and showed the marks of his punishment, and how his hands had been pierced. But who saw all this? Why, a distracted woman, as you say, and one or two of the same imposture, and some dreamers, who fancied they saw things as they desire to have them, the same that has happened to innumerable people." "If he would make manifest his Divine power, he should have shown himself to them that derided him, and to him that condemned him, and indeed to all; for surely he had no reason to fear any mortal blow now after he had died, and, as you say, was a God." "When he was neglected in the body, he was continually preaching to all men; but when he should have given full assurance to all men, he shows himself to one woman and his associates." "When he was punished, he was seen of all, but when risen, by one; the contrary to which ought rather to have been." "If he would be hid, why was there a voice from heaven declaring him to be the Son of God? And if he would not be hid, why did he suffer, why did he die? Is it not exceeding absurd, that you should desire and hope for the resurrection of the same body, as if we had nothing more excellent, nor more precious?" "Omitting many things that might be alleged against what they say of their master, let us allow him to be truly an angel. Is he the first, and the only one, that has come? or have there been others before? If they should say he only, they are easily convicted of falsehood; for they say that others have often come, and in particular that there came an angel to his sepulchre, some say one, others two, to tell the woman that he was risen; for the Son of God, it seems, could not open the sepulchre, but wanted another to remove the stone. And there came also an angel to the carpenter about Mary's pregnancy, and another angel to direct them to take the child and flee." "At first they" (the Christians) "were few in number, and then they agreed. But being increased and spread abroad, they divided again and again, and every one will have a party of his own." We can thus see from the extracts we have read from this heathen writer, allusions that prove the earliest existence of the facts that constitute the very substance of Christianity.

The following is an extract from Porphyry, who wrote his work against Christianity about the year 270. He is speaking of the conversion of Origen to Christianity. He says, "An example of this absurd method may be observed in a man, whom I saw when I was very young, who was then in great esteem, and is so still for the writings which he has left behind him; I mean Origen, whose authority is very great with the teachers of this doctrine. For he, being a hearer of Ammonius, who was so eminent in our time for skill in philosophy, in point of learning made great improvements by the instructions of that master, but, with regard to the right way of life, took a quite different course with him. For Ammonius, a Christian by birth, and brought up by Christian parents, as soon as he was arrived to maturity of age, and had gained a taste for philosophy, returned to the way of life prescribed by the laws. But Origen, a Greek, and educated in the Greek sentiment, went over to the barbarian temerity; to which he devoted himself and the principles of literature which he had received; as to his life, living as a Christian, and contrary to the laws; with regard to his sentiments concerning things and the Deity, a Greek, and joining Greek sentiments with their absurd fables." It appears from the following extract from the same writer, that the prophecy in Matthew xiii. 35, was in some copies at that time ascribed erroneously to Isaiah. For Porphyry says, "Your evangelist Matthew was so ignorant as to say, which was written by the prophet Isaiah, 'I will open my mouth in parables, I will utter things kept secret from the foundation of the world.'" He also speaks thus of the Gospel of St. John, "If the Son of God be Word, he must be either outward Word or inward Word. But he is neither this nor that. Therefore he is not Word." And speaking of our blessed Lord, he says, "And now people wonder that this distemper has oppressed the city so many years, Esculapius and the other gods no longer conversing with men. For since Jesus has been honored, none have received any public benefit from the gods."

I must give another short extract, from Julian the apostate, who says, writing about the year 360, "I think it right for me to show to all men the reasons by which I have been convinced that the religion of the Galilean is a human contrivance badly put together, having in it nothing Divine; but amusing the childish, irrational part of the soul, which delights in fable, they have introduced a heap of wonderful works, to give it the appearance of truth." "That Moses says God was the God of Israel only and of Judea, and that they were his chosen people, I shall demonstrate presently; and that not only he, but the prophets after him, and Jesus, the Nazarene, say the same; yea, and Paul also, who excelled all the jugglers and impostors that ever were." "That God from the beginning took care of the Jews only, and that they were his chosen lot, appears not only from Moses and Jesus, but from Paul also; though this may be justly thought strange in Paul; but upon every occasion, like a polypus upon the rocks, he changeth his notions of God; at one time affirming that the Jews only are God's heritage; at another time, to persuade the Greeks and gain them over to his side, saying, 'Is he God of the Jews only? Yes, of the Gentiles also.'" "Jesus, whom you celebrate, was one of Cæsar's subjects. If you dispute it, I will prove it by and by. But it may as well be done now. For yourselves allow that he was enrolled with his father and mother in the time of Cyrenius. But after he was born, what good did he do to his relations? For they would not, as it is said, believe on him. And yet that stiffnecked and hardhearted people believed Moses. But Jesus, who rebuked the winds, and walked on the seas, and cast out demons, and, as you will have it, made the heaven and the earth, (though none of his disciples presumed to say this of him except John only, nor he clearly and distinctly; however, let it be allowed that he said so,) could not order his designs so as to save his friends and relations." "But Jesus, having persuaded a few among you, and those the worst of men, has now been celebrated about three hundred years; having done nothing in his lifetime worthy of remembrance, unless any thinks it a mighty matter to heal lame and blind people, and exorcise demoniacs in the villages of Bethsaida and Bethany." "But you are so unhappy as not to adhere to the things delivered to you by the apostles; but they have been altered by you for the worse, and carried on to yet greater impiety. For neither Paul, nor Matthew, nor Luke, nor Mark, have dared to call Jesus God. But honest John, understanding that a great multitude of men in the cities of Greece and Italy were seized with this distemper, and hearing likewise, as I suppose, that the tombs of Peter and Paul were respected and frequented, though as yet privately only, however, having heard of it, he then first presumed to advance that doctrine." "But you, miserable people, at the same time that ye refuse to worship the shield that fell down from Jupiter, and is preserved by us, which was sent down to us by the great Jupiter, or our father Mars, as a certain pledge of the perpetual government of our city, you worship the wood of the cross, and make signs of it upon your foreheads, and fix it upon your doors." This was written in the 4th century, when superstition began, and he noticed the superstition. "Shall we for this most hate the understanding, or pity the simple and ignorant among you, who are so very unhappy as to leave the immortal gods, and go over to a dead Jew?" "You have killed not only our people who persisted in the ancient religion, but likewise heretics, equally deceived with yourselves, but who did not mourn the dead man exactly in the same manner as you do. But these are your own inventions; for Jesus has nowhere directed you to do such things, nor yet Paul. The reason is, they never expected you would have arrived at such power. They were contented with deceiving maid-servants and slaves, and by them some men and women, such as Cornelius and Sergius. If there were then any other men of eminence brought over to you — I mean in the time of Tiberius and Claudius — when these things happened, let me pass for a liar in every thing I say." "But why do you not observe a pure diet as well as the Jews, but eat all things like herbs of the field, believing Peter, because he said, What God has cleansed that call not thou common? What does that mean, unless that God formerly declared them to be impure, but now has made them clean? For Moses, speaking of four-footed beasts, says, Whatsoever divideth the hoof and cheweth the cud is clean; but whatsoever does not do so, that is unclean. If then, since the vision of Peter, the swine has chewed the cud, let us believe him; for that would be truly wonderful, if, since Peter's vision, it got that faculty. But if he feigned that vision, or, to use your phrase, the revelation, at the tanner's, why should you believe him in a thing of that nature?"

The next extract I will give is a short one from Josephus, the Jewish historian, who recorded the ruin and downfall of Jerusalem. He was a Jew. This passage has been disputed by two or three, but I think the evidence in its favor is irresistible. If Josephus had been silent on the great occurrence of the age, it would have been even more significant than his saying any thing about it. If Josephus, who writes an account of every thing that happened to the Jews prior to the downfall of the capital he loved, had been silent about Christ, it would have been the most ominous silence that historian ever preserved. But that he wrote this passage is evident from the context, and from other points which I need not now enter on. He says: "At that time lived Jesus, a wise man, if he may be called a man, for he performed many wonderful works. He was a teacher of such men as received the truth with pleasure. He drew over to him many Jews and Gentiles. This was the Christ; and when Pilate, at the instigation of the chief men among us, had condemned him to the cross, they who before had conceived an affection for him did not cease to adhere to him; for on the third day he appeared to them alive again, the divine prophets having foretold these and many wonderful things concerning him. And the sect of Christians, so called from him, subsists to this day." He also says in another part, "Bringing before them James, the brother of him who is called Christ."

We have had laid before us, first, extracts from heathens; second, from inveterate opponents of Christianity; and, lastly, from a Jew; all demonstrating that the facts of Christianity occurred and were written and accepted from the very moment when they were proclaimed. And if you believe not Moses, the evangelists, and the prophets, let me ask you who are sceptically inclined to believe Celsus, Porphyry, Julian, Josephus, and Pliny, and Trajan? And thus we produce evidence from all sides and from all sources, so far, I think, irresistible and conclusive.

Our next inquiry is, did these writers of the New Testament record truly, and honestly — we do not speak now of their inspiration — the facts that they witnessed, the truths that they knew? We answer, the reading of the Bible is the best evidence. The style of truth is always artless. Ask any clever barrister at the bar; and he will tell you at once that he can see through a got-up story; that he can at once detect latent proofs, which the common eye could not see, that it has been prepared for the occasion, and is destitute of reality. But let the most inquisitorial inquirer examine the writings in the New Testament, and he will see there is an air of artlessness, a candor, an ingenuousness about them, a sincerity so transparent that it is impossible to doubt that these are the words of soberness and of truth. The writers of the New Testament, and this is so remarkable, never suspected that they would be disbelieved. A person getting up a story not real, would be constantly slipping in hints, incidents, remarks, arguments, to show that he ought to be believed. But the sacred penmen seem never to have suspected that they would be disbelieved for a single moment. And yet they record the most stupendous miracles just as if they were most ordinary things. Can we suppose that a novelist, a writer of an ingenious tale, would ever record miracles unprecedented and unparalleled in their grandeur, as if they were ordinary things? What is remarkable, the evangelists do not once, from beginning to end, pronounce a eulogy upon the chief subject of the book —

that is, Christ. Now take a writer of a biography, or a writer of a history, or a tale; and you will see how often he pronounces eulogies on his hero, how often he praises him. But here the sacred evangelists are perfectly silent. They record in the four Gospels what Jesus said, what Jesus did: they utter no exclamations of surprise, no wonderful panegyrics upon him that wrought them; they give the simple, artless record of conscious and eternal truth.

They do not conceal — as we have seen in the case of Moses, to go farther back — their own sins. And yet never did the most inveterate Jews, or the most bitter Gentiles, from Pliny to Porphyry, Celsus, and Julian, charge them with a moral offence. Do you not recollect that Pliny says they made them take an oath to be all that was holy and pure; and they were put to death simply because they professed a religion that was not then established by law — the religion of Christ. It is important to notice that these men that wrote this book, and who preached its truths, had nothing in the world to gain by it. When you find men persist in something by which they have nothing to gain, but every thing to lose, you have therein at least evidence of their sincerity. We do not say this will prove the truth of their propositions; but it does prove at least the fact of their sincerity. The apostles had no hope of temporal gain; they were the subjects of a King, whose first palace on earth was a stable, whose first throne was a cross, whose only crown was a crown of thorns about his bleeding brow; and who told them when he asked them to follow him, "The foxes of the earth have holes, and the birds of the air have nests; but the Son of man hath not where to lay his head." What could induce men to adhere to such a religion, but the clearest evidence and the ineradicable conviction that he was the Son of God, and that what he taught was eternal truth? But it may be said they did not anticipate such treatment.

They were warned long before what they had to expect. They were told distinctly and often what penalty they would have to pay for their adhesion. Jesus said, "They shall deliver you unto councils; they shall scourge you, and put you out of the synagogue; and ye shall be hated by all men for my name's sake." The time did come; they were cast into dungeons; they were sewn up in the skins of wild beasts, and fierce dogs set upon them; they were covered with pitch, and made torches to light Nero, driving in his chariot through the imperial gardens; and they endured it all, they stood it all. Now what could have enabled them thus to endure? I admit, martyrdom does not prove the truth of the cause. It is not the breath that a man gives out that makes the martyr; it is the cause in which he gives it out. But still, if you find men brave every reproach and cruelty, not merely because they believed in a dogma, but because they witnessed to a fact, that gave them no *éclat*, that could bring them no gain; that brought them, on the contrary, to the dungeon, the fagot, and the flame; the inference from all this is irresistible that they wrote what was true, and were sincere when they did so. Or, in the words of the poet,

> "Whence but from heaven could men unskilled in arts,
> In different ages born, in different parts,
> Weave such agreeing truths? or how, or why,
> Should all conspire to cheat us with a lie?
> Unasked their pains, ungrateful their advice,
> Starving their gains, and martyrdom their price."

Let us enter on another proof that this book is what it pretends to be — God's book — let us refer to the miracles that were done. These miracles were undoubtedly wrought; friend and foe attest that they were; thousands were called upon to witness them, and did witness them. Mahomet did not work a single miracle, and for the very obvious reason that he could not; and therefore prudently and wisely he would not risk the spread of his faith, and the claims of his mission, upon the ground of miracles. We should naturally expect that miracles would be done when a new creed, or new faith, was to be introduced into the world, demanding the acceptance of mankind. For what is a miracle? It is not a mere freak of power; a rare and extraordinary display, like a rocket, to blaze before the senses, and elicit admiration and astonishment, when wrought for truth; it is the hand of omnipotent power, holding up the bright light of an external truth. The miracle is simply the credential of the document. What the seal is upon a lease, or deed, the miracle is upon the Bible. And when people say, Would it not be better to have the miracle repeated? we answer, if you once place your signature and the impression of your seal upon a deed or lease, lawyers would not think of asking you to come back and repeat it once a year, or once in six years, or twenty years. Once done, its significance lasts. So a miracle once done as an appendage to the document, is never exhausted. Now we have clear and unimpeachable evidence that miracles were done. But by whom? Evil spirits could not have done Christ's miracles, because there was such beneficence inherent in them. The wicked one would not have done them. "A kingdom divided against itself could not stand." Men could not have done them, for they wanted power to do what was superhuman. God himself therefore must have wrought these miracles; and because he did so, it is evidence that the book they authenticate is the book of God. The God of truth would not stoop from heaven to authenticate a lie; or put forth omnipotent power to make one believe a worthless falsehood. The very fact therefore that God wrought the miracles, is proof of his authenticating the truth of the document. Besides these, we have still a standing miracle in the regeneration of the individual heart. That is a miracle as great as Paul or Peter ever wrought. The suspension of the laws of nature is the outer miracle; the suspension of the laws of mind, or the reversal of the machinery of mind, that is, its transformation, regeneration, and renewal, is a miracle as startling and striking, and it takes place every day.

Another question, not unimportant in this discussion, is, have we now the sacred writings uncorrupted, just as the apostles left them? We answer, not a shadow of a shade of a doubt of it. The first specimen of evidence is the fact, that we have two ancient manuscripts in Greek. One of these MSS. is in the British Museum, where you may have permission to see it, called the Alexandrian MS. It was written, probably, in the 4th century. We have also the Vatican MS. written in Greek, in probably the same century. Some think that they were written even earlier than that period. Now then, we have two Greek MSS., both of the New Testament — of which alone I am now speaking; one in the British Museum, and the other in the Vatican at Rome. And if you will compare the one in the British Museum with any Greek Testament published by Bagster, of Paternoster Row, you will see how faithfully our *textus receptus* is copied. In the first century of the Christian era a translation took place from Greek into Syriac; of which a translation has been given in English, now in my possession. And that translation having been made in the 1st century, can be compared with our Bible now: and if you will compare it, you will find how entire the coincidence is. The *Italic* version was a translation of the New Testament into Latin, and was written in the 2d century; revised and corrected by Jerome in the 4th century; and in its modern shape by Clement and Sixtus —

called the Clementine and Sixtine editions — it constitutes now the Latin or Vulgate version adopted by the Church of Rome; ours and it are substantially one. I add another interesting fact; if the whole New Testament were to perish for ever, I will engage, from the writings of Chrysostom and Jerome, Lactantius, and Augustine, and Basil, and the other fathers of the first four centuries, to bring nearly every text contained in the New Testament out of their pages. Some they quoted to explain, some they quoted to explain away, some they quoted to illustrate. I will take friends and foes, writers for and writers against Christianity during the first four centuries of the Christian era; and, suppose the Bible to be lost or destroyed, I engage to gather almost every text in the New Testament out of these writers alone. Well, all this is evidence that the text as it is in our Bible was written by the apostles, and existed in the very earliest days of the Christian era. There are but two translations now that claim any importance. There is the Roman Catholic translation, and there is ours. It is not worth entering into comparisons, but if I were to do so it would show that ours is the most accurate. And I believe that if ever there was a miracle in modern times, it was the translation of the Authorized Version of the Bible in 1611, by our authorized, as they are called, translators. It is so venerable in expression, so true, so just to the original; not, I admit, without imperfections; but if every mistranslation of our New Testament were altered, on what side would the alteration be? On the side of evangelical Christianity, and Protestant truth. We instance such a passage as this, Tit. ii. 13, "Looking for that blessed hope," it is in our version, "and the glorious appearance of the great God and our Saviour Jesus Christ." This is not a just translation. The literal and exact translation is, "Looking for that blessed hope, the glorious appearing of Jesus Christ, our great God and

Saviour." This is the literal and true translation. And if every translation, where there is a defect, were altered as it should be, it would only be more visibly corroborative of all that we value as Protestant and evangelical Christians. And, with regard to the Roman Catholic version, I will mention one fact, and I do not mention it at random, for I am ready to prove it, having carefully gone into it. During the last thirty years, there have been more than two thousand alterations in the Roman Catholic version of the English Bible. There are two versions; the Douay is that of the Old, and the Rheims is that of the New. And what do you think is the result? That this infallible church, which, I presume, pronounced it an infallible English version, has altered some two thousand translations; and nearly every one of them has been an adoption of the Protestant translation in the Protestant Scriptures. This infallible church has altered her infallible translation; and the alterations have been the abandonment of her own, and the adoption of ours. And, I have no doubt, she will go further if she only become more enlightened. To show the faithfulness of our version, and to give an instance of inconsistency in the Roman Catholic translation, I may add, wherever the expression, μετανοειτε, occurs in the Greek New Testament, which means repent, it is rendered in the Latin translation by the classic phrase *agite pœnitentiam.* If you translate this literally, it would be, "do penitence." The Roman Catholic church accordingly has translated it, "do penance." But any one who knows Latin, or French, or Italian, is aware that to translate literally is often to translate into nonsense. This expression, *agite pœnitentiam,* in the Latin is a peculiar phrase corresponding to such as these: *agite vitam,* a Latin phrase, meaning *to live,* not *to do life: agite otium,* a Latin idiom, meaning *to rest,* or to be at rest, not *to do rest.* So *agite pœnitentiam* means *to repent;*

it does not mean *to do repentance.* And, therefore, I must conclude that church has adopted the literal translation of the Latin idiom just to get a pretence for what she calls the sacrament of penance. But still you would naturally expect of her learned divines, that having adopted this translation, they would preserve consistency. But mark the inconsistency. In the part where the people are to do it, it is, " do penance;" but in a subsequent chapter the expression occurs, " Christ is exalted a Prince and a Saviour to give " — it is the very same Latin translation, *pœnitentiam,* " penance." Well, of course she will translate it " penance," as in the last. No, she renders it, " exalted a Prince and a Saviour to give repentance." Why this alteration? Because the Roman Catholic church says that the people are to do penance; but if it were stated, that Christ gives penance, the humblest Irish peasant would say in his cabin, If Christ give us penance, why should I be asked to do it? So grossly has that church perverted God's holy word. But you need not be afraid of a comparison between the two translations. The Roman Catholic translation of the Bible contains so great a number of errors, that no man, with the merest smattering of Latin or Greek, can ever hesitate one moment to condemn much of its distinctive rendering.

We have thus seen a few outlines of the evidence that can be brought forward in favor of this book; the object and result of which is to show that we are not credulous, but the very reverse. The more I reflect upon this book, I feel its existence as a whole is proof that God has been with it, and the wing of his providential care spread over it at every moment. Every hostile element has assailed it; every adverse force has tried to undermine it. But since Moses wrote — that early servant, — and since Jesus died — that rejected Lord, — what a transformation has been achieved over the length and breadth of the world by the influence of this blessed book! Homer among poets, and Plato among philosophers, have left no such deep impression as these fishermen of Galilee, these publicans of Jerusalem. The harp of David thrills many a heart that the Grecian bard's cannot touch: and the reasoning of Paul convinces many an infidel that the logic of Plato has never been able to reach. Nations have passed away; tribes have withered down to their very roots; systems have ceased, without a priest to continue their succession, without a shrine to commemorate their existence, without a monument to mark their birth and their decay; genius and learning have all passed away, or gone down to the dust, and have left scarce a footprint upon the sands of time; but this blessed book defies the effects of time, repels the corrosions of decay. The frail parchment, or rather the frailer paper, has held fast its trust, when inscriptions upon stone have been washed out, and brazen monuments have melted, and the everlasting granite has crumbled to decay. What is this, but evidence that some one greater than man has ever been with this blessed book? It speaks now more tongues than ever it spoke at Pentecost. It gives names to our babes, it hallows our weddings, it gives comfort at our funerals. It is in the prince's cabinet, in the pedlar's pack, in the sailor's hammock, in the soldier's knapsack. It colors every tongue; its glad music is heard more or less in every conversation. It has crossed broad seas; it has climbed rugged hills; its wing has not been numbed amid Polar snows, nor has it fainted under equatorial heats. It remains still in all its pristine magnificence and purity, the treasure of many a home, the warmth of many a fireside. Extinguish this book from the world, and there would be a chasm so terrible that humanity would rush into suicide as a deliverance from the awful sensation of it. Can this book be human? Is it possible to show that this book is not of God? But we must turn round upon the infidel. We refuse to stand upon the defensive wnen we can be upon the aggressive. Our own government is a precedent. They do not wait here and let the emperor of Russia come and land upon the Thames, or at Portsmouth, or Plymouth; they go out to meet him, and have become justly the aggressors, in order to be the triumphant defenders. The infidel disbelieves that the book is Divine, and believes it is human. We believe that the book is Divine, and we disbelieve that it is human. The infidel asks, Is it likely that your Bible came from God? I do not stand to defend; but I turn round, and say, Is it likely or possible that this book came from man? It is your business to prove that it came from man. And I will therefore ask you to be the defendant, and put you in the position of defence. I have an easy task to prove that this book is from God; you have an impossible task to prove that this book is from man. But if it came from man I would ask, how is it so different from the former religions of man? How does it ascribe the creation of the world to God? Where did it learn the resurrection of the body? how such pure morality? Where did it gather such grand descriptions of the future life? Will you explain to me how a handful of fishermen and publicans of Galilee, in spite of prejudices, in spite of learning, in spite of power, in spite of influence; with no learning, with no influence, with no prejudices in favor of it, wrought miracles? And if you say they did not work them, will you explain how they made the most learned believe that they actually did so?

I assert boldly, without qualification, it requires enormous credulity, anile credulity, stupid credulity, to be an infidel; it requires but common sense, and honest and impartial inquiry, to hold that this book has God for its author, truth for its matter, eternal joy for its happy and its blessed issue.

# CHAPTER VII.

## PROVE ALL THINGS.

"Truth crushed to earth will rise again,
Th' eternal years of God are hers;
But error wounded writhes with pain,
And dies amid her worshippers."

"Prove all things; hold fast that which is good." — 1 Thess. v. 21.

In our last chapter we learned that there is evidence for all the facts and doctrines of Christianity, from the days of our Lord onward to the latest centuries, external to and independent of the New Testament Scriptures at all. I quoted the memorable correspondence of Pliny and Trajan; the testimony of Josephus, not unimpeached, but really vindicated as true; the remarks of Celsus, and Porphyry, and Julian; all condemning the truths of Christianity, but, by an overruling Providence, guided in their condemnation of the doctrines to embosom in that condemnation the assertion, and therefore evidence, of the facts. So that if we wished to construct a creed external to the Bible, and without calling in the aid of a single writer of the patristic ages favorable to Christianity, we might gather the leading tenets of our common Christianity out of the writings of Josephus the Jew, Julian the apostate, Porphyry the infidel, from the letter of Pliny to Trajan, and Trajan's reply to Pliny.

Now this is a point of some importance; and if it does not add any thing to our knowledge, it disposes of the sceptic's cavil. The sceptic prefers, why it is difficult to say, a heathen-witness to an upright, honest, and consistent Christian one.

We will now briefly allude to and vindicate some of those great truths that are revealed within the book. We tarried outside the book in our last. To-day we will enter inside, and investigate some of those great doctrinal truths which have been perverted or misunderstood; and that need only to be faithfully evolved and plainly stated in order to be fully and triumphantly vindicated. The prescription, "Prove all things," need not be made to the man of pleasure. Eat, drink, to-morrow we die, is the sum and substance of his creed. It need scarcely be addressed to the thoughtless; for such will say, We have no time to think of these things. We are so busy with the shop, and trade, and traffic, or our profession, that we have no time to think upon the subject at all. Strange, indeed, are such apologies: a man trembling on the borders of eternity every moment has no time to think what the issue will be which a single step may irretrievably precipitate! Our common idea is that we are walking towards the precipice of death; and that we can calculate, to-day we are so many miles distant, to-morrow so many fewer, the next day so many fewer; till we reach the very edge. But this is not the fact. We do not walk towards the precipice; we are walking along the slippery edge of the precipice; and know not what step may place us where all recovery is beyond our reach, because all is fixed; and all repentance impossible, because no place is found for it, though sought with tears. Nor will these words be accepted by the formalist. If we say to him, "Prove all things," his answer will be, The calendar is my rule of faith; whatever saint's day, or whatever festival, or sabbath it is, that is all I think about; and having said my prayers, and sung my hymns, and heard the sermon, I have done my duty, and am quite happy; and must be happy hereafter. It is in vain that we address those that are overconfident, unless we have first shaken their confidence. They think all is right, they have never investigated; but like the ostrich in the desert when pursued by the fleet Arab steed, they hide their heads in the sand or dust of absolute indifference or ignorance, and fancy that because they cannot see the avenging pursuer all is well, and will be well for ever.

But there is a class to whom we may address these words, "Prove all things;" and to that class, we specially appeal. A member of the church of Rome would probably feel the text as addressed to him to be an insult. He would say, It does not matter that an apostle has said so; the pope has substantially said, Prove nothing, but believe every thing I say! He objects to private judgment altogether. And yet, strange enough, the Romanists object to private judgment, while they are working by private judgment to lead us to adopt their system as the best. What strange conduct; to object to private judgment as the most mischievous inhabitant of the human breast; yet to make use of private judgment to carry us over the threshold of the church into the midst of its superstition.

I do not assume that the text is a call to entertain every wild notion that seeks hospitality in our minds, and give a candid investigation to all its objections or its demerits. If we were to indulge in this ceaseless process of ceaseless testing, we should be always proving, and could scarcely be said to be ever holding fast. But many things are daily presented to us which we are forced to discuss. Notions will spring up in our minds, either weeds indigenous to our nature, or sowed by the enemy when men sleep, that we are obliged to canvass and to dispose of. There are many doctrines in the word of God that need to be clearly seen that they may be heartily grasped, and carried out into vigorous daily practice. And, besides, the word "prove" holds a sense which I have scarcely yet assigned it. It is in the original *δοκιμαζετε*, a word applied by goldsmiths to the testing of metals. A goldsmith has gold with a certain alloy in it; it is either fifteen, seventeen, or twenty, or the *maximum* twenty-four, carats fine. He tests it, and he then tells you the exact amount of alloy of silver or copper that is in the gold, and thereby the exact value of the gold. The word here translated "prove" means, test, separate the dross from the metal, the alloy from the gold; hold fast the precious gold, let go, as speedily as you can, the worthless, the comparatively worthless copper. We have the word employed in this sense by the Apostle Peter, where he states, in 1 Peter i. 7, "That the trial of your faith, being much more precious than of gold that perisheth, though it be tried" — that is the same word; and if it were translated as it is in my text, it would be, "though it be proved" — "with fire, might be found unto praise and honor and glory at the appearing of Jesus Christ." Error is never so dangerous as when it is the alloy of truth. Pure error would be rejected; but error mixed with truth makes use of the truth as a pioneer for it, and gets introduction where otherwise it would have none. Poison is never so dangerous as when mixed up with food; error is never so likely to do mischief as when it comes to us under the pretensions and patronage of that which is true. And this prescription, too, shows us that our creed, our religion, does not shrink from inquiry. You may depend upon it, a doctrine that dreads light, a religion that shrinks from discussion, is like a gilt trinket in a goldsmith's hand, which he will neither test nor place in broad daylight. Our religion shrinks not from discussion. It is not the rationalism, it is true, that puts reason on the throne of God; nor is it, on the other hand, the fanaticism that substitutes feeling for fact; nor is it a gloomy asceticism that crushes instead of encouraging and elevating human nature; nor is it a lawless system that emancipates from all control. But it is the consecration of man's noblest powers; the concentration of all he is to the elucidation of God's word; and the deep persuasion that, like pure gold, that word will come forth from the ordeal brighter and more beautiful than before. But it does happen, and it is important to state it, that there are current in this realm two Bibles; one bearing the superscription that we love, of royal authority; not making it true, but recommending it as true; and another bearing the *imprimatur* of Papal authority, called the Vulgate Version of the word of God. Both these versions, I admit, differ in their translations of the New Testament in very few respects; and I would feel the utmost confidence in arguing with a member of the church of Rome, not from my Bible, but from his own. In fact, in his translation, there are some passages wickedly wrong; there are other passages even more beautiful than our own. For instance, in one verse, our translation is, "When Christ had made an end of sin." In the Roman Catholic version it is, "When Christ had exhausted sin;" which is a finer translation. At the close of the Book of Revelation in our Bible it is, "Blessed are they that do his commandments, that they may have right to the tree of life." The Roman Catholic has taken another reading, which I think the better reading, and it is: "Blessed are they that have washed their robes in the blood of the Lamb, that they may have a right to the tree of life." In these two respects, I think it is superior to ours; but then in others it is lamentably defective. But on this I dare not here enter. The two Bibles differ not so much by diversities of reading; but in the fact that in the Roman Catholic Bible there is a large collection of Books that we have not. There is the Book of Tobias; the Two Books of the Maccabees; there is the Book of Ecclesiasticus, not Ecclesiastes, but Ecclesiasticus. Romanists say these Books are as much inspired as the Gospel of St. John. We have rejected them, and if we have not, we ought, and the sooner we do so the better. But I believe most Protestants have rejected them, and hold them to be uninspired. Our first inquiry is, are these Books part or parcel of the Bible? Prove them to be so, and we accept them and hold them fast; if you cannot, we ask, what business have they there at all? First, to the Jews were intrusted the oracles of God. Whatever sins the Jews were charged with, they never were accused by our Lord or by the apostles of adding to or taking from the Bible. The Jews, to whom were intrusted the oracles of God, never accepted the Apocrypha: they never regarded it as a part of the Old Testament Scriptures. The Old Testament is written in Hebrew, with the exception of a portion of Daniel, which is in Chaldee; the Apocryphal Books never were Hebrew, they were originally in Greek. That is a strong presumption against them. Again, our blessed Lord and the apostles quote from almost every Book of the Old Testament; never once from a single Book of the Apocrypha. And, in the next place, what is singular, the Second Article of the New Articles of the Creed of the church of Rome, says, "I will never take an interpretation of Scripture unless according to the unanimous consent of the Fathers." Now it happens that the Fathers are almost unanimous, and at one, in one thing; that is, they almost all reject the Apocryphal Books of the Old Testament. During the first four centuries of the Christian era the Fathers almost unanimously reject the Apocryphal Books. One takes the Book of Esdras, and regards it as inspired; but almost all have rejected the Apocryphal Books altogether as uninspired, and forming no part or parcel of the word of God. I will mention what will be very startling to a member of the church of Rome; the present pope, Pio Nono, took a solemn oath that he would regard the Apocryphal Books as inspired. Pope Gregory the Great, in the sixth century, says that one of the Books of Maccabees was not inspired. And yet Gregory the Great was infallible, according to the church of Rome; and Pio Nono is also infallible, and yet they differ, the one directly contradicts the other! So much for these books, which we believe, on the strongest and most conclusive external evidence, to have no claim to inspiration. If we proceed to their interior contents, and examine them, the evidence against them is irresistible. It is true, these books contain some remarks that go far to support Roman Catholic views; but it is singular enough that the writer of the Book of Maccabees says at the closing chapter, and in the last two or three verses, "Which if I have done well, and as it becometh the history, it is what I desired, but if not so perfectly, it must be pardoned me." Now can you conceive an inspired writer begging forgiveness for the imperfection or errors he perpetrates in his narrative? The evidence, internal as well as external, therefore, is conclusive against their claims. These books are not in any shape inspired. I have often deeply deplored, (and I say it not to disparage a sister communion, but to state a truth,) that in the lessons prescribed for reading in the English church, I admit not on Sundays, but on weekdays, there should be quoted a single lesson from these Apocryphal Books. I admit that an Article of that church says most truly, that these books may be read for moral instruction, but they are not to be regarded as Holy Scripture proving doctrines. The distinction is broad and palpable. But still, I question very much whether they are worth much for moral instruction; at least I can show that lying and suicide are approved in the Apocryphal Books; and the lessons that are good in themselves lose their excellency and their value when we know that the same writers inculcate unsound and very destructive sentiments and opinions.

Having seen that these books do not belong to the Bible, let us make some remarks upon another subject, which will convey information upon points that in these days it is very important to understand. I allude to the Creeds. Are we to accept all that is in the Apostle's Creed, the Nicene Creed, the Athanasian Creed? Are all these true? Are they inspired? Ought we to receive them as if they were the word of God? I answer with respect to the Apostles' Creed, first, it never was composed by an apostle, or by the apostles, individually, or as a body. The Apostles' Creed is not given in the same words — and I have very carefully and very diligently searched them out — in any writer of the first four centuries. For instance, one father gives the creed in one shape; another father in the fourth century gives it in another shape. And those two clauses, singular enough, which our Tractarian brethren have made so much of, namely, "I believe in one Catholic church, and in the communion of saints," were not originally in the Apostles' Creed; they made their first appearance about the middle of the fourth century, and were incorporated nearly four hundred years after the apostles were dead and buried. If this document be regarded as what some have said, an unbroken tradition; evidence of its fracture I think is too transparent for a moment to be disputed. If it be regarded as a Divine document, it is plain that there is no evidence for that at all. Lastly, if it be regarded as a human document, very briefly, and very beautifully, and very justly describing the leading doctrines of Christianity, as such, and because according to Scriptures, we accept it, as we would accept the Shorter Catechism, the Thirty-nine Articles, or any other valuable document, important as a Scriptural epitome of truth. The Nicene Creed, it is well known, is the Apostles' Creed expanded; the Athanasian Creed, based on both Creeds, if I may use the expression, was drawn up to meet the Arian heresy, in the fourth century. Now the Athanasian Creed contains the most precious truths; but I think it is a pity that it condemns where we had better pray. The less man judges, and the more man prays, the better. If it had said, "The doctrine of the Trinity is a vital article, and ought to be held, and must be held, by every true Christian," it would have stated truth. But when it seems to assert he shall be damned who cannot comprehend the minutest metaphysical distinctions which it gives, I think it is trenching upon ground which had better be left alone, and deciding and judging where we had better leave all in the magnificent latitude in which it is left in the word of God. Not that there is any doubt of its main doctrines; the Deity of our Blessed Lord, the Deity of the Holy Spirit, Three Persons and One God — these constitute the very foundation of Christianity. I do not say that there is a word in the Creed that is wrong. One only regrets that nice metaphysical distinctions, which university men alone can determine, but that ordinary men cannot all understand, should be pressed as the *criteria* of everlasting life or of everlasting death.

Another topic on which error prevails, and to which I will very briefly allude, is the word church — the church. This word, the church, that we hear so much about, has a meaning. What is in it which we may hold fast? Is there any thing in its popular use that is wrong, which we should repudiate and reject? I need not describe the origin of the word *church*. The word "ecclesiastical" comes from the original Greek *εκκλησια*; but the word *church*, which is the English pronunciation of a more musical word, the *kirchen* of the German, the *kirk* of the Scotch, is softened as it is supposed, though this may well be doubted, into the word *church* of the English. And this shows very beautifully too that our religion in this country did not come from Rome; because the Romish word *ecclesiastical*, which most would have thought we should have retained, we have let go; and the Eastern phrase *κυριακη*, or *kirk*, or *church*, we have retained. The origin of the word *kirk*, or *church*, is from *κυριακη*, the Greek word which means, the Lord's house. Whenever, therefore, you say *kirk*, or *church*, you mean, "the Lord's house;" a very beautiful phrase, and of Eastern origin, indicating that Britain's Christianity was not received from Rome, as our pretended archiepiscopal ruler in Westminster asserts; but is derived from an Eastern source, and can be demonstrated on other good grounds to be so. Having seen the origin of the word, what is the church? Some say it means the clergy. Hence the phrase, Such an one has entered into the church, meaning that he has been ordained, or taken holy orders. Now the clergy are not the church; they are the officers, not the army; they are the pilots, not the crew; they are the clergy, but they are not the church. The church is the company of God's believing and redeemed people. In the next place, this word church is not an outward or external polity. The church may be Episcopal, it may be Presbyterial, or it may be Congregational; just as a man may wear a black coat, or a blue coat, or a red coat, and yet remain a man in spite of all and notwithstanding. The discipline of the church is its clothing, the doctrine is the life and vitality of the church; the discipline of the church is temporary, the doctrine of the church is everlasting. In the next place, the word church, as occurring in the New Testament Scriptures, meant originally a political and deliberative assembly. In the historian Thucydides the words frequently occur that "they were not able ποιειν εκκλησιαν," translated into the language of the House of Commons, "were not able to form a House." It was the deliberative assembly in which political matters were discussed, and a vote was taken, and a determination come to. Again, you read the phrase frequently ουκ εγενετο εκκλησια, literally translated in our modern language, "there was no church;" but in the customs of Greece it meant, "there was no house;" there was not the requisite number of members for representative deliberation. So that the word meant simply a political assembly met together to discuss the affairs of the realm; and in no sense did it mean originally a sacred assembly. And even in the New Testament it is used in a sense very different from sacred. The tumultuous mob that met in the playhouse of Ephesus, for whom the town-clerk said he was likely to be called to account for its riotous proceedings, as described in the Acts of the Apostles, is called, the church. But it would be absurd to translate it *church* in the modern sense of that word; and therefore it is justly rendered, a crowd, or an assembly. All this brings us back to the beautiful definition of what a church is. "Where two or three are met together," says Christ, "in my name, there am I in the midst of them;" or translated into modern phrase, "there is a true branch of the church universal." What is it that makes a home? A mother. What is it that makes a palace? A queen. Take away these two, and the charm of the one and the splendor of the other are gone. The greatest architect in the world may build the most splendid house that suns ever shone upon; but if our gracious queen do not choose to live in it, it is just the architect's grand house, but nothing more. But if she is pleased to take up her royal residence in the humblest hut on the banks of the Dee, that hut is instantly transformed into the dignity of a palace. And so, in the same manner, an orator may collect a crowd; but it is Christ descending into the crowd that makes it a church, and out of the tumultuous assemblage consecrates a company of true believers. Another question has arisen about the officers of this body called the church; the ministers of the church, what are they, and who are they? Let us prove what is true here; let us hold fast what is good, and reject what is evil. First, the ministers of the church are not priests; in no sense or shape are they so. And I just stop to explain that the word *priest*, which occurs in the Rubrics of the English Prayerbook, does not mean what its readers may imagine. It is not the translation of the original Greek *ιερευς*, "a sacrificing priest;" but *πρεσβυτερος*, "a presbyter." Hence in the Saxon, *prest*, and in the English, *priest*. A better word, I think, would have been *presbyter;* but still, as it is there, let us ascertain in what sense it is employed. We say in the Christian ministry there is no such officer as a sacrificing priest; and for the very obvious reason, there is no altar for him to officiate at. There is no such thing as an altar in the English church, there is no such word in the Thirty-nine Articles; and anybody who pretends to be a priest in the church of England has nothing to do, and is therefore to be pitied, because there is no place for him to officiate, and no function for him to fulfil. And in the next place, he has no sacrifice to offer. The Sacrifice was offered 1800 years ago; and those accents still ring through the length and breadth of Europe, and they will ring in multiplied echoes and yet more eloquent reverberations, "It is finished;" there is no more sacrifice for sins; Jesus hath died once for all. Who is the minister? He is simply the ambassador of Christ: not only or merely the teacher of the people, but the ambassador from the Lord Jesus Christ. Were any one to say, I am a priest, I would instantly say to him, Then you are not an ambassador of Christ. And if he said, I am an ambassador of Christ, then I would logically say, You are not a priest. The two cannot be in one, for this reason; a priest is one that transacts with God something on man's behalf; but an ambassador is a being that comes from God, and transacts with me on God's behalf. And therefore, the priest cannot be the ambassador; and the ambassador cannot be the priest. Then who is the minister? Whether he be ordained by the Scotch presbytery, or by the English bishop, or the Congregational board, seems to me not an essential and vital element. These are things that have been discussed in every age, and on which no conclusive light has yet been thrown. It does appear that in the New Testament there is plainly and clearly revealed the flock; clearly and plainly the Divine institution of the ministry; clearly and permanently the ministry existing till Christ shall come again, and take the ministry into his own hands. Essentials this book leaves definite, sharp, and fixed; details it leaves for circumstance, for country, for latitude, and for clime. And as to the notion that some have grafted on it, called the apostolical succession, historically it is not true; Scripturally it is not known; logically it can be demonstrated absurd. But instead of giving my own opinion, I will give the short opinion of the most powerful intellect of the age; I mean the present Archbishop of Dublin, Dr. Whately; a man of consummate power, great mind, vigorous intellect; and though one must differ with him in some things, yet one rejoices that those things in which we differ, the progress of the Irish church missions has very much diminished. However, on this subject he is a very competent authority. Now what does he say? He says, "There is not a minister in all Christendom who is able to trace up with any approach to certaintv his own spiritual pedigree. The sacramental virtue (for such it is that is implied — whether the term be used or not — in the principle we have been speaking of) dependent on the imposition of hands, with a due observance of apostolical usages, by a bishop, himself duly consecrated, after having been in like manner baptized into the church, and ordained deacon and priest, — this sacramental virtue, if a single link of the chain be faulty, must, on the above principles, be utterly nullified ever after, in respect of all the links that hang on that one. For if a bishop has not been duly consecrated, or had not been, previously, rightly ordained, his ordinations are null; and so are the ministrations of those ordained by him; and *their* ordination of others (supposing any of the persons ordained by him to attain to the episcopal office); and so on, without end. The poisonous taint of informality, if it once creep in undetected, will spread the infection of nullity to an indefinite and irremediable extent. And who can undertake to pronounce that, during that long period usually designated as the Dark Ages, no such taint ever was introduced? Irregularities could not have been wholly excluded without a perpetual miracle; and that no such miraculous interference existed, we have even historical proof.

Amidst the numerous corruptions of doctrine and of practice, and gross superstitions, that crept in, during those ages, we find recorded descriptions not only of the profound ignorance, and profligacy of life, of many of the clergy, but also of the grossest irregularities in respect of discipline and form: We read of bishops consecrated when mere children — which is a matter of fact; — "of men officiating who barely knew their letters; — of prelates expelled, and others put into their places, by violence; — of illiterate and profligate laymen, and habitual drunkards, admitted to holy orders; and, in short, of the prevalence of every kind of disorder, and reckless disregard of the decency which the apostle enjoins. It is inconceivable that any one, even moderately acquainted with history, can feel a certainty, or any approach to certainty, that, amidst all this confusion and corruption, every requisite form was, in every instance, strictly adhered to, by men, many of them openly profane and secular, and unrestrained by public opinion, through the gross ignorance of the population among which they lived; and that no one not duly consecrated or ordained was admitted to sacred offices. Even in later and more civilized and enlightened times, the probability of an irregularity, though very greatly diminished, is yet diminished only, and not absolutely destroyed. Even in the memory of persons living there existed a bishop, concerning whom there was so much mystery and uncertainty prevailing as to when, where, and by whom he had been ordained, that doubts existed in the mind of some persons, whether he had ever been ordained at all." Well, this is of a bishop in his own church. If we go back a little and look further we shall find Tillotson — the able and accomplished Tillotson — was never ordained a deacon at all. Secondly, he was ordained a priest or presbyter by Sidserf, a Scotch bishop, the worst sort of bishop of all; who came across the Tweed, and gave ordinations in the diocese of another bishop, where he had no business, for money; and all ordination for money is null and void. Well, Bishop Tillotson became an archbishop; and as an archbishop he ordained others. I need not infer the consequences. But it is worse than this. By resting the claims of this blessed gospel and the ministrations of the clergy upon such a ground as this, you generate a year of superstition, and it ushers in a year of infidelity and scepticism. And you will always find that, whether at Oxford or at Paris, or elsewhere, the age of superstition has its recoil in an age of infidelity and scepticism. So much then for the ministry of the gospel.

The next topic we will refer to is the sacraments of the church. Some there are that disregard them; some that seem to me to disparage them; and there are a few true Christians, notwithstanding, who rescind them altogether. And the opposite extreme to this is that of those who make them substitutes for Christ, and one of them an idol to be actually adored. Now, reading the New Testament, we see at once that baptism is a simple and precious sacrament, signifying a person's adoption into the visible church, not necessarily the true church, and committing him when young, and if old and baptized as an adult, to profess Christ, to hold fast the gospel, and adorn the doctrine he professes. The other, the Lord's supper, is the sign of the necessity of our spiritual union and communion with Christ; a ceaseless profession of our attachment to him, a declaration before the world of our trust in his precious death, and sacrifice, and atonement; and doing so, we avow ourselves to be the followers of the Lord Jesus Christ. But it is not a sacrifice for sin. Baptism is not regeneration in every case in which it is administered. And the sure way to destroy the sacraments is to lift them above the place in which Christ has put them, and give them a dignity, a position, and an authority that do not legitimately belong to them. It is a great mistake to think that by excessively venerating an institution you help to keep that institution in its proper place. The sure and certain rebound is the degradation of the institution altogether. The path of safety is obedience to the prescription of Christ; any other is sure to end in folly, in sin, and in ruin.

A great truth on which I would also wish to make some remarks, is the subject of the atonement. No more precious truth is in the Bible. Christ died for our sins, a sacrifice, to secure salvation to the chiefest of sinners. But many persons say, If all our sins be forgiven in the atonement, then we need not mind how we live. Others say, If all our sins are forgiven by the atonement, there is the greatest inducement to live a holy, a pure, and a righteous life. One makes the atonement a covert for his sins, or instead of nailing his sins to the cross to be crucified, he hides his sins behind the cross to be indulged in. Such is an illustration of the awful sentiment of the apostle, "because grace has abounded he thinks sin, therefore and thereon may abound also." But he who holds that the atonement is the highest inducement to practical morality, answers what the apostle asks, "Do we then make void the law?" and thereby he shows that the atonement was held to be in the apostle's days what it is held to be in ours; and that the same objection is not new, but very old. "Yea, rather, we establish the law, instead of making the law void." It will be found that they that look to the atonement for the pardon of every sin, look to the Spirit that taught them that atonement for the extirpation of the love of every sin. Some think the atonement so wide in its effects that every man upon earth is pardoned. If so, universal salvation, as it seems to me, must be the issue. Another class so narrow the atonement that they make it available only for a small section, their own sect or party; or, to take a Scriptural word, but in this sense a misapplied one, an atonement to be preached only to the elect. When we open the Bible we find that the gospel says, not Christ died for the elect only, not Christ died to save the whole world; but that Christ died for sinners, the chiefest of sinners. And instead of discussing the extent of the atonement, let us prove by our practical acceptance of it, that to us it is the wisdom of God and the power of God unto salvation.

On the work of the Holy Spirit there is a great deal of mistake. Some people think that the Spirit ought still to work miracles, and that in the Christian church there ought to be miracles as plentiful as at its birth. The answer that we make is, first, we know the Holy Spirit is still in his church, for the fruits of the Spirit are still found among his people. If the Spirit be here sanctifying the hearts of his people, and giving birth to the fruits of the Spirit, then we must infer, not that he has lost the power to do a miracle, but that he does not will that there should be miracles. The answer therefore to those that say there should be miracles is, Show that there are miracles. If a miracle is an appeal to the senses, when we see a miracle we shall be satisfied. But let us see if it be not absurd to expect a perpetual miracle. At present, for instance, the grass growing, the earth moving, the sun rising, the tide ebbing and flowing, are as much expressions of God's almighty power as the resurrection of Lazarus from the dead — there is not the least difference. But because we see these every day, we call them the ordinary phenomena of nature, and cease to call them miracles. But if the sun were to begin to-morrow to rise in the west, and set in the east; if the tides were to reverse their course, and rivers all to roll upwards to their fountains, we should instantly say, "God's omnipotence has intervened, and it is a miracle." But our children and our children's children, being accustomed to it, would look on the sun rising in the west as one of the ordinary phenomena of the world, and not to be classed with extraordinary miracles. So that if miracles were continuous, they would lose the intended effect, by ceasing to be regarded as miracles at all. We may rest assured, it is not omnipotent power that men need to make them Christians. "If they believe not Moses and the prophets, neither would they believe if one were to rise from the dead."

The great doctrine of justification by faith is not exempted from errors. Some say justification includes good works;

others say that justification excludes good works. Now both persons speak truth; but each speaks half a truth, which is sometimes a whole falsehood; a profile view of a human countenance is often not a true view. Both these parties speak what is true; and yet speak, in some degree, what is false. Justification does exclude works, and yet justification does not exclude works. It excludes works from our title, but it includes works as the evidence that follows our title. We are justified by Christ's righteousness alone as the ground of our acceptance; but the evidence before the world that we belong to Christ and believe on him, is the good works of charity, and mercy, and love, that ever follow. There is no real justification before God in heaven unless there be a real consistency of life before man upon earth. And yet the good works are not in our title, but external to it. We insist on and accept of good works as strongly as the objector, only we put the good works in their proper place, and Christ's merits in their proper place.

Another doctrine, which has been very much objected to, is God's sovereignty. It is said, If God be sovereign, can we be responsible? Do we not read, "I will be gracious to whom I will be gracious"—"No man can come to me, unless the Father, who has sent me, draw him?" And if God's sovereignty be so absolute, does not this take away our responsibility? I answer, No man was ever admitted into heaven except with his own will, freely, fully, heartily expressed; and no man was ever plunged into ruin without, sooner or later, knowing, even as he lived and loved to muffle every rising conviction, that he was going there. So that God in his sovereignty does not drag man to heaven, or force man to ruin. But when he brings man to heaven, what does he do? "He works within them to will and to do of his good pleasure." He changes the will, makes it willing, and then he saves in our willingness, and not in spite of that willingness.

The doctrine of election has been mixed up with much alloy, and misconceived of men. That there is such a doctrine we think nobody that opens his Bible can for one moment dispute. Such a passage, for instance, as that of the apostle in the Epistle to the Ephesians, the 1st chapter, at the 4th verse, is decisive, "According as God hath chosen," or elected us, "before the foundation of the world" — not since it — "that we should be holy" — not foreseeing that we should be holy — "and without blame before him in love." Then if God has elected men to everlasting life, we may live as we like; we need give ourselves no trouble? I answer, that is your reasoning; but, because it is plausible to you, it is not necessarily correct. And the best proof that your logic is not right, is that wherever election is referred to in the Bible, it is always referred to as followed by active piety and devotedness to God. For instance, "Work out your salvation with fear and trembling." There some stop. But the Holy Spirit adds, "Because it is God that worketh in you to will and to do of his good pleasure." And if to choose or elect a man to heaven be right at all, it was right to determine to choose him ten thousand years ago as well as ten months ago. If the thing be right, it matters not whether it was determined before the foundation or since the foundation of the world. But instead of discussing the metaphysics of election, remember that the answer to the question, "What must I do to be saved?" is not, "Believe in election;" but, "Believe on the Lord Jesus Christ, and thou shalt be saved." Election is not a doctrine to be touched, or discussed, or fairly understood by men who are not yet Christians at all; it is a doctrine to be enjoyed in its sweetness by true believers; because it teaches them this, If I have lost the near, the dear, the beloved, it was not chance, but the purpose of God. If I am placed in peril, in the van of the battle, in the midst of contagion, I know that all is arranged, I enjoy the comfort and all the conscious safety of it. And thus election to a believer is a sweet spring of comfort. But election dabbled with and canvassed by men who have not learned the alphabet of Christianity, only puzzles them and keeps them from pondering truths more suitable to their case. We cannot comprehend it — this is very true; but it is declared in the Bible, and therefore it is the mind of God.

Another mistake is sometimes perpetrated on the subject of faith. Many persons say faith now takes the place of works. The old law was, "Justified by works;" the new law, they say, is, "Justified by faith;" and they substitute the word "faith" for the word "works," and then as before. Now that is not the fact. Faith has no more merit than works; it is no more the ground of our acceptance than works. If it were so we should be now saved by intellectual acumen, sifting and believing truth, instead of being saved by good works, paying the price of heaven, and so reaching it. But that is absurd; it would now be orthodoxy of creed as the ground of salvation, instead of orthodoxy of life as of old. How then does faith save us? It saves us as the instrument. If you put money into the hand of a poor man, it is not his hand that he thanks, but you. If you give bread to a starving man, it is not the trencher on which it lies that he thanks, but the donor. And when you obtain eternal life through faith, it is not faith that you thank, but the gift of that righteousness which is unto all and upon all; and faith you recognize as a divine and precious instrument, that concurs with you in regarding Christ as all and in all.

Some people have a very erroneous idea of the study of a portion of the word of God called prophecy. They say, "Oh, it is so perilous, a field of snares and pitfalls, that our best way is never to read it at all." Others say again, "It is so plain and luminous, that we can see the future as transparently as we see the present." Both go to extremes. Not to read what God has thought fit to inspire; not to read that of which God has said, "Blessed is he that readeth," seems to be monstrous. It is not Protestant. But on the other hand, to attempt to play the prophet instead of the humble interpreter, and to predict future events instead of simply proclaiming what is written, is a very different thing. But surely a Christian man and a Christian minister may say, "Fallible as I am, liable to mistake, still more liable where the field is difficult and the subject is dark, and the future is the scene of operation; I may yet say, if these principles of interpretation be correct — and I speak as to reasonable men, judge ye — if my reasoning, deductions, and explanations be correct, then such and such dates reach such and such periods, such and such events are at hand;" this is rational, submissive, and dutiful. It is one thing to foretell; it is quite a different thing to forthtell. And even when we forthtell, we must not dogmatize where much is confessedly obscure, but be content to read, and pray, and knock, and wait, if peradventure God will open up the truth more fully.

In proving all things, recollect there is a distinction of some value. Some questions are worth proving, some are not worth proving, and we have no time, in this rushing and impetuous age, to spare for needless ordeals. For instance, whether the church should be Episcopal or Presbyterial; whether you should pray with a liturgy or without one; whether you should kneel at the Lord's table or sit at the Lord's table — are questions for the preference of taste, not for controversial and bitter discussion. Men have prayed with a liturgy as well as those who have prayed without one. Christians have commemorated their blessed Redeemer kneeling as devoutly as those that have done it sit ting. It is not the form that is of value; "My son, give me thine heart," is the great requirement in every act and exercise. Far better to expend your energy in testing and deciding great questions, than in quarrelling about minute and evanescent details. And, in the second place, learn from all of this the great doctrine of personal responsibility. It is not, Believe your priest, and he will take the charge of your soul. It is not, Believe the church, and the church will be answerable, if anybody is answerable. Christianity is a personal thing between the individual and Christ, and you can no more denude yourself of your responsibility, than you can denude yourself of your immortality. In the next place, let us learn that the Bible is a very plain and intelligible book. If it be a book for the people, it is intelligible. The Bible was written to the laity; its Epistles are addressed to laymen; and it is to laymen that an apostle says, "If we, or an angel from heaven, preach any other gospel than that ye have received, let him be anathema." The Bible, therefore, is intelligible; the Bible ought to be in the hands of the people; and thank God, the shewbread that was stored in the holy place of old, for the few, is now the daily bread of growing millions. Thank God, that the lamp of a nation has now become the light of all mankind. As long as we keep within that book, we are invincible; the moment that we go for our religion outside of it, like Samson shorn of his hair, we become frail like other men. No antiquity must weigh one straw with you in ascertaining what is true. Many say, That is the old religion, and this is the new; you answer, The inveteracy of error may equal the antiquity of truth. No degree of age turns error into truth. Our real question ought not to be, How old is it? but, How does it accord with God's holy word? All that is old is not true; all that is true is really old. In the next place, no minister upon earth, however gifted, eloquent, or good, must be to you the standard of truth, the rule of faith, the oracle which you are to obey. You may hear often a minister you love; you may listen to a preacher whose instructions do you good; and it is the best test of all preaching, that they do so. But if you take what he says, because he says it, then you will be a follower of that minister, and his name entailed upon your sect will be your only heritage. But if you take what the preacher says, not because he says it, but because to your minds and consciences he has proved it by God's holy word to be true, then you have got an apostolical succession of the noblest stamp. Like the Bereans, you are more noble than the rest; for when an apostle preached, they searched the Scriptures, whether these things were so; and therefore many of them believed. Investigation leads to Christianity, not to scepticism.

# CHAPTER VIII.

## ABSTAIN FROM ALL APPEARANCE OF EVIL.

"Know nought but truth, feel nought but love,
Will nought but bliss, do nought but righteousness.
——— All things are known in heaven
Ere aimed at on earth."

"Abstain from all appearance of evil."—1 THESS. v. 22.

IN this passage there are suggested two distinct ideas; suggested, if not contained, in it. The Greek word used here for *appearance* is *ειδος*, it means often a form, a shape; sometimes the shape of a thing when the substance is present; and not unfrequently the shape or appearance of a thing when the substance is not actually present. If the word be used in this sense of shape or kind, it would mean here, "Abstain from all kind of evil;" that is, from every shape, development, and form of it; from every thing that is evil in whatever shape it appear; whether in the shape of dishonesty, of untruth, or in any other shape; abstain from it. But this strikes us as somewhat like tautology or unnecessary repetition of what the apostle has said before. To abstain from all evil, would have expressed sufficiently the idea, without using a word at least equivocal in our understanding of it, from all appearance of evil. It seems, therefore, far more probable that the meaning is, Abstain from, strongly abjure, avoid by every possible means, every thing, as far as you can, that, innocent in itself, may be construed by the world to be evil; that a censorious, uncharitable, and cavilling world may plausibly pronounce to be evil. To do, it is difficult and always successful, but to attempt, it is a duty. And if I point out where misconstructions are possible, or probable, or where your peril lies; though I cannot prescribe the absolute prevention or infallible remedy; yet if we can learn the direction in which our danger lies, we shall have made at least one step towards the cure, or anticipation of the evil. The reason why the apostle prescribes, "Abstain from all appearance of evil," seems necessary to follow as a counterbalance to the frequent warnings of the Bible, against resting in the letter, or rebukes of mere formalism, or being too much taken up with outward aspects, forms, and appearances of things. We are justly reminded in the Bible, that "God is a Spirit; and they that worship him must worship him in spirit and in truth." "He is not a Jew who is one outwardly; but circumcision is that of the heart and the spirit, not of the letter." And again, "My son, give me thy heart." These expressions, and others analogous to these, are so often used, and the lofty duties they embody so frequently insisted on, that it does seem as if something relating to outward appearance, were wanting to balance and perfect the economy of the Christian character. Inner character is the chief thing, but not the only thing. "Abstain from evil; abstain also from all appearances that may, justly or unjustly, be construed to be evil." At least, "as much as lieth in you." "If it be possible, as much as lieth in you, live peaceably with all men;" you cannot always be at peace with all; but you are responsible for the spirit, and for the aim, and for the efforts that you make to attain it. So here, "Abstain from all appearance of evil." You will not always succeed in a censorious world; you will not always appear perfect even among true Christians but your responsibility is exhausted in humble, prayerful, consistent efforts, not only to be all right, holy, and beautiful within; but, as far as possible, to let the inner light so shine upon the outer world, that the world shall have no occasion to suspect there is error, by not being able to detect the appearance, or the semblance of it.

I assume that this prescription is addressed not so much to unconverted, that is, ungodly and unchristian men, as to true Christians. The prescription for the world would be, "Abstain from all evil;" but the Christian treads a higher level, he lives amid a purer light; and therefore the prescription to him has a delicacy and elevation that the Christian mind alone can appreciate; and therefore he is not only to "Abstain from evil," but, "from all appearance of evil." You may be in God's sight, what a Christian is, pure in heart; but it is also most desirable and highly expedient that you should appear pure in outward appearance before the world. You may be in God's sight sincere; but it is desirable that you should be seen of men to be so. You may be honest before the Searcher of hearts; but it is not immaterial that nothing should be done, however indirectly, or however slightly, that should lead a carping and a caviling world to suspect or infer dishonesty where there is none; or to allege insincerity where there is pure and disinterested sincerity only. Far be it from us, as it was far from the mind of the apostle, to inculcate a punctilious attention to external details, or a ceaseless and scrupulous regard of postures and appearances. If the mind is absorbed with these, our pathway through the world will be zigzag, tortuous, and difficult. But while giving attention to the interior of the temple, we should not disregard its steps and its portico. While thinking of the heart, we should not be insensible to the value of the best vehicles and exponents of the heart's life, desire, and aim. We must not make the outer life the main thing; yet we should try that the outer life may be blameless and without rebuke in the midst of a corrupt and a perverse generation. Let us try to ascertain the importance of this prescription, from considering it, first, in reference to our actions; secondly, in reference to our words; and lastly, in reference to our spirit; and in all these three respects we shall see how we, as Christians, are exposed to peril, and stand in need of Divine direction to enable us to avoid what may appear to be evil. There is not a *trait* that a Christian can develop, an act that he can do, or a word that he can speak, that may not be twisted into evidence of evil against him. There are men in this world resembling the tarantula spider, that sucks poison out of the sweetest flowers; who search human life as old Zoilus searched the poems of Homer, in order to find out defects and faults. There are spirits in this world that do not care to find out and study beautiful and perfect character; but like wasps that dash at the incipient decay of the ripest fruit, they seize on the least appearance of imperfection and find enjoyment there. This is too much the character of the world; we need to know it in order to be prepared to meet it. We must not expect that any thing we do will be construed in its noblest light by everybody, and on every occasion; this is hopeless. There are nobler spirits in this world, not indeed sanctified by grace, yet so magnanimously generous, that they will never form a bad opinion of a single act, if they can construe it into good. But these are rare exceptions, few and far between. The vast mass is too much like the restless sea, liable to be moved by every gust of passion, receptive of all strange impulses, and prone to take our good and speak evil of it. Let us suppose the case of a true Christian; he desires not to insulate himself from the world; let him, on the highest grounds, and from the purest motives, and for the noblest ends, mix with the world, eat with the men of the world, take up his place and engage in conversation in the public walks of the world. How will this be construed by many? They will forthwith whisper, "It is your choice, not your sense of duty. You like the company of the rich, the great, the fashionable, the powerful." The appearance will justify it: you may be actuated within by a pure motive, but the appearance without will justify the impression that uncharitableness will be sure to form. It will exaggerate the appearance that is real; it will construct a heavier superstructure upon it, than fairly and justly it will bear. Knowing this, we are not to cease to do our duty because the world misconstrues it; but we ought to be on our guard that the appearance may not extend beyond the exact appearance of a pure, an inner, ingenuous, and noble mind.

In our daily avocations in the world we are, perhaps, very busy; we work hard from morning to night; our own conscience tells us, that we are trying to pay every man, to use the common phrase, twenty shillings in the pound; and determined to owe no man any thing, except, according to the prescription of the apostle, to love one another. To find bread for ourselves and ours, we work hard on the weekday, and appear constantly in the sanctuary on the sabbath day. The appearance too surely will be misconstrued. It will be whispered in every company, You are avaricious; it will be said, He is making haste to be rich. Others will say, He is laying up treasure on earth during six days, while he pretends upon the Sunday to be laying up only treasure in heaven. You cannot avoid, though you may dilute the construction. Ungenerous, unjust, untrue, it may be, and it is; but it will be made nevertheless. It is difficult to prescribe how to avoid it. Nevertheless persist in the onward path of what you feel to be true and Christian; yet be on your guard against the appearance of evil. Know that you are liable and open to the misconstruction of the uncharitable, do all you reasonably can in order to neutralize, or to arrest, or prevent the misconstruction of a censorious world. In dress, your desire may be to appear as the rest of mankind, to dress as other people dress, to appear as becomes your position in life and your station in society; to go neither before the fashion, nor to lag behind it — the desire that seems to indicate the most common sense. But you will probably be construed by the world as one giving excessive attention to these things; as more anxious about outward appearances, and less desirous of the beautiful and holy spirit of Sara, who thought more of the ornament of a meek and a quiet spirit, than of gold, or jewels, or costly array. Such misconstruction is inevitable; you cannot help it; the appearance may seem to justify it. But knowing the risk of such imputations, you must, by the exercise of good sense, — which is a very valuable thing, — and under the influence of Divine grace, try so to dress, that none shall notice any thing very peculiar or singularly distinctive. A perfect speaker of our language, speaks English in such a way, that nobody can say from what county he comes; and a person of thorough taste, so dresses, that nobody notices any peculiarity of class. Dress like the rest of mankind, giving as little occasion for animadversion, or misconstruction, as you possibly can.

In contributing to religious or charitable objects, and trying to relieve the physical, the moral, or the spiritual wants of mankind, you are open to every tone of unjust or ungenerous remark. Perhaps you are denying yourselves a luxury, that you may give to a charity. The world sees the gift to the charity, it does not see the self-denial that is its secret spring. It cares not to discover that you are doing without something in your drawing-room, in order that you may give something more to cheer and raise the homes of the poor. You give in all likelihood more liber ally than your neighbors; and what will be your neighbors' construction? They will say, He is not thinking of his family; he is worse than an infidel; he is not laying up for his own; or he has some selfish object; or he is courting human *éclat*. You cannot avoid the misconstruction, it will be made in spite of its injustice, it has been made from the beginning; all that you can do is, while manfully doing what you feel in God's sight to be right, to try so to dilute what may appear to be evil, or so to modify the outward aspect of your acts, that your good shall not be evil spoken of.

We have studied our subject in one aspect. But suppose we reverse the medal and view the obverse; and we shall see that we do not escape censure by adopting the very opposite course. Instead of mixing with the world, in order to do the world good, we will suppose that you isolate yourself from the world; that you shun the society of gay, and witty, and talented, but very worldly people; that you interpret most rigidly the text "Come out from it, and be separate." Will this appearance help you to escape the world's censure? I venture to assert, you will hear it recorded in the newspaper, if you are worth the newspaper's notice, or spoken of in some small *coterie*, Such a one is fast sinking into asceticism; he is gradually developing into a Quaker; he is forgetting his duty to society and mankind; he is likely to take the cowl and become a monk; his life is sour, and morose, and ascetic. If you mix with the world, trying to do the world good, it will say, You are fond of company. If you avoid the world in order to save your own feeling from sinking to its zero, they will say, You are ripening for a cell. Take either course, and the appearance will be misconstrued by a censorious world, in the direction that tells against you. Or instead of laboring hard in order to pay your debts, I will suppose that you are so deeply impressed with unseen and eternal things, that you take no thought for to-morrow; you try to live utterly above the world — to tread a higher, a holier, and a nobler level. Will the world's tongue let you alone now? Will this appearance be to you a defence and a shelter? Alas! you will find it all the very reverse. They will say, He is inattentive to his business; he is neglecting his duty; he is preaching, or praying, or going to church or chapel, instead of minding his own proper business. So that whether we take one alternative or the other, the appearance still will be liable to misconstruction. Or, instead of dressing like the rest of mankind, and according to the station in social life as fairly becomes you; you dress very severely, and with extreme simplicity. You think this is best and most convenient. What will they now say? Such a one is so singular; he is so niggardly that he does not dress as becomes his rank; and he is beginning to think that religion consists in wearing his coat shaped in this way; or the color of his robe of that hue; or in wearing neither jewel nor diamond, nor ornament at all. The appearance will be made to justify the construction; but the construction may not be the less uncharitable on the part of the world, or unmerited on yours. But you must be prepared for it; it is part of the cross; it is in our commission. Our liveliness will be construed as frivolity; reserve will be charged as rudeness; caution will be regarded as cunning; prudence will be set down as worldliness; in short, in every direction you will find you are exposed to have the appearances construed, not in the direction that you mean them to indicate, but in the distorted, and perverted, and crooked direction in which the world chooses to twist them.

Having thus seen how inner character and outer conduct may be all pure, and holy, and righteous, and yet the appearances be misconstrued; let us turn our attention to conversation, or to speech, another phase of human conduct, and see how liable or likely it is to be misconstrued also. You are mixing in the world, as I have specified; you converse with your friends freely and pleasantly; and you are anxious to be as agreeable to those with whom you mingle as possible; and perhaps to be useful also to all you can reach. What will be the construction of a censorious world? Because your conversation is not directly religious, they will say, it is therefore light, frivolous, gay, vain. But it does not follow, because the name "God" is not mentioned in conversation, that the conversation is therefore irreligious; nor does it follow, because the name "God" is mentioned in conversation, that that conversation is religious. There are phrases most holy that often cover hearts most irreligious; and there is language free and unaffected, in all the simplicity of candour, ingenuousness, and truth, that, in the sight of God, and in the estimate of a discerning man, is noble, and true, and holy. We are, perhaps, deeply interested in some great question; we feel anxious about its success; we are constitutionally earnest; it may be, rapid in our conceptions, and very decided in our way of expressing them. Then what will be the construction of the world? Its construction will be from the appearance, This is passion. He is a man of fervent and impetuous feelings; he has a strong temper; he does not know how to restrain it. There may have been no temper in it; but the simple and full expression of what one feels deeply, who has never learned, according to the maxim of Talleyrand, that language was meant to disguise sentiment, but, according to the prescription of our Blessed Master, that the meaning of language is, to let be known exactly what you think and feel. Or we are speaking, for instance, against deadly error, against Romanism, or Socinianism, or Infidelity; and if there be any meaning in the Bible, it is our duty to do so. If these systems be right, it is utterly impossible that we can be so; and if they be wrong, to speak against the thing that is wrong does not mean to abuse the person. Of all systems of controversy, whether on the platform or in parliament, that of abuse of persons, and smart retorts uttered at the expense of individuals, is the most obnoxious and abominable. But surely it is possible to denounce in unsparing terms what you know — not what you believe, but what you know — and what you can prove to be deadly error; and yet, in denouncing the error, to have the most unfeigned and earnest affection to him that holds it. You may be denouncing some great error, and speaking intensely of its character and its issue. Your language is warm; there is no sin in that. Your expressions are decided, because you have not your opinion to gather, it has been made up upon fair, and deep, and thorough investigation. But worldly men that think it is no matter what a man believes, and that it does not matter what way you try to get to heaven, will say, You are insulting such a man's religion; you are indulging in uncivil, uncharitable, and illiberal aspersions. This is painful censure, unjust though it be, and in order to avoid it as much as possible, let us always clearly discriminate between the person that we love, and the deadly error that we hate, and feel it our duty to protest against and to rebuke. On the other hand, and singular enough, if, instead of speaking in that way, you try to be most courteous, most forbearing, most tender; and to show, by your language, that while you are deeply opposed to the error, you feel earnest affection to the person; other men will say, You are compromising the truth; you are giving up the strong stand that you ought to maintain; you are making too great advances towards error. Or you are speaking, again, of the sentiments and the conduct of other men. And you may speak your impressions. This is a license, call it so if you like, or rather liberty, of a British subject, that of all public men, who are public property, he may speak freely alike of their defects and their excellences. And the difference between us and France, and Austria, and Italy, and some other countries, is, that here people may discuss their differences — call a public meeting, state what they are, and come to a resolution, and there is an end to it. But in those countries where no such liberty lives, the sparks that must be repressed smoulder in the depths of society; free discussion is prohibited; and a revolution at intervals is the necessary and natural issue. In discussing the opinions and sentiments of public men, or of those who are taking a prominent part in public matters, you speak fairly and honestly, but the appearance of your free and faithful speech will be misconstrued; they will say, You are slandering, or you are envying, or you are very jealous of the greater power and excellence of another person. And if, again, you should be silent, and not venture to speak evil of anybody when you cannot speak any good; they will say, You are silent on public faults of public characters; it will be said, you are compromising the truth; you are anxious to make your way as quickly as you can, and therefore to get everybody on your side, and to give offence to no one. And the appearance would actually justify it. So that wherever we speak, in public or private, it is impossible altogether to avoid misconstruction. A preacher quotes a Greek word in his sermon; an achievement which any boy acquainted with the Greek Grammar can accomplish. The critics in the magazines and religious journals pronounce it a parade of great learning, and acquaintance with the Greek tongue. Or again, a preacher who happens to belong to the Scotch church remarks upon the excellence and beauty of much of the English liturgy; and on many parts of it he cannot speak too eulogistically; instantly he is set down in a Scotch newspaper as a candidate for a bishopric. Or he makes an incidental remark on dissent and dissenters — how godly and truly pious a man is such a dissenter! Forthwith he is set down as courting popularity with the masses. Does he express his opinion that such a bishop may be a Christian, or that a duke may get to heaven? He is seeking the favor and the patronage of the great. Does he say any thing about the worth of the humbler classes; what silent springs of excellence deep down are there undetected; what noble characters sweep crossings; what holy and pious hearts beat in hovels on which the sun has never shone? Then he is becoming a democrat. Does he say that the Crystal Palace should not be opened on Sunday? He is resisting and opposing the enjoyments of the people. Does he preach Calvinism? He is a fatalist. Does he preach Arminianism? He is a legalist. Does he think prophecy, which God gave for our reading, and pronounces a blessing on those that read, ought to be studied? Then he is assuming to be a prophet; fixing the very day and the very year of the end of the world. In short, let a man say what he likes, and in the most careful and the most courteous terms that he will, it is impossible to avoid appearances that will be misconstrued. Knowing, therefore, the peril, all that we can or ought to do is, as far as lieth in us, to try and arrest or dilute its liability to misconception. It was while studying these thoughts, and putting these thoughts together in my mind, that for the first time in my life I felt the profound philosophy and depth of a single statement of St. James. "For in many things we offend all. If any man offend not in word, the same is a perfect man." How true! He must be perfect; for it is almost impossible so to speak that somebody shall not misconstrue it, or take offence at it. These misconstructions of appearances are not in the least degree to make us compromise. The duty of an ambassador of Christ, is to proclaim the message which he can prove to be true, regardless comparatively of all consequences. But still, knowing the peculiar atmosphere in which we move, the peculiar exposure under which we lie to misconception, and that mere appearances may thus have been the grounds of very grave mischief; it becomes us to act with an eye without, though the main introspection must be within; and to speak in the pulpit or elsewhere with some reference to words, as well as with a main reference to thoughts. And though I would not say, that the preacher ought therefore to read his sermon in order to avoid misconception, he ought to be very careful in his words as well as thoughts. We must not bring in the preacher guilty for a word; or because he uses an expression which you think too strong, or that may be misconstrued or misapprehended. The hearer must not judge uncharitably; but, in the exercise of that charity which the apostle lauds and praises, and not more than it deserves, and which is the highest, because Christian, courtesy, let us "Rejoice not in iniquity, but rejoice in the truth; bear all things, believe all things;" believe only good, unless there be irresistible proof of evil; "believe all things, hope all things, endure all things." What a magnificent world would this be if charity were its life, the law and the limit of its living!

Having thus seen how appearances in our conduct and conversation may be misconstrued, let us notice very briefly appearances in our spirit liable to misconstruction. This is more delicate, and less easily detected and distinguished; but still, here appearances too will be, and must be, and have been, perverted by misconstructions. For instance, one has great decision of character. He sees things by intuition, he pronounces at a glance. He is set down instantly as precipitate and rash. Another man is very cautious; his caution leads him to delay, he is set down and characterized as vacillating and weak, as behind the nineteenth century, not up to the age. Our efforts to rise above the ordinary level, to maintain our course on elevated ground, and live in inner communion with God, will be misconstrued. Superiority to the censure of the world will have an appearance that the world will pronounce to be *hauteur*, pride, self-conceit. True humility will be construed into meanness of spirit; enthusiasm, which is worthy of an apostle, will be called intemperate zeal; warmth of heart and genuine affection will be liable to be misconceived as frivolity; buoyancy of spirit will be set down as lightness of mind, gravity of spirit as dulness; tenacity of principle will be called obstinacy; reserve will be branded as cunning, and silence will be thought indecision. When I think over all these liabilities of outward appearances, the appearances even of what is good within; when I weigh these liabilities to misconception; I am reminded of that sentiment in the Gospel of St. Matthew, which sums up almost all we have said in very few words. "John came neither eating nor drinking, and they say, He hath a devil. The Son of man came eating and drinking, and they say, Behold a man gluttonous, and a wine-bibber, a friend of publicans and sinners. But wisdom is justified of her children." How true is that! What a wonderful book is the Bible! What striking lights are in every page of it! What perfect wisdom in every remark! The age is behind, never before it. All I have said may be summed up in these words, — that if you come neither eating nor drinking, they will say, "He is an ascetic. He hath a devil."

If you come eating and drinking, they will say, "He is a glutton, a friend of publicans and sinners."

In closing these remarks, let us learn how much of our own comfort depends upon appearances. Not what we are, but what we appear, shapes and determines the world's judgment of us. The world cannot see our motives, because it cannot search the heart; it can only see our outward appearance; and by its tone, its depth of shadow, or by its brilliancy and sharpness of outline, the world forms its opinion of us. It is very distressing to a mind conscious of integrity and fairness, to be represented in colors the very opposite of what it feels; owing mainly, it may be, to our disregard of, and inattention to, appearances. To be reflected as we are, is to a Christian mind a source of satisfaction, never of pride. But to have a character in the world derived from appearances more favorable than we really have a right to, is no enjoyment; and a character derived from appearances in the world the very opposite of what we are conscious of, must be to a sensitive mind extremely painful. How, then, are we to act? Let us first see that we are good, and subordinately to that, that we appear good; that we have right principles rooted within, and next, not disregard the appearance of those principles without. Let us never forget, that we are in the midst of an alien, uncharitable, censorious world, with a strong sympathy with what is evil, and a desire that everybody above its own temperature should be reduced as low as itself. Knowing that what we appear is liable to be misconstrued by that world, Christians must pay attention to appearances; although their deepest and their profoundest attention must be given to principles within.

Our usefulness in the world is very much dependent on appearances. This is a very important though a very much forgotten thought. Let there be a case where the appearances without are the result of evil, unquestionable evil, within; let there be another case, where all is right within, but where the appearances without are very much the same as in the former case. The effect of the latter is just as injurious as the effect of the former. Though in the latter there may be no inner evil, yet there is a disregard of outer appearances; though there may be nothing evil to represent within, yet it may be just as injurious to others as an evil appearance which is in itself only the true and exact exponent of bad that is within. And let us never forget that outward appearances of character are ceaselessly operative. We exercise a more powerful influence by what we appear, than by what we say and do in the world. What was the reason of the depth and greatness of the impression that Jesus made upon the public mind? It was not wholly his speech; it was not his miracles; but the fact that no man lived like that man, and therefore no man spake like that man. It was that quiet, solemn, and heavenly life that struck so deep an impression on the world around it. Now what we design, or what we feel, man cannot see; but what we appear to be, everybody can see. And if we are careless of outer appearances, we are careless of an element that is moulding and shaping the mass of mankind either for good, or for misery and ruin. But some one will say—I do what is right; and I do not care what the world or anybody may say. In such a sentiment there is much that is magnanimous and noble; it would be absurd and wrong to deny it; but there is something in it, too, unsound and doubtful. You say, I do what is right; and I do not care what the world thinks. Is that proper? If people speak evil of you from malice, from envy, from ill-will, or uncharitableness, then you ought to be deeply grieved that men should be so wicked as to do so; and you ought to feel the instant obligation of our Blessed Master's prescription, "Pray for them that despitefully use you." On the other hand, if the cause of their unfavorable judgment be something indiscreet in your conduct; something in appearances that are not as they should be, though all may be right within; is it not matter of great grief to us that, Christians as we are, we have by our mismanagement, or indiscretion, or disregard of appearances, generated a conviction, or impression, among mankind, injurious to that cause with which we are identified, and lowering to ourselves as Christian men? And besides, on the other hand, we are all members of the church universal. We are epistles, seen and read of all men. Our conduct will be construed as the result of principles, and if we suffer from disregard of appearances, the whole church of Christ will suffer; the name by which we are called will be injured, and its march across the world will be so far impeded.

Another will say, I do what is right; and I am not, therefore, responsible for consequences. There is much in this most just, most noble, worthy of being recollected; but there is a sense in which it is not true. We are not responsible for the consequences of what is truly felt, truly spoken, and justly and truly expressed in our conduct: but we are responsible if — notwithstanding all is excellence within — we either speak indiscreetly, or act imprudently, or develop appearances which are liable to misconstruction. Such offence in the world, is not the offence of the cross; but the offence of our indiscretion, our imprudence, our want of care, of vigilance, of caution. It is possible to be responsible for the issues of our conduct; not indeed for the issues of truth, or of doing our duty; but responsible for issues that arise not from the truth we hold and the principles we love, but from our indiscreet, passionate, or compromising expression or reflection of them. See therefore, here, a reason of the inefficacy of many a true Christian in the church of Christ. There are many Christians who are constitutionally very odd and strange. Christianity does not turn Peter into Paul, or Paul into James; it seizes the man as the fall has left him; and day by day works out and develops from that man that which God has determined him to be. When one becomes a Christian, he does not lose his hot temper at once. When a natural man becomes a Christian, he does not cease to have his own peculiar temperament or to have many lingering defects. We all know that there are thoughts in our minds, sympathies in our hearts, that we would not wish the world to know; but God knows; and these are the evidences of the remains of a nature not yet utterly subdued and sanctified. We find many a true Christian in the world, impetuous, extravagant, full of zeal without knowledge, of fervor without discretion; or very obstinate, or very bigoted, or very stupid. And what is the result? Men have ears to hear, and eyes to see; and these ears and these eyes come into contact with the outer appearances only; they cannot see the inner worth of the man. They see the faults that remain, not those that are gone; and men form a judgment of what Christianity is, by the obstinacy — the stupidity — the indiscretion — the zeal of this specimen, as they call it, of what Christianity makes a man. You see therefore, the inefficiency of many a good man in the church of Christ, is owing to his not abstaining from all appearance of evil.

Let us learn finally the value of a sound judgment, a tender conscience, ceaseless vigilance. We are sentinels, we are soldiers; we are surrounded by enemies. Be sensitively anxious, first, to what you should be; and next, to what you appear to be. Do not only ask, What am I? which is most important; but ask also, How will this appear to others? What impression will this leave upon Christian men? What opinion will this generate in a world that is carping, cavilling, censorious, uncharitable? A sailor when he is steering his ship, not only looks to his compass, but makes allowances for currents in the ocean, and acts and steers accordingly. You must not only think of your main route, and of the main character; but you must recollect there are many currents, and strange eddies in this world; you must not only determine to be and do right, but you must also ask, What impression is this appearance likely to leave? What effect will it have? It is the duty of Christians to be very slow to judge. When you know how many appearances may be the acts of indiscretion, not the just exponents of inner character, you ought to be very slow to judge. We shall not find out till the judgment-day how many grave infirmities are compatible with being true Christians notwithstanding. And if so, we shall find there is much, oh! much, to forgive in the best; and there is much, oh! much, to pity rather than condemn in the very worst. Do not pronounce unfavorable judgment upon your brother or your sister from an indiscreet word, from an incidental appearance that does not suit your taste, or from a hasty act. Do not overestimate appearances in others; do not underestimate their importance in yourselves. Do not infer too much from appearance in a brother; do not attach too little to appearance in yourselves.

How much need have we of the Holy Spirit, not only to give us clean hearts, but clean hands; not only to create in us right spirits, but to hold up our goings, that our footsteps slip not.

## CHAPTER IX.

### THE PERORATION.

"O may thy Spirit seal our souls,
And mould them to thy will;
That our weak hearts no more may stray,
But keep thy precepts still:

That to perfection's sacred height
We nearer still may rise,
And all we think, and all we do,
Be pleasing in thine eyes."

"And the very God of peace sanctify you wholly; and I pray God your whole spirit and soul and body be preserved blameless unto the coming of our Lord Jesus Christ." — 1 THESS. v. 23.

VERY justly and truly does the apostle, who lived near to his Lord, and saw all things in his everlasting light, close his prescriptions for daily life with fervent prayer: "The very God of peace, not only make you rejoice evermore, pray without ceasing, in every thing give thanks, quench not the Spirit, despise not prophecy, prove all things, abstain from all appearance of evil, but even sanctify you wholly; and I pray God your whole spirit and soul and body be preserved blameless unto the coming of our Lord Jesus Christ." It is not the least important feature, that every prescription given for practical duty, precious in itself, should conclude with earnest prayer to the Giver of all good things, for strength to do it. The loftiest duty is possible with grace; the least is all but impossible without it. It is the duty and privilege of preachers and ministers of the gospel to begin to pray after they have ceased to preach. Preaching without prayer may illuminate the intellect; but only that preaching that is sealed and sanctified by prayer will be owned of God to touch the heart, and to leave plastic and transforming influences there. If we bid men do, but never tell them of the secret and fountain of their strength, we shall treat them as Pharaoh did the Israelites in Egypt, giving clay to make bricks, but no straw to bind them. These practical prescriptions which we have been studying, do not imply, because addressed to us, inherent strength in us by nature to do them: they do however imply responsibility and obligation. It is when we have heard them stated in all the length and breadth of their purity and their obligation, that the very difficulty we feel it to generate, not despair, or indolence, or neglect; but earnest, persevering supplication at the throne of grace. When God says, "Do this," the command does not imply in us by nature inherent strength to obey, but it does imply obligation to obey. Our sense of inability to do, is the very first step towards doing. Because, if I am convinced that I am bound to do this, but feel that I cannot do this, and hear that God's strength is made perfect in weakness; if I am sincere and earnest in my convictions, I shall be fervent in prayer to God that he would give me strength and grace equal to my obligations.

In considering this, the prayer of the apostle, let us first notice the great work that the apostle prays may be consummated in the heart of his converts, namely, that they may be sanctified wholly, and preserved blameless. Let us notice, in the second place, the subjects of this sanctification; the soul, the body, and the spirit. Let us next consider the limit of the process, and its perfection at the coming of our Lord Jesus Christ; and lastly, the author of it, "The very God of peace." First of all, in this closing prayer, we have the great work, the sanctification of all the people of God. What is sanctification? The Shorter Catechism describes it very beautifully. Justification is an *act;* something that is done, and done for ever, incapable of increase, and beyond the range of decrease. But sanctification, says the same admirable document, is a *work* of God's Holy Spirit. It is not an act, but a process, that begins like the infant light of the awakening morn, and shines through the grey and the misty dawn, until it reach the full and unclouded splendor of a meridian, and in this case, an everlasting noon. Sanctification is a process. Its beginning is here—its progress for ever. Let us see what its strict and literal meaning is, as employed in Scripture. Its first essential idea is that of separation; the Hebrew word *kadosh*, and the Greek ἁγιος, corresponding to it, and the Latin *sacer*, though naturally translated *holy* and *sacred*, yet very often are translated by a word meaning the very reverse. The Hebrew word *kadosh* is applied to a bad and depraved person; the Latin word *sacer* is applied to that which is cursed, as *auri sacra fames*, "the accursed thirst of gold." And, the reason of this is, that all three words mean in their original use merely that which is separated; it may be separated to evil, or separated to good. The radical meaning is simply separation. And therefore, in studying the meaning of the word *sanctification*, we must look first at its radical idea, which is separation. "I am the Lord thy God, which separated you from all people, that ye may be a holy people." Hence the apostle speaks of being "separated unto the gospel." "Come out, and be ye separate;" or set apart, or, if you like, ordained. The very first characteristic of genuine sanctification in the case of every child of God is separation, not mechanical, but moral, from all that is evil, unholy, and impure. And among all the separations frequently referred to in Scripture, the most common one is separation from the world; from its service, its affinities, its sympathies, its preferences, its delights, and its joys; as far as they are tainted by the world's contagion, and peculiar to the world as enmity to God and to his law. It may be a baptized world, it may be a refined world, it may be a polished, an educated, and a cultivated world, but it is the world still; and from all that is still evil in it, and alien to the spirit of the gospel, it is not only the Christian's duty, but his holy instinct, to separate himself and stand apart; not indeed with contumelious contempt, but with sorrow and regret; and while protesting against its evil, doing our best meekly to correct it. Many will separate from the world, and then let the world alone; but this is the spirit of a Cain, not the spirit of an Abel; "Am I my brother's keeper?" is an inhuman thought. Just in proportion as you feel constrained to protest against what the world is doing, you are the more solemnly bound to try to lead the children of the world to a more excellent, holy, and Christian way. The monk abandons the world mechanically, and leaves it as far as he is concerned, to wend its way to ruin as it may; while he goes into his sequestered nook, and vainly thinks he can rise above its influence and be holy, and happy, and pure. But were he successful, this would not be Christianity. The apostles were in the world, but not of it; they tried to do the world good, and to make it better for their having passed through it; their very footprints were cheering guides. If all the salt of the earth were to be withdrawn, if all the lights of the world were to be put under bushels, then the very world that needs their presence most, would be beyond the reach of their rays; and instead of Christianity being practically an offer, wide as the wide world, it would cease to be addressed to the many, and reach only a few, and the world would lose its only opportunity of hearing the glad sound, and becoming wise unto everlasting life.

The next sense of sanctification, is to be made holy; is to make that holy which is unholy. This denotes not an external or conventional, but an internal and real, transformation. To be holy, or to be a Christian — that is, an anointed or consecrated person — is not retreat from duty, because duty is difficult; but the inspiration of duty, because duty devolving upon us. It is not an outer robe, but an inner character. It is the saint grafted on the man, the heart of nature quickened from above by the grace of God; till they that were the servants of Satan are transformed into a chosen generation, a royal priesthood, a peculiar people, that they may show forth the praises of Him who hath called them from darkness into his marvellous light. This holiness or sanctification we have called a process. Its commencement is regeneration; its close is perfection; and its fulness is when the age to come shall have burst upon the earth, and all things shall be made new. But it has a beginning. Regeneration is its initial act, the heart is born again; and from this it proceeds from strength to strength, from grace to grace. The entrance of the Holy Spirit into the heart, is the first step or stage in this sanctification. There is the child in Christ, who was born again yesterday; there is the full-grown man in Christ Jesus, who has lived and adorned the gospel for forty, fifty, sixty years. One is at one stage, the other at another; but each illustrating the truth that the light shineth more and more unto the perfect day. In each case, the grain of mustard-seed in the heart grows up until it becomes a majestic and a sheltering tree. But it has been objected by some, Is not this ceaseless and continuous progress in sanctification, or separation from all that is sinful, and conformity to the

Lord Jesus Christ, contradicted by the personal and practical experience of many of the people of God? Is not, some say, the machinery often reversed? Does not the current of grace often flow backward in its channel? Are there not some who were Christians a year ago, truly growing in grace, who have since ceased to grow, and are retrograding rather than advancing in the way that leads to heaven, and in the character that fits for it? I answer, once a true Christian, born again by the Spirit of God, it is impossible he can ever go finally backward; it is barely possible such can ever stand still. It is absolutely certain that in some shape or direction he will advance and send forth the influences of inner and divine life; and though he may not appear to thousands, nay, not appear to himself, yet really and truly he may be advancing in likeness to Christ and in fitness for the kingdom of heaven. Quite true, the first feelings of joy that thrilled his spirit when he learned the distinguishing and peculiar truths of the gospel, have all departed. It is right that they should do so; it was not meant that they should continue. But they may have left behind them an abiding growth, a steady progress. The effervescence is gone, but the pure wine remains. The excitement of conviction may have settled down into solid and solemn conversion; and though there may not be now blazing light, sparkling joys, yet the whole temperature of his Christian character may be materially raised. Passion has become principle. There may be progress as a whole, though there may not be continuous progress, stage by stage. On some days the plants grow rapidly; on other days they do not advance at all. But very often while the plant itself is not growing visibly as measured by a scale, it may be striking deeper its roots: it may be collecting and husbanding or sowing the elements of growth, and so preparing for mightier future efforts the secret sap that is its vitality and its power. The tide does not rush up to its accustomed mark at once. It advances so many yards one way; it retires a little, and seems as if it repented of its approach to the land, and wished to retreat again to the secret and silent depths of the sea. But if we wait a little, another wave comes with more majestic and onward sweep; and in the course of six hours we find there has been on the whole, though not at every minute of the six hours, progress towards the shore. Many a Christian who thinks he is not growing at all, may be growing in the most important sense of the word. He that is growing more acquainted with the weakness, and the sinfulness, and the waywardness of his own heart, is no doubt thinking that he is going back, but he may be really making preparation for going forward in the noblest sense of that word. We may be growing downwards in lowly humility, not less important in its place than growing upwards in conformity to the Lord Jesus Christ.

Our progress in sanctification may very much determine the place of dignity we are to occupy in the age of glory and of happiness that is to come. Justification is our title to heaven, absolute, perfect, and complete; so that the greatest saint of the greatest maturity, and the lowliest and humblest Christian who was born again yesterday, have both the same title, without any distinction or difference, to everlasting joy. But there is another requisite besides a title to heaven. There is fitness for heaven; the one just as essential as the other, and the one never separate from the other. For where God the Father shows his electing love, there God the Son exhibits his redeeming love, and there God the Spirit sets forth his sanctifying and regenerating love; the last just as needful as the first. If I had a title that would enable me to cross the threshold of the better land; but if I could not breathe its air, mingle in its songs, enjoy its fellowship, hold communion with its King, I should feel it an uncongenial clime, and myself a stranger where others find a home. It is necessary, therefore, not only that I should have a right and a title to heaven, which is complete in my Lord; but that I should have a fitness for heaven, which the Holy Spirit gives me in regeneration and sanctification. Every Christian is equally entitled to cross the threshold; but every Christian is not equally fitted for the same sphere or place of dignity, and greatness, and glory. "One star differeth from another star in glory;" one gem on the walls of the heavenly city from another gem. The everlasting temple is composed of living stones, laid in successive tiers; but the apostles and prophets are laid next and nearest to the foundation stone. Regeneration is the starting point of an endless approximation, but the race is not finished throughout the ceaseless ages of eternity to come; heaven itself will be what earth is, ever running the race, but without its fatigue; ever looking unto Jesus, the author and the finisher of our faith, but without an intervening cloud. It is thus that sanctification, and our progress in it, may determine, not our right to heaven, but our place in heaven. And there is something most interesting in this; that he who has prayed most fervently and frequently now; who has given most diligence to add to his faith virtue, and to virtue temperance, and to temperance patience, and to patience brotherly kindness, and to brotherly kindness charity; that he who has made by grace, on the footing of his acceptance in Christ, the greatest progress in conformity to Jesus, shall still, by grace, but through his fitness for it, occupy a loftier place, and taste a richer joy, and tread a sunnier table-land, in the rest that remaineth for the people of God. Here is the highest encouragement, not indeed to seek heaven by our doings, or merit access by our deservings; but by grace, and through that Spirit who is given to earnest prayer, to seek to be fit for the highest place in heaven. Whatever a person undertakes, he should do it with all his might; whatever we seek to fit ourselves for, we should seek to excel in. If you are a soldier, try to be the best and bravest in the battalion; if a sailor, seek to be the best and ablest on the deck; if you are a tradesman, determine to be the best in the parish. And if you be a Christian, why should you not aim to be the greatest, the wisest, the holiest, and therefore the happiest here and hereafter.

After the apostle had prayed that they may be thus sanctified, he specifies what is the special subject of the process of sanctification; namely, "soul, body, and spirit." I do not pause to make distinctions of a metaphysical kind. I assume that he desires in this prayer, that all which constitutes the man may receive the influence, the sanctifying influence, of the Holy Spirit of God. It is the apostle's prayer, that the mind may comprehend and appreciate in all their brilliancy those glorious truths that are foolishness to the natural man; that all the splendor of heaven may be brought into the darkest nooks of the mind, that it may see plainly what it now sees obscurely; and delight in growing knowledge in which the world can feel no pleasure and covets no share. In the words of the apostle; "The eyes of your understanding being enlightened; that ye may know what is the hope of his calling, and what the riches of the glory of his inheritance in the saints, and what is the exceeding greatness of his power to us-ward who believe, according to the working of his mighty power." There is not a Christian mind that does not need more light, more sympathy with truth. And it is a blessed thought, that the Holy Spirit not only converts and sanctifies the heart, but enlightens, instructs, and convinces the mind. He prays that the heart may be sanctified, and presented blameless; that it may be regenerated by the Spirit, may have sympathy with all that is pure, be sensitively receptive of every holy and happy impression, and have that deep, and pure, and abiding thirst for God which can be satisfied only when time and things temporal are no more. That the body also, and every organ of the body, may be the willing instrument of the mind and the heart in the service of God; that we may be living epistles; not only be good, but seem good; that holiness to the Lord may be inscribed upon the eye, upon the ear, upon the tongue, upon the hands, and upon the feet; and the whole body a sacred fane, every organ a consecrated vessel, and all the faculties and affections of the soul the ministering priests and Levites within, that present to God the ceaseless and fragrant incense of a living and acceptable sacrifice, which is our reasonable service. We are here plainly taught, that all these constituents of man are destined to appear when Christ himself, who is here referred to, shall appear. It is not true that the body is to be despised, cast away as the raiment that we have worn out, and have no further use for. The body of a believer is redeemed by the same precious blood with which his soul is redeemed; and the one shall appear at the resurrection morn, and in obedience to the bidding of him that redeemed it, just as surely as the other. There is not a sailor that sleeps beneath the waves of the Baltic, or the Black Sea, whose only *requiem* is their ceaseless chime, who, if a believer, shall not hear the sound of the last trump, and come forth from the silent waters, no more in the dripping garments of his grave, but in the radiant form of one ready to meet the Lord. There is not a Christian traveller, whose windingsheet is the sands of the desert, who shall not hear that sound and come forth. And there is not a martyr in the Catacombs at Rome, nor a sleeping saint built into the everlasting pyramids, who shall not hear the roll of the last trump; and his body, ransomed by precious blood, shall become again the bright, the holy, the beautiful companion of the consecrated Levite within; and so shall both be for ever with the Lord. It is this blessed hope that inspires us to keep, not only our minds, and our hearts, and our consciences, but our bodies, blameless. Every organ of that body is Christ's; every atom of its dust is his; none of it belongs to Satan or to decay. Satan, and the lust of the eye, and the pride of life, and the love of the world, have no right to a particle of it. It is wholly Christ's; his image is struck on it, his superscription is legible on it; his Holy Spirit is in it; and bright hopes of being for ever with the Lord it may now cherish and rejoice in. Therefore we pray that our whole body, soul, and spirit, may be preserved blameless. We need thus to pray; for what is beyond the reach of sin amid the inhabitants of heaven, is exposed to sin in our case. What is innocence in the lower creation may be guilt and criminality in us. And therefore we are to watch, we are to wait, we are to pray, not only that we may not be blameworthy, but that we may appear and be blameless before God, and before man.

The apostle's prayer is, "that ye may be preserved blameless unto the coming of our Lord Jesus Christ." I doubt if the translation here is correct. It is in the original, εν παρουσιᾳ; "And the very God of peace sanctify you wholly; and I pray God that your whole spirit and soul and body be preserved, or kept, blameless *in* the coming of our Lord Jesus Christ." Our translators have had *unto* suggested to them by the word *kept*, or *preserved;* but the strict meaning is, "*in* the coming;" meaning that perfection of Christian mind, Christian heart, and life, is not obtainable yet, but that it will be. Perfection is a certainty, but it is a certainty embosomed by hope, not yet held fast by faith. And any one that supposes he has attained absolute perfection now, either deceives himself, or deceives the person to whom he says so.

But the very lowliest and humblest and weakest Christian may look forward to that blessed period when all shadows shall be scattered from his mind, when all evil passions, that domineer over or oppress his heart, shall be laid; when his body, relieved from the infirmities, the corruptions, and the traces of evil and of the fall, shall be rebuilt, reconsecrated, and restored; and, in the beautiful language of the apostle in another Epistle, "We shall be made a holy church, without spot, and blameless. That he might present it unto himself a glorious church, not having spot, or wrinkle, or any such thing; but that it should be holy and without blemish." When is this to be? When Christ comes, and presents the church thus to himself. I may mention, in passing, one Greek word used by the apostle in that passage is very remarkable. "Without blemish" — *αμωμος*. The heathen god of laughter was Momus; and it was supposed of him in heathen mythology, that the slightest thing, which the common eye could not see, his acute eye saw, turned into ridicule, and laughed at. Now the apostle's idea is, that Christ's church, the company of believers, the bride, shall be so holy, so spotless, so perfect, in mind, in body, in spirit, that even the god of the heathen that turned into ridicule specks that were invisible to others, shall see nothing in that holy and spotless Apocalypse that he can seize, or turn into a source of laughter. It is a most expressive thought; and indicates the magnificence and glory of that church which Christ shall present unto himself. Angels, startled at the glorious spectacle; the cherubim and seraphim, noticing a white-robed company in the realms of the blessed, that are not natives, but colonists and immigrants, will ask the question, startled by the strange spectacle, Who are these, and whence came they? And the answer given will be, "These are they which came out of great tribulation; and have washed their robes, and made them white in the blood of the Lamb."

The Author of all this — "The very God of peace — sanctify you wholly." "The very God of peace!" What a beautiful characteristic of our God is this, "The very God of peace!" The Author of peace, the Giver of peace; who delights in peace; "justified by faith in whom, we have peace with God, through our Lord Jesus Christ." And this tells us, that wherever peace reigns amidst the nations of the earth, there, even if it be national and natural peace, is a reflection, half spent in its transit, but still a reflection, from the God of peace. Mr. Howells used often to say in Long Acre chapel, that if he saw two dogs at peace with each other, he saw there "the very God of peace;" that one atom of peace left in a world that has plunged into war with God is a trace of the lingering mercy and favoring goodness of our God. Wherever there is peace, therefore, there is a reflection of his presence; and wherever there is war amid the nations of the earth, on one side or on the other, — the right side God knows, and it is not difficult often for us to determine on a national scale, — there is evidence of the answer to the question, "Whence come wars and fightings among you? Come they not from your lusts, which desire, and have not?" And if God be the very God of peace upon the earth, he is eminently so in the church of Christ. If war is unjustifiable in nations, oh! how inexcusable is it in those that profess to be Christians! There are sections of the Christian church, true Christians, who are opposed to national war on any terms, or on any grounds, defensive or aggressive; but if we come into their chapels, or stand on their platforms, how often do we find they are at war, exterminating ecclesiastical war, with each other! Now give me national war, which has many of the materials of grandeur and heroism, rather than that most horrible of all, ecclesiastical wars. The worst battles, next to those fought in lawyers' offices, have been fought on professedly

Christian platforms. If we hate war, the war that breaks out with consuming fury amid nations, we should remember that nations ought to look to churches for the example they are to follow; and if war begin at the house of God, how can we expect that there will be peace amid the nations that know him not? God is the very God of peace; and peace on earth ought to be the first recognition of his sovereignty. But the reason, perhaps, of this special attribute introduced here by the apostle, is, that all the prescriptions he has given, are dependent upon our acceptance with God, and our justification by him. St. Paul says, in the fifth chapter of the Epistle to the Romans, at the first verse, "Therefore being justified by faith — we have peace with God." And the apostle, accordingly, in praying that the God of peace would sanctify them, assumes that they are justified, and therefore that they will be, as he prays they may be, wholly sanctified.

We are frail, and need such prayers as these. We need to pray for ourselves, that he who has begun in us the good work, would carry it on to the end. And what a blessed thought, that he who is the Alpha, is the Omega; that he that begins, concludes; that he who is the Author, is also the Finisher of our faith. It needs a Divine hand to sow the incorruptible seed; it needs a Divine sunshine to ripen and mature the fruits; it needs a Divine hand to weed the soil, and keep the fair flowers from perishing. It is literally true of grace, as it is of nature, that "in God we live, we move, we have our being." We must therefore pray to him, if we would persevere, that he would preserve us, soul, body, and spirit, blameless, unto the day of his coming. Here too is a precedent for ministers of the gospel. Paul, in this Epistle, has preached the glorious truths of the gospel of Christ, and followed those truths with practical prescriptions of the most precious kind. But he, the eloquent and the gifted, so felt that all he had done would be utterly without fruit if left to itself, that he closes this most eloquent and impressive appeal with earnest and fervent prayer. He felt, "Not by might nor by power, but by my Spirit." The best peroration to the most eloquent sermon, is fervent prayer that God would follow it with his heavenly blessing.

But whilst God is the Author of all this sanctification, let us not forget that there are *media* of it. God works by means; and our blessed Redeemer has told us, in his own prayer, the means of our sanctification. "Sanctify them through thy truth; thy word is truth." It is through the truth that we are sanctified. We are not sanctified in ignorance, in indolence, or in infidelity; we are sanctified through belief of the truth. All the truths that God has revealed, have this sanctifying tendency, "Elect according to the foreknowledge of God through belief of the truth unto sanctification." Again, we read, "Seeing all these things shall be dissolved"—that is a revelation of God's truth—"what manner of persons ought ye to be?" Again, "As he that hath called you is holy, so be ye holy in all conversation and godliness." "Born of incorruptible seed." And if the truth, then, be a medium or means of our sanctification, how important it is that we should come into contact with a faithful ministry! Men are rational, responsible, and susceptible of impression; and God works by these, and through these, to generate that character which is ripened day by day for heaven and for eternal joy. And when we sit under a faithful ministry, we hear motives, hopes, precepts, prescriptions, promises, doctrines; all of which are consecrated by God to be a ministry to the soul for conviction and for conversion. The farmer sows the seed; but if no rain and no sunshine light upon it, there will be no harvest. On the other hand, God gives the sunshine, the rains, and the dews; but if there be no seed sown, there will be no harvest. The terrestrial toil, which is ours, or the means, and the celestial blessing, which is God's, must both go together; that through the truth, and by the Holy Spirit, we may be sanctified and made fit for the kingdom of heaven. God uses also for our sanctification, not only truth, but losses, and crosses, and afflictions, and trials. I believe all these things in providence are consecrated, just as all these truths in the Bible are directed, to the believer's growth in grace. Many have been brought into close contact with the eternal world by seeing one loved and cherished entering there, and its gates closing behind him. Many a one who has lost the riches of this world, has learned in the loss for the first time to grope, and ultimately to find the unsearchable riches of Christ. Loneliness created by death, by loss, by separation, has been often blessed to be acquaintance and friendship with God. And many a believer has been constrained to say that he felt in his sad hours what he never dreamed of in his happy ones, that God made him, that eternity must receive him, that a Saviour died for him. And thus a Christian's losses, and sorrows, and trials, are, by God's grace, made to work together for good to them that love him. "The tree," says the poet,

> "Sucks kindlier nature from a soil enriched
> By its own fallen leaves — so man is made
> In heart and spirit from deciduous hopes,
> And things that seem to perish."

We must not, therefore, be satisfied with any height we may have attained, or progress we have made in the Christian life; but ever forgetting the things that are behind, stretch forward to those that are before. Still give all diligence to "add to your faith virtue, and to virtue temperance, and to temperance patience, and to patience brotherly kindness, and to brotherly kindness charity." The living belief that God has planted in the depths of our heart, must, if it be real, grow in vigor and effloresce into all that is beautiful and holy. No Christian, however great his acquirements upon earth, however close his conformity to God, must ever be satisfied with any thing short of entire conformity to his image, and the enjoyment of the dignity of God's freedmen, and the liberty of Christ's servants even in the world that now is. Earnestly and often let us pray that the Sanctifier may dwell in our hearts. Prayer is the expression of wants that we feel, and of desires for attainments that we have not. And if we desire that all the beautiful, interesting, and important prescriptions we have studied, may be practised by us, we must earnestly pray that the very God of peace may sanctify us wholly; and that spirit, and soul, and body may be preserved blameless unto his coming. Live in this world as not your home. It is the field of conflict; a camp as much as a nursery; often the one, often the other. Set your affections upon things that are above, strive after things that are before. Grow in grace, and in knowledge of our Saviour Christ Jesus. Do not regard the world as a workshop, in which you are to toil for bread to feed the body; but as a porch of heaven, a vestibule of eternity; ever aspiring, ever praying, and ever rejoicing in the assured hope that one day we shall be like him, "for we shall see him as he is."

# CHAPTER X.

## BUSINESS.

"In laborer's ballad oft more piety
God finds than in Te Deum's melody."

"Not slothful in business; fervent in spirit; serving the Lord." — ROMANS xii. 11.

BEHOLD a practical prescription devolving primarily upon those who have enjoyed great privileges, and learned precious truths. The doctrines of the gospel must be translated into precepts. We have to learn that the loftiest truths that are revealed from heaven, necessarily, if truly and rightly received, blossom into the fairest practices that can adorn and beautify the earth. We need direction in our worldly life, for our living, acting, toiling in the world; we need to see that religion must inspire, and regulate, and sustain all our conduct in every department of the world. We may not be slothful in our worldly business, but diligent, and yet fervent in spirit; the inner fervor of the heart inspiring the outer labor of the hand, — serving our Master who is in heaven, the Lord Christ.

There is a general tendency among us all to divorce religion from business; to give religion exclusive jurisdiction in the church or the chapel; and to give business exclusive jurisdiction in the market or on the exchange. Our tendency is to assign religion wholly to our Sundays, and to assign business wholly and exclusively to our weekdays; to regard religion as a department proper enough in its place, and business as a totally distinct and independent department, proper enough in its place. Religion is for our Sunday life; and business, we think, is for our daily life. We would not for the world bring the ledger into the house of prayer; and then, with a strange consistency, we will not for the world bring the Bible into the counting-house. In all this there is a radical mistake; there is a great flaw in such reasoning, and in such apportionment. It assumes, as I have said, that religion is a department distinct in itself; finished and final on its own day, in its own place; but that it has nothing whatever to do with the varied spheres and provinces of social life into which the Christian is called, to discharge the duties and responsibilities of the world. Those that think so, seem universally to feel that a consecrated place is suitable for the one; and that the market and the exchange are only suitable for the other: that religion is the business of priests, or clergymen, or ministers; that business must be the religion of merchants, and tradesmen, and commercial men; in short, that religion is a sort of transcendental, rarefied air, very suitable to breathe on consecrated heights, on Calvary, on Mount Zion, or on Mount Tabor; but that it is too thin an air to be breathed upon the low levels of ordinary life; or to be allowed on any terms, or for any consideration, to penetrate into the places where this world's transactions are carried on. In short, religion, in the estimate of these men, is locked up on the Sunday night in the sanctuary; and all she says and all she taught they think it is their duty devoutly to forget, as soon as they have closed their Bibles, left the church or the chapel, and entered on the more serious, the more grave, and we fear, in many minds, the more important, duties and obligations of the world. Now the consequence of all this is very serious; it is really a fatal error; the practical results of it are extremely mischievous. We come to regard the church as holy, and we do well in that; but we also come to regard the exchange as altogether profane. And whilst we would insist upon the fulfilment of all the precepts of the decalogue in the consecrated place, and on the floor of the church; we do not at all care to drag these precepts, as we say, into the profane parts and provinces of this present world. We think Christianity too delicate, too dainty a thing, too easily ruffled, injured, done violence to, to bring her into everyday life, or to soil her robes by suffering her to appear in the markets of this present world. The result is, the market is left to herself; trade becomes mere gambling, commerce degenerates into something intensely secular, intensely atheistic. You have the holy place, with its holy influences; but you think it is more appropriate that the place you have chalked out as profane — namely, the world — should not be troubled by the holy, the sanctifying, and directing influences of the religion of Christ. Hence the Protestant will stoutly contend for an open Bible in the house of God, in the pulpit, and in the pew; but very many of these very Protestants will say to the Bible, when it knocks at the doors of their counting-houses, "Hitherto, but no further." They think the Bible an admirable book open and unclasped in the house of prayer; but it would disturb the counting-house, it would injure the ledger, it would affect our profits at the end of the year; it would not allow us to say, This is good, when it is bad. We will contend as stoutly as Martin Luther for the open Bible in the sanctuary; but we will contend as stoutly against its introduction into the house of business. We want to die with the Bible, we want to cherish the hopes of the Bible; but we want to do business altogether without the Bible, and independent of it, and as if no Bible were actually in existence. You can see almost by my statement of it, how outrageous such sentiments as these are, and how unnatural, unscriptural, and unjust. We not only thus degrade business, but we do double wrong; we dishonor religion itself. We seem to honor it, but really we deeply dishonor it. We lift religion up to a lofty place; we enthrone her upon a lofty summit; and we praise, and magnify, and adorn her; we build cathedrals in her honor, we chant hymns to her praise; we call her great, and good, and noble; but we cannot admit that religion shall come down, and mingle in our homes, our houses, and our markets. We say to religion on the Sunday, "Hosanna in the highest;" but on the weekday, Away with it, away with it, it is not proper it should be here. It is far more honor to Christianity, to this blessed gospel, and to the Lord of the gospel, — and doing more homage to it than building cathedrals, and celebrating her praises on Sunday, — to invoke her to leave the lofty place where we have carried her, to come out of the sanctuary where we have tried to shut her up, and to bid her come down, and tread the path of daily and of public life; till cottage hearths become holier than ancient altars, and the humblest peasant's home more sacred than the grandest cathedral. It is not by enthroning religion on Sunday in the sanctuary; but it is by bringing religion into the counting-house, the exchange, and the market, that we really honor her. It is not by studied service, by early matins, by twilight vespers, by chimes of holy bells that summon us three times a day to come to worship, that we do homage to Christ. True, such is thought religion; in Rome it is pronounced so; by the imitators of Rome it is felt that you may spend the evening in the opera if only an hour before you come to vespers; and that in the morning, you may do any thing you like, provided you have come only first to matins: if you attend to religion in consecrated places, in canonical hours, that is being religious; and as for the intervals between, you may follow the lust of the eye, the pride of life, and the love of this present world. Now it seems to me that to be truly religious is not to go to matins, nor to vespers, nor to go to church on Sunday (though this last is right and dutiful); but it is to bring the motives, the hopes, the precepts, the spirit of religion into all our walks and ways in the world, till our whole life becomes religious. True Christianity is not a nun, to be locked up within cloistered walls; but she is a wife, a mother, the nearest and the dearest in all the walks and vocations of this present life. She is not to be your light upon Sundays, but your guide upon weekdays. Piety does not retreat from business, but it seizes business, sanctifies it, and makes it sacred. The gospel of Jesus is not to be a voice crying in the desert, like that of John the Baptist; but if I understand religion, it is to open a shop, it is to freight ships, it is to keep accounts, it is to write up your ledgers, it is to wear an apron till it be as holy as a bishop's sleeve, and to wield a spade as responsibly and devoutly as a monarch sways a sceptre. The true characteristic of religion is to go down into every thing, rise up to the highest, till, like the atmosphere, it embraces all in its beneficent and its beautiful folds.

Such is the meaning of being fervent in spirit, serving the Lord; and yet, not being slothful in business. We do not want to make sabbath days worldly; but to make weekdays holy. We want religion, and the Bible requires that true religion shall move with the whole force and splendor of a celestial presence wherever man goes; on the deck, on the battle field, on the exchange, in the market, in the counting-house — everywhere. Religion is not a profession; it is not a subject for a special day; it is not a thing tied down to a place, restricted within a time. You came to the church on Sunday to learn religion; to feel its motives, to deepen your impressions, to get an answer to your prayers. But you have not done with religion; when the Sunday is finished, you only begin to have to do with religion. You have been as pupils on Sunday; you are to go out as practitioners on the Monday. You have been apprentices to-day, learning the lessons that you want to know; and you are to go forth on Monday, and all the days of the week, practising those lessons as you may be able. But this is in perfect contrast to the idea which I have referred to; namely, that religion is something to be kept entirely aloof from the world; like the electricity in the electric jar, to sparkle on the Sunday; indicate its existence there; but on the Monday to be entirely repudiated, laid aside; it is, and ought to be, held like the electricity throughout the whole universe, that balances the orbs, gives fertility to the soil, and keeps all in harmony and order. I ask of you, what in religion would you exclude from business? What grace would you exclude from your counting-house? Not truth, surely; not justice, surely; not love, not honesty, not integrity. These, you say, ought to be in business; and if these ought to be in business, where are the roots? Planted in business soil, these graces will soon wither and crumple up; but planted by the fountain of living waters, they will grow fresh and green; and not only be the stay, the cohesion, but the ornament of your character and conduct in the world. Would you exclude prayer from business? Surely not. Is your own right hand able to do all? Are you lord of the winds and commander of the waves? If these are above your control, does it not seem proper you should pray to Him who can control them? Is praise unbecoming in the counting-house? If you have been blessed, if you have been prospered in the world, if you have been successful in business, surely it is natural, it is instinct, it is duty, to praise him who has blessed you, and none can curse you; and blessed your basket and your store, and made you merry. The church, sometimes seen on the continent of Europe, built in the middle of a market-place, is a very beautiful type, whether meant so or not, of Christianity enthroned in the market as well as in the church; sanctifying, directing, guiding, and inspiring all; till business becomes sacred, weekdays become holy; and God is blessed and adored by hand and foot, and everywhere, and on all occasions.

But let us look very briefly at the component parts of this beautiful connection. We have, "Not slothful in business," or, diligent in business; we have next, "fervent in spirit;" we have lastly, "serving the Lord." I have shown that religion and business are to be like woof and warp, constituting together human life; not two separate things; but the one sanctifying, toning, shaping, directing, the other. True religion is not one department, and business another; but while business is not to enter into religion, and profane it, religion insists upon entering into business, and sanctifying it. And this will not make business worse, or the man of business lazy; on the contrary, when fervent in spirit, serving the Lord, it is possible, nay, it is duty, to be not slothful in business. In examining the passage, not to be slothful in business, we can see how much it is in keeping with other passages of Scripture. What does an apostle say? "If any man will not work, neither should he eat." It is as much a duty to be a hard-working, industrious merchant, tradesman, physician, lawyer, as it is to pray, to read your Bibles, and to praise God. The one is just as really a duty as the other. Labor existed in Paradise before sin entered into our world; only it was labor then without its harassing fatigue. Labor must exist now. You have children to provide for, you have your bread to earn; and that which was the recreation of innocence in Paradise, is become the necessity of mankind outside of it. And if any man will not work, not only should he not eat, but as a matter of fact, he will get nothing to eat, unless he have recourse to begging, which is dishonorable, or to stealing, which is dishonest. And besides, whatever it is a man's duty to do, it is his duty to do with all his might. If it be right, you are to do it with all your might; if it be wrong, you are not to do it at all. And therefore a Christian merchant, if he be a true Christian, is not to be lazier, or less attentive to his business, than the most grasping, covetous, money scraping miser that is to be found on the Royal Exchange. He is just to be industrious as he, in seeking fresh markets, in improving the texture of the material he prepares, in calculating all the contingencies of trade, in looking out for the best profits, in trying to make the best bargain. He is not to be behind on the Exchange, or in the market; it is his duty with all his might to do whatsoever his hand findeth to do. And I need not quote as proofs of this from the Bible such passages as these: "He that loveth pleasure shall be a poor man;" that is, he that playeth instead of working will come to poverty. Again, "Love not sleep, lest you come to poverty." He that sleeps in the morning, instead of being up and looking after his business, will come to poverty. What intense good sense are in these ancient aphorisms of Solomon! "He that is slothful in work is brother to him that is a waster." They seem not to belong to the same class; yet the profligate, who extravagantly squanders his money, is only the creation of the lazy and the indolent man, who does not use proper efforts, and employ proper diligence, in earning his money. But it is a singular fact, that prodigality and indolence, extravagance and laziness, are very often found together. A Christian merchant need not be indolent. On the contrary, if he be a Christian, and a merchant, or a tradesman, or whatever he be, he ought to try to be the very best, and the most successful in the parish; and if he do not, I would have him clearly understand, it is not the gospel nor its requirements that prevents him from being so.

But in spite of all this, he is to be fervent in spirit. That is to say, he is to maintain communion with God. While his hand is busy at the spade, or at the loom, or at the counter, or with the pen, or with the lancet, his heart is not to be wholly there, but he is to be lifted up above it. This world is not to cool the warmth of his spirit; but the warmth of his spirit is to raise the temperature of this world and of all that are about him. He is to carry the fervency of a sanctified spirit into the most commonplace facts of this present world. This religion must warm our business life; our business life must not freeze our religion. And do you think that the man that is truly a Christian, or who maintains this fervor of spirit, will be lazy? — do you suppose that this will obstruct his business? Do you think that it will ever be an apology on his lips or in his mind for inattention to business? I believe the very reverse. God's great law is, " Seek first the kingdom of God and his righteousness, and all the rest will be added." If you maintain this fervency of spirit, instead of finding it interrupting or obstructing your business, it will give impulse, vigour, energy to it. Like the ancient patriarch, you will go out with your sack to get corn; and will return with the sack filled with the corn; and you will find hid in the sack, not, literally, a golden cup as he did, but something more precious than all, a full sack filled with this world's success, and buried in the midst of it the blessing that maketh rich, and addeth no sorrow. Thus shall we discover that it is possible to maintain fervency of spirit, and yet to be not slothful, or to be diligent, in business. Look around at the nations of the earth at this moment. The nations that are the most successful in trade, are they not those where Christianity has risen highest? America and Britain probably transact more business, to use the ordinary phrase, than all the nations of the world besides. Where there is the greatest fervor of Christian spirit there is the greatest success in mercantile enterprise; for a Christian, as an individual, has in his Christianity the very elements of industry. Whatever withdraws man from the dominion of the senses, from excess of wine, from revellings and banquetings, — and Christianity does this, — will give him more time to spend in application to the calls and claims of business. A Dorcas, when sewing garments for the poor, no doubt had first to use diligently the time given her in preparing her own. He that toils most for others has necessarily first toiled most for himself. It is the Christian that has the best idea of the value of time. He has learned to estimate time, to see its preciousness, to calculate its shortness. We therefore in this world, as well as in the things of a better world, work while it is called today, knowing that night cometh, when no man can work. If there were nothing else in Christianity than its sabbath, it alone would be a guarantee that the Christian who enjoys it will be the more diligent in business. Sabbath day rest is refreshment after the six days' toil, and a new impetus to the mind to undergo the fatigues of the week that is to follow. The least slothful in business will be the most fervent in spirit; or rather, reversing it, the fervent in spirit will not be slothful in business. The heart that is where Christ is, will ever wield the busiest, and generally the most successful, hand.

In both we are to serve the Lord. "Not slothful in business, fervent in spirit, serving the Lord." The last prescription in the clause is explained in such passages as these.

"Servants, be obedient to your own masters, as unto Christ; not with eye-service, as men-pleasers; but servants of Christ, doing the will of God." See here what gives dignity to the most menial servant. Let your situation in this world be the humblest and the most menial; you fulfil its duties, not because there may be a harsh or a tyrant master over you, but because you are doing the work that Christ has assigned you. Your sense of responsibility to Christ consecrates all you do; and you do not feel humbled, but dignified and ennobled, in doing the lowest service, for you serve the Lord Christ. "Whatever you do, do it heartily, as to the Lord." If you sweep a crossing, if you keep accounts, if you serve a mistress or a master, do it heartily, not as unto them, though that is right; but look above them, and feel it is a duty that you are fulfilling as to the Lord. And again, "Whatsoever you do, in word or in deed, do all in the name of the Lord Jesus Christ." But you naturally say, We shall find next week that we shall be so overwhelmed with the pressure of business, we shall be so busy from early morning to late at night, that we can scarcely get time to think about religion.

I do not prescribe that when you are making an article of commerce, or summing up your accounts, or prescribing as a physician, or drawing up a case as a solicitor, or pleading at the bar as a barrister, at every moment, and at every step, and continually, you are to feel a sense of God's presence. That cannot be. You are so absorbed, as common sense shows, doing the thing that is given you, that you cannot have the thought of God and religion like a continuous presence. But, nevertheless, you may be doing all to the Lord, and doing it wholly for him. For instance, a father goes into a distant land to toil, because he cannot get bread for his family at home. He labors in that land. He is busy, perhaps, sowing or ploughing for twelve hours together. He thinks of nothing but of the furrows, the seeds, or of the plough, or the harrow, and all the demands of agriculture. But, nevertheless, the reason for his being there, the motive power of his being there, is to find bread for his family and his children. So you may be busy all day in traffic, in commerce, in business, in trade. You may not, from six o'clock in the morning till six o'clock at night, have the thoughts of religion, because you are utterly absorbed in the business that is before you. But the reason of your doing that business, when you look back, and the reason why you are engaged in that business, when you look forward, is that you may do God's will in that sphere, place, and province in which his providence has placed you; and while fervent in spirit, and diligent in business, you are serving the Lord Christ. Or, to take another illustration, a minister of Christ may be anxious to find out the meaning of a Greek or a Hebrew word. If you call upon him, he is searching two or three hours into different writers to ascertain the derivation and application of this word. For at least half a dozen hours, that minister may have been preparing his sermon, and yet he has been so busy in searching out that word, its derivation, its application, its usages, that he has had no time or spare thought to think of any thing but of this one Hebrew or Greek word, and all its applications. Nevertheless, the reason why he makes the search, and his joy when he has concluded the search, arises, ultimately, from his desire to win souls, and to spread the kingdom of Christ. So with you; you may be in the world, whatever your situation or employment may be in that world, serving Christ, whilst you are utterly absorbed for the hour or two in the business that is before you. And if you were not to attend to that business with all your energy, you would soon lose your business, and the opportunities of doing service to Christ's cause, or good to mankind. It is a grand mistake in the world to think that you can only be religious when engaged in religious work. That is not true. You are religious when you are building, or ploughing, or sowing, or reaping. If any thing were to go wrong, or any temptation urged to do wrong, you would fall back upon the grand governing motive, "Serve the Lord Christ:" but for the time you are engaged wholly in the work; and it is not irreligious to do it with all your might, when the motive for which you do it, and the end to which you do it, is a Divine one. It is not true, that doing religious work is necessarily being religious. A man may spend twelve hours every day in building a church, and may be an absolute heathen or an atheist. Another man may spend sixteen hours a day in building a warehouse, and may be doing a most holy and religious work. It is not the work that makes the workman holy, but it is the workman's heart that consecrates the toil, and makes all he does to be serving the Lord Christ.

Do you say, All that is very well in the pulpit, or at a communion table, but we cannot carry it into business. Now I am showing how you may carry into your business your religion, and that your religion will not lead you to be slothful, lazy, unsuccessful, but the very reverse. Whenever, therefore, I hear men say, I failed in my business because I paid so much attention to my church or my chapel, I at once answer, that is not true; there is not an atom of truth in it. And you may depend upon it, it was not your attention to your church and your chapel, but something else. No man ever became less industrious because he became really pious. Let us never plead religion as an excuse for inattention to business. That is a lazy apprentice, and not a religious apprentice, who says, I went to the prayer-meeting, and therefore I could not attend to my master's order. That is indolence, and not piety, that says, I have failed to do this, or I could not execute your message in the proper time, because I turned aside to distribute a few tracts, or went to talk with a pious man. Religion bids you do your duty to your master diligently, not slothfully; with all your might; and this is religion, when you do it. To make the pretence of distributing tracts, or a conversation with a religious man, an excuse for inattention to your master's orders, or for not executing those orders with all your might, is either direct hypocrisy, or it is a grievous misconception of what religion is. Never plead that business keeps you from religion; still less that religion, at all events, keeps you from business.

Do not put off religion, piety, the fear of God, acceptance of the only Saviour, devotion, and dedication to him, till after you have become rich, and retired. The secret why many say, I have no time to attend to religion till I have despatched this business, or got this matter off my hands, is their making haste to be rich. Religion is to be in business, not after business. It is to be the life of business, not a postscript to business. It is to direct, sanctify, sustain, ennoble business; not to be a separate thing to be attended to afterwards.

And lastly, in the midst of all your diligence on earth, never forget, "What shall it profit a man, if he gain the whole world, and lose his own soul?" Do not so look to business, that you forget the great, the essential, the primary thing, salvation. And do not make religion, or the things that belong to your peace, a plea or pretext for inattention to your business, and undutifulness to your master, or disobedience to those that are set over you in the world. And in our daily life, and in our Sabbath life, in the counting-house, or at a communion table, or at our daily meals, may the Lord bless us and keep us; may the Lord make his face shine upon us, and be gracious to us; may the Lord lift up the light of his countenance upon us, and give us peace, through Christ Jesus.

## CHAPTER XI.

### FEAR NOT.

" And thou, too, whosoe'er thou art
That readest this brief psalm,
As one by one thy hopes depart,
Be resolute and calm.

Oh fear not in a world like this;
And thou shalt know ere long,—
Know how sublime a thing it is
To suffer and be strong."

" Fear thou not: for I am with thee: be not dismayed; for I am thy God." — Isa. xli. 10.

Men are liable to be afraid when they find themselves in the midst of perils, whether by sea or by land. They need a prescription against fear, not a prescription against feeling. If we are in the midst of battle, exposed to shot and shell, or on the deck no less exposed, we cannot but feel, because we are flesh and blood; yet though we feel, we may not fear, because we are Christians, and the promise is applicable to us always and everywhere, I am with thee; "I am thy God; I will strengthen thee, yea, I will help thee, yea, I will uphold thee with the right hand of my righteousness."

We live in startling times. Peril surrounds and envelops us like an atmosphere. The first showers of the last judgments, predicted to come on the earth, begin already to baptize it. Look where we will, there are clouds and darkness in this world, but look where we ought, and there are bright beams of the unutterable glory, each pointing to the blessed truth, "Lift up your heads, for your redemption draweth nigh." But, without specifying what may be the features of this age, which is needless and unnecessary, we know that in every age, in every part of the world, on every level of daily life, "through much tribulation," of some sort, "we must enter into the kingdom of heaven." Some men's tribulation is in the sick frame; that of others lies in their family; the tribulation of others is more secret and unseen, but no less real; and the tribulation of many may be sorrowful sympathy with the whole world that lieth in darkness and in the wicked one. But in some shape or other, if we be Christian pilgrims with our faces in the right direction, through much tribulation we must enter into the kingdom of heaven. Our blessed Lord, the great Captain of the faith, has said, "In the world ye shall have tribulation;" if he had stopped there, ours would be a sad and sorrowful lot. Blessed be his name! he adds what neutralizes all, "but in me ye shall have peace." Precious thought! Look to the world, and within the world, and you are dismayed; but look beyond the world to Him who is enthroned far above it, and in Him you shall have peace. The Stoic — of the old heathen sect, or denomination of heathen mythology — believed that man became excellent in proportion as he became hardened into granite. His idea was, that to feel was disgraceful, undignified, undutiful; and that the perfect man, the true, the good man, neither felt, nor laughed, nor wept; was neither pained, nor pleased; but lived as if these things were mere fables, fancies, or dreams. Now he must have had a great deal of hypocrisy to enable him to say he did not feel these things; and he must have undergone a very great hardening process, and made great progress in it, before he could approach within a thousand miles of that strange state which was thought the very *acmé* of philosophical perfection — insensibility to pain or pleasure. But the Christian prescription runs not thus. It has no sympathy with the Stoic. It does not destroy the man in order to evolve the Christian, as Zeno proposed to destroy the man in order to eliminate the Stoic; it accepts the man, and elevates, sanctifies, inspires him. Christianity does not refuse to say, "Weep." What would be the use of bidding a man not weep? It is a relief to his sorrows: there is no grief like that which cannot weep: when grief is bitterest, tears dilute and lessen it. Hence Christianity says so beautifully, "Weep; but weep as though you wept not;" and "Rejoice; but rejoice as though you rejoiced not." Is there not here, as elsewhere in this book, common sense? Are not these truths, that come home to our hearts as essentially true, real, and human; and evidences, in their place and measure, that the book that is pervaded by such maxims as these, is a book that Stoics not only never read, and Peripatetics never knew, but that philosophers of any sect never wrote, that God, in short, inspired? The bravest man is not always the most hardhearted. I have heard of surgeons who were employed in the severest operations because they were supposed to be the most insensible; but I have heard of other surgeons, possessed of most tender and sensitive feeling, who nevertheless had that thorough grasp, and practical control, as it were, of their own sensibilities, that they could steel and stretch them for the moment to the stern duty that devolved upon them. The man who has fine feeling, and yet can act as if he had none, is a far nobler type of character than the man that has no feeling at all. It has often been remarked, that the bravest soldiers and the most heroic sailors are not the mere brute animals that have nothing but muscles and flesh and blood, and no feeling,and still less the miserable Russians, who are intoxicated with alcohol in order to bring them up to the charge; but men who feel most keenly; yet at the same time seeing duty as plain as daylight, they nerve their hearts for the discharge and the fulfilment of it. There appeared in the papers the other day a letter written by a soldier in the East to his family at home, giving an account of his being for the first time in action. He said that at first he felt as one naturally feels, and as the bravest must feel; but these first sensibilities passed away. In an assault on Bomarsund, he saw perfectly well that it was a bullet from his *Minié* that laid low a Russian opposed to him. He had just time to go up to the wounded Russian soldier he knew he had shot; and on seeing him he says, I had no feeling when I fired; I had no sensibility to disturb me; but when I saw the wound that I had made, and looked into that dying man's eye, I wept bitterly, and like a child, at what I had done. Now here was a man that could do his duty as a hero only could, and yet had all the tenderness of a woman, all the sensibility of a child, and not the least brave, or the least nerved for his responsibilities in the field. Men may have keen feeling, and yet do their duty; they may weep, and yet act as though they wept not; may feel, and yet feel as though they felt not; may rejoice too, and yet rejoice as though they rejoiced not; and so the beautiful combination of the tenderest humanity and the loftiest Christian principle constitutes that perfect man, which ancient philosophy longed for and never saw; perfect in Christ; perfected in us in proportion as we approximate to him, the great model of all excellence.

Let us try to enumerate some of the things of daily life that man is apt to fear; the things that we all meet with, and must in some degree feel, but which none of us need fear. Let us not take a human catalogue, but a Divine one. They are given in the eighth chapter of the Epistle to the Romans, at the thirty-fifth verse, where we find the whole list of what man has more or less to go through. "Who shall separate us from the love of Christ?" he says; "shall tribulation?" That is the first distress. The second, "persecution;" the third, "famine;" the fourth, "nakedness;" the fifth, "peril;" the sixth, "the sword." From the thirty-eighth verse; "death — life — angels — principalities — powers — things present — things to come — height, depth, nor any other creature." You can think of these things; some of them you meet with; all of them you must feel when they overtake you; none of them you must fear; for in them "I am with thee; I will help thee; yea, I will uphold thee with the right hand of my righteousness." The first is "tribulation." The word *tribulation* is the translation of the Greek θλιψις; literally, "pressure," the kind of force applied to the grape in order to squeeze the juice out of it for fermentation. The word "pressure," is very familiar to us all. "The money market," they say, "is tight;" or, "There is a pressure in the money market." Again, "I am pressed for money;" or, "I am pressed for time." The apostle says, "Fear not pressure." When the worldly man, who does not know the truth, or love the Saviour, is subjected to the pressure of circumstances, he desponds, despairs, or destroys himself. But when a Christian is under this pressure, like the aromatic plant that gives out its most fragrant perfume the more violently it is trodden upon and pressed, a Christian appears under heavy pressure more beautiful and more like Christ than before. Feel, but fear not. The second is "distress." The word which we have rendered *distress*, is, literally, *tightness*, or narrowness, or straitness of place. It is translated into the popular phrase, "I cannot turn myself round" — "I do not know how to turn myself. I cannot see an outlet; I am shut in, and can see no means of escape." Now what are you to do? "Feel not" I dare not prescribe; that would be absurd; that would be saying, "Do not be men;" but "Fear not" I may prescribe, for that is God's own blessed prescription. The Israelites were once in this straitness of place. There was the Red Sea before them, too deep for them to wade; there was Pharaoh with all his chariots thundering in their rear. If they went back, they would be put to the sword; if they went forward, they would be drowned. Then what were they to do? The answer was given, just the answer that Paul gives as the ground of "fear not" — "Stand still and see the salvation of God." Now I know it is a very difficult prescription. It is exceedingly easy to bustle, to do something; but it is the most difficult of all to stand still, to wait, and wait patiently, resting on the Lord, knowing that he will bring it to pass. But we have many texts that justly and truly express this state of things. They said, "Neither know we what to do; but our eyes are upon thee." So the apostle says, "We had the sentence of death in ourselves" — that is, there was no help in ourselves — "that we might not trust in ourselves, but in God, that raiseth the dead." Now it is exceedingly useful to a Christian man to be shut into this narrow place; because when he is at his wits' end, when he sees that he can do nothing upon earth, then he begins to look up to Him who can do all from heaven; and he learns to wait upon God when there is nothing else to wait upon, and to lean upon the rod and the staff of the Son of Jesse when all human props have been utterly swept away. Such discipline as this is good; we need it; and when God sends it, it is well.

The next trial enumerated by the apostle is "famine." There are three great plagues with which God punishes sinners, chastens Christians, pestilence, and famine, and war. It is a very delightful thought to us, and I hope one that has made our hearts all thankful to God, that we have had in the autumn of 1854 the most splendid harvest that our country has reaped for many a year. And if in the present state of the world abroad, and of public health at home, a famine had smitten us, nobody can conceive what the issues might have been. God, therefore, in the day of his east wind, stays his rough wind; and if he takes away one blessing, he compensates by the gift of another. But famine, nevertheless, may come, as well as war, or plague, or pestilence; and when it does come, to whom must we look for bread? Alas, what a miserable inscription is that which I read on the Hotel de Ville at Brussels. On the very front of that exquisite Gothic edifice, it is written up in large letters that all may read from the *marché*, —

A BELLO, FAME, ET PESTE, MARIA, LIBERA NOS;

that is, "From plague, pestilence, and war, Mary, deliver us." Think of that being written on the most public edifice of that beautiful capital! But that litany we do not pray; Mary has no power to answer it, there is not the remotest probability that she hears it; we are certain that we are not to pray to her; we look far above her; we know the blessed assurance, "He that hears the cry of the wild raven; — he that clothes the grass, which to-day is, and to-morrow is cast into the oven, will he not clothe you, O ye of little faith?" In famine long before now he has made the heavens rain down bread; he has made the rocks melt into cool and refreshing water; and he has made the wild ravens carry food, rather than his prophet should want bread. If these be facts, remember God's arm is not shortened, that he cannot do these things again; his ear is not heavy, that he cannot hear our prayer still; and therefore should gaunt famine come, feel it we must, it is human nature to feel it, and no philosophy can appease hunger; but though we feel it, we will not fear; but we will trust, because God is with us, and he has promised to strengthen us: and if nature refuses, he can act and work above nature, and do exceeding abundantly above all we ask.

The next trial is "persecution." These are days in which, as far as we can see, there exists no persecution on any side or by any party. The only people now that would indulge in the luxury of persecution have not the power; while those that have the power have no disposition, because taught the more excellent way. Persecution is the greatest blunder Satan ever perpetrated upon earth. He lost his mind, and his ingenuity, and his talent, when he originated that prescription for putting down truth. If you will read all history, you will find that persecution never put down a truth, and it never permanently backed up a lie. It fails in both directions. There is something in man's honest mind that will not submit to be crushed, and beaten, and driven to conviction. He may be persuaded; he cannot, and he will not, and he ought not, to be forced into an opinion. But persecution may come; and all its awakened terrors may again be inflicted upon us. We know that the germ and principle of it are still nursed most carefully and closely in Rome. Its emissaries have the will if they had the power to make short work of all opposition to it. But they have not got that power, and I might almost say they never will. But still, persecution may come from other quarters, and in some shape; and if it should not come, we shall be thankful. But if it do come, we will not fear. Jacob in his exile saw a brighter vision than in his home: John, in the desert Patmos, on the bosom of the Ægean Sea, saw brighter visions than he ever did in the college of apostles: and there is no dungeon so dark, no cell so deep, no prison walls so thick, that God cannot enter there. John Bunyan saw in his prison a brighter glory and enjoyed a greater inspiration, than ever apostle, or bishop, or presbyter, for eighteen hundred years before, had seen or realized in palace or cathedral.

The apostle adds another — "nakedness." What does he mean by this? The practice was, when the Christians were treated according to the tender mercies of Nero and Domitian, to strip them naked and to tie them up in the streets, for the sun to burn them by day, and the colds to freeze them by night; and to be made a gazingstock and a mockery, and the subject of insult, and scorn, and sarcasm to all spectators. But the Christians, nevertheless, were not ashamed of it. There is no shame in nakedness to which they were subjected; there is shame in sin only. After all, what is clothing on which men pride themselves? The furs of wild beasts, the feathers of wild fowls; the silk, the product of a poor, filthy worm; and the precious pearl, the mere product of an oyster-shell. These are not things to be proud of; nay, they are proofs of our fall, not marks and remains of our aboriginal glory. There is no greatness in these, there is no shame in the want of them. And what puts them all in the right place, Solomon in all his glory was not arrayed like the wild field flower that the peasant treads upon, and takes no notice of. Now the martyrs, exposed all night and all day naked to the scoff and scorn of their malicious and malignant enemies, were in nakedness. They rejoiced, notwithstanding, that they were counted worthy to suffer for his name's sake.

The apostle adds "peril," as another of those things which we are not to fear. We have a description, or rather a catalogue of the perils which he passed through, in 2 Corinthians xi. 25. "Thrice was I beaten with rods, once was I stoned, thrice I suffered shipwreck, a night and a day I have been in the deep; in journeyings often, in perils of waters, in perils of robbers, in perils by mine own countrymen, in perils by the heathen, in perils in the city, in perils in the wilderness, in perils in the sea, in perils among false brethren; in weariness and painfulness, in watchings often, in hunger and thirst, in fastings often, in cold and nakedness." Many parts of the apostolical succession men claim to have now; but it is rather remarkable they do not claim this; they do not seem to wish to inherit this part of the succession—perils, and nakedness, and famine, and cold, and hunger, and all by sea and land. The apostle felt these, unquestionably felt them; but in his worst perils by sea and by land, though he felt, he feared not; for he heard, what we may feel, the blessed promise, "When thou passest through the waters, I will be with thee; and through the rivers, they shall not overflow thee: when thou walkest through the fire, thou shalt not be burned, neither shall the flame kindle upon thee." Now these are true, these promises are real; God means them to be believed and to be acted on by us.

"The sword." The sword is the *acmé* of persecution; it evidently means martyrdom. And that sword, martyrdom itself, we are not to fear. Feel it we must; life is precious; to die is unnatural; but fear it we should not. The ancient Christians, such was their faith, such the intensity of their peace, coveted martyrdom; and felt they were honored when they occupied the van of the Christian army, and were exposed to death itself for Christ's sake.

"Death"—whether it come by martyrdom, or in the course of nature—feel you must; fear it you must not. It separates the friend from friend, the protector from his *protégé*, the patron from his client, the proprietor from his estate, the child from his parent, the soul from the body; but not the believer from Christ Jesus. Feel it you may;

but fear it not. To a Christian death is life; he dies that he may live; he goes through the deep ravine of death freely, that he may rise to the sunlit crag that shines and sparkles without a cloud above him and beyond it. The funeral bell that tolls the death of a Christian to the ears of survivors, is only the bridal peal that hails in heaven his marriage to the Lamb. Fear not death.

The apostle adds another — "life." Death you can understand our fearing; but life — what does the apostle mean by fearing this? It is often easier to die than it is to live; and hence men have rushed into death rather than bravely face the difficulties of life. We live in an age when the struggle for existence is so great as almost to make us forget the existence that is beyond. Many a one in this great city is struggling amid the waves of trouble, and in a sea of which he can neither feel the bottom nor see the shore. The age of competition, when the tendency is to make the world a workshop, and every man a crank, or a cog, or a pinion, or a fly-wheel, in the machinery, and to use up human nature just as machinery is used up, only giving it food as men apply oil and grease to the axle-tree, to enable the machinery to keep on; this horrible notion is the tendency of our age; and the tendency against which we should most firmly and decidedly fight; the tendency of them that have to increase what they have, by exhausting utterly them that must work. I do not pity any man for being hard worked; every one ought to work hard; and I have no pity for the subject of hard work. That is all right. But then there is excessive work, that human flesh cannot stand; that must soon wear it out, and make it to be used up. That is treatment that man ought not to be subjected to; and yet it is the tendency of the present day. I hope that at last there is the wakening of a better spirit; I hope that men are appreciating what is the truest interest of both parties. If you want to make the most of a horse, do not work him seven days, but only six; and you may depend upon it that he will be more valuable to you — ten per cent. more valuable. And if you want to make more of a servant, work him a great deal less instead of a great deal more, and you will find that you will gain by it instead of losing. But whether this happen to you or not, fear not — be patient — suffer and be strong. Deliverance may be nearer than you expect; and at all events, this world is not our all; it is but the path to a brighter and a better.

The apostle adds, — "Angels, principalities, or powers;" these also we are not to fear. We do not fear demons, or evil spirits; they are kept in chains. We need not fear good spirits, or angels; for "are they are not ministering spirits unto them that are the heirs of salvation?" He adds, "things present." Men often fear the present more than they feel the past or fear the future. Sickness, weakness of faith, sorrow, distress, many a cup of bitterness, many a battle, fears within, fightings without — feel them, but fear them not. "Things to come." When we look at the past, we see much to be thankful for; when we taste the present, we feel much to lead us to trust still; when we look into the future, our fears often conjure up phantoms that are dissipated the instant we enter upon it. And at all events, the future is not come; fear it not; and not even feel it, for we have nothing yet to do with it.

The apostle appends, "height and depth, or any other creature;" neither the height of prosperity nor the depth of adversity; neither the height of honour nor the depth of shame: there is nothing on the loftiest pinnacle of the temple to which Satan can carry us; there is nothing in the deepest crypt or dungeon into which he may precipitate us, that should make us fear. The whole universe is the friend of him who is the friend of God; all things help him who is a son of God; all things are in alliance with him who is in Christ Jesus.

What then shall we fear? Tribulation? If we suffer with him, we shall also reign with him. Famine? He will give us living bread and daily bread. Nakedness? We are clothed with the righteousness of Christ. Peril? Christ is our shield and our safety. The sword? Absent from the body is present with the Lord. Banishment? The whole earth is filled with God. Death? "Oh death, where is thy sting? Yea, though I walk through the valley of the shadow of death, I will fear no evil; for thou art with me; thy rod and thy staff, they comfort me." The curse of sin, the condemnation of sin? "The blood of Christ cleanseth from all sin." Fear not, for I am with thee; I will never leave thee; I will never forsake thee. I give unto them eternal life, and none shall be able to pluck them out of my hand." "In all things," says the apostle, "we approve ourselves as the ministers of God; in much patience, in afflictions, in necessities, in distresses, in stripes, in imprisonments, in tumults, in labors, in watchings, in fastings; by pureness, by knowledge, by longsuffering, by kindness, by the Holy Ghost, by love unfeigned, by the word of truth, by the power of God, by the armor of righteousness on the right hand and on the left, by honor and dishonor, by evil report and good report; as deceivers, and yet true; as unknown, and yet well known; as dying, and, behold, we live; as chastened, and not killed; as sorrowful, yet always rejoicing; as poor, yet making many rich; as having nothing, and yet possessing all things." What an eloquent passage! what a noble statement! how full, how comprehensive! Therefore fear not life, nor death, nor principalities, nor powers, nor height, nor depth, nor any other creature. Christ intercedes for you: "Satan hath desired to have you that he may sift you as wheat; but I have prayed for you, that your faith fail not." Christ is with you: "Lo, I am with you always, even unto the end of the world." His dying prescription is for you; "Let not your hearts be troubled; ye believe in God, believe also in me." The promise of a triune Jehovah is yours; namely, "I am with you." The basis of our triumph over every fear is, God present with us. We have felt that in suffering to be quite alone, is to aggravate our grief; to have one human being that can sympathize with us in suffering, is in some degree a comfort. And when a man has no human being, (I speak to common experience, and to what all feel,) even to have a faithful dog is better than to be utterly alone. Such is man's dislike in trial to be alone, that he ever seeks some one to be with him. Now, says God, not a faithful dog, — not sister, brother, husband, wife, or friend, — that is not good enough for you, that is not enough for me to bestow; but, in all, and in any, and in every of these conditions, I, the mighty God, the everlasting God your Father, in whom you live, and move, and have your being — I am with thee. What a blessed promise is that! His presence is with us everywhere and always; omnipresence enveloping us, omnipotence paving the way for us, infinite wisdom directing all, infinite love embosoming us and all ours. "I am with thee" — that is Christ's own promise — "Lo, I am with you always." "Where two or three are met together in my name, there I am in the midst of them."

But what is the nature of this presence? Very briefly we may observe, it is not God's essential presence. In one sense God is everywhere; in the height, in the depth, on the ocean, in the uttermost ends of the earth, in heaven and in hell — everywhere God is present. And therefore the promise, "I am with thee," as the mere essential presence of God, would be of no comfort. But it is what may be called God's especial presence, his presence as a father with his son, as a mother with her child, as a protector with his *protégé*. It is that presence which Moses alludes to when he says, "If thy presence go not with me, carry us not up hence;" it is, his special, cheering, protecting, preserving presence. Now that presence, says God, shall be with every Christian. It may not shield you from all that will give pain; but it will inspire you with fearlessness in the midst of all. This presence is not with us in the sanctuary only, but in the shop, in the counting-house, in the street, on the quarter-deck, on the field of battle. And that man that goes into the midst of battle as soldier or sailor, and has with him this blessed conviction, "My God and my Father is with me," will not be less brave, but more so: and he will have a sustaining element within him, that the mere reckless and thoughtless man has not. And so, if we are exposed to famine, or pestilence, or plague, or any other peril: — if, as a physician, I go into the infected chamber of typhus, or where plague or pestilence ravens by our neglect, I must feel, I know the elements I have to contend with; but if I be a Christian man, I can take this blessed thought with me, "I am with *thee*." But mark the specialty of it. We can easily understand God being with us in the bulk, as it were; but God is with the individual Christian as close, as near, as truly, as really, as he is upon his throne, or as he is with the greatest saint in glory. He does not say, "I am with man as a whole;" but "I am with *thee*" — close to thee as thy humanity; really, and truly, and actually, I am with thee. In all places — in the closet, in the sanctuary, in the family, in the tents of Mesech, and in the tabernacles of Kedar, on Pisgah and on Tabor; — everywhere and always thy God is with thee; in all time of your tribulation, in all time of your wealth, in the hour of death, and in the day of judgment, on earth and in heaven, in grace and glory.

Blessed Lord, fulfil thy promise, and be with us, each, all, now and evermore; for Christ's sake. Amen.

# CHAPTER XII.

## THE LIGHTS OF THE WORLD.

"Ye with mild radiance, every hour,
From your dear Saviour's face benign,
Bent on you with transforming power,
Truly, if faintly, shine."

"Ye are the light of the world. A city that is set on an hill cannot be hid. Neither do men light a candle, and put it under a bushel, but on a candlestick; and it giveth light unto all that are in the house."— MATT. v. 14, 15.

SUNDAY light is meant to be carried into daily life, the one is the inspiration and direction of the other: we receive on the first day a supply for the remaining six days. Christians are the lights, not of the church, but of the world — not of sabbath days, but of weekdays — not of sabbath life, but of daily life. When Jesus addressed a few rugged fishermen of Galilee, and one or two publicans professing Christianity, and said to them, "Ye are the light of the world," does it not seem as if the world into which they were sent to give light was then in darkness? Was it really so? Was our Lord ignorant of polished Greece? Had he never heard of imperial Rome? Had he seen or heard of none of the monuments of artistic magnificence and of exquisite beauty unrivalled in former ages?

The world had then a statuary, whose very remains are now carefully treasured up in our Museums, the admiration of cultivated taste. It had then paintings, so beautiful and so perfect that the very birds of heaven pecked at the grapes upon the canvas as if they were growing upon the vines of the earth. And it had poetry too, so rich that the very fragments of it, which have been drifted down the centuries of the world, are at this moment stored and studied by all who wish to see what bright thoughts in eloquent words human genius can convey. There were in the world gifted and eloquent orators; there was persuasive eloquence, advancing science, and literature, and civilization, of no ordinary greatness. All these existed at the moment that Jesus said to his followers, in language that thousands would have shrunk from, "Ye" are the light of the world. Jesus knew of all these attainments of the earth, and he could appreciate their excellency and beauty too. He that could see and seemingly admire the exquisite tints upon a violet or a rose, who could prefer to all the artistic magnificence of Solomon himself the fair lily of the garden, or the wild field flower, we may depend upon it, had a taste that could appreciate, and did appreciate, those efforts of the brush and the chisel to recover what was lost in Paradise, a perfection that had passed away like a dream, and left scarce a wreck behind it. But whilst he was aware of all, and could exactly estimate all — he only could see, because he only could fathom, its utter emptiness and unsatisfactoriness, for nothing of all this cast light on the deepest problems that agitate the heart of man. Socrates, and Plato, and Apelles, and Homer, and Sophocles, could reflect no light upon questions intensely momentous. What must I, a poor sinner, do to be saved? had neither echo nor answer from ancient oracles. Not beauty, but bread will feed me; not the arts and sciences, but a blessing from my Father can do me the highest good. Jesus scanned the wide world with that eye that took it all in; and saw in all the glory that shone from the temples and academies of Athens and Corinth, a pale day that would soon end in everlasting night; he heard in the eloquence of the most gifted orators of ancient days, words that had no echoes in the hearts and consciences of a hungry, an ignorant, and a perishing people; and he beheld, in all the paintings of its painters, and in all the statues of its statuaries, the fugitive attempts to embody still more fugitive impressions; — there was beauty to the eye, but no nutriment to the heart. Under all this exterior also there lay deep corruption; amid all this splendor there was great moral wickedness; and Jesus, with the foresight of a prophet, and with the wisdom of a teacher, and the truthfulness with which man never spake, turning from beholding the magnificent panorama of artistic greatness and grandeur, said, "Ye, the fishermen of Galilee —" not ye, the painters, the poets, and the sculptors of the world — "are the light of the world." And he spake truly. If he had not said it, it still would have been true. For what do we find? When we look beneath the surface of the beauty and glory on which the ancient world prided itself, which modern sceptics quote as a proof that we are not indebted to Christianity for all that we most admire, we find lurking the most revolting immorality. Some of the religious rites of the cultivated Greeks were so abominable that they would now be prosecuted by the public magistrate: the names of the most illustrious ladies of the days of Socrates and Plato are not remembered with admiration and approbation now. Athens, in its meridian, in the very age of Pericles, had a population of six hundred thousand, and out of the six hundred thousand, five hundred thousand were slaves, that might be hanged, or drowned, or stoned at their master's bidding. The arts concealed, they did not extirpate, slavery. At first you admire this exterior loveliness, but the moment you look down below, you see what a frail, worthless, and superficial thing is the richest outward splendor among a people without the living and sustaining power of inward and true Christianity. The arts and the sciences may beautify the outward path, they cannot make the path of immorality to be abhorred. They may adorn much that is good, or they may conceal with a meretricious splendor much that is false; but they cannot secure a true and pure morality. They may make an academy, they cannot constitute a people. Arts are not the parents of whatsoever things are pure, and just, and beautiful. Painting, poetry, science, music, are fit to be the handmaids, they never can be the mothers of all that truly adorns and really elevates mankind. They may beautify the capital of the pillar, they cannot be its strong and everlasting foundation. In all the cities of Greece and in all the provinces of Italy, there was no such thing as a home; therefore there was no such thing as a people. Christianity has given the first, and through the first it has generated all the dignity and greatness of the second.

It is the light of Christianity, or Christ reflected upon the world, alone, that solves the deepest questions, and answers the most anxious inquiries of mankind. The object of light is to disclose what would be otherwise unseen. What do we see in this light? The very first object this light discloses is God. The ideas of God entertained by even the most gifted of ancient times were extremely distorted and imperfect: but if we look at God in the light we now have, his greatness, his goodness, his mercy, his justice, his holiness, his character, shine out grand and noble; not comparison, but contrast, to every conception of his glory that was entertained before. The sun can only be seen in his own light; Deity can be seen in his own eternal splendor only.

A Christian now has an idea of God the heathen nations never dreamed of. Heathendom, in fact, was midnight; Mahometanism is a smoke that darkens the air; Romanism is a portentous eclipse at noonday; but Christianity is the light that shines in darkness, and reflects its beams upon every problem that man feels most deeply important, and gives the sure answer to every question that needs an answer in the yearning heart of nature. One great question, for instance, has long been felt, How shall man, a sinner, be justified before God? No oracle but that of the Bible gives an answer to it. Another question has often been asked, What is the way to heaven? No light from ancient shrines, or altars, or temples, or tripods, gives us the least explanation. Will God pardon the sins of them that believe, confess, and forsake them? To that question Heathenism can give no reply. Take any one subject, the deepest and dearest in a dying hour, and where can we get light upon it except from this blessed book, from this holy and precious religion? So much has this book done for us, that the problems that perplexed the academy in ancient times are now the aphorisms that are taught in Sunday schools. The great questions that philosophers could not solve, a Sunday school child now will clearly and distinctly explain. Our children know more, and understand more about God, about conscience, duty, heaven, and responsibility, than all the philosophers of Greece and Rome put together. What has made this alteration, whence is this vast superiority? The light of the everlasting gospel is the reason of it. The least in the kingdom of heaven — that is, in the present day — knows more than the greatest beyond or before it. The Parthenon, with all its unrivalled magnificence, before God and before an enlightened mind, sinks into utter meanness and contempt beside that living temple growing up in the age in which we live, built of living stones, upon Christ the Rock of ages, whose builder, and maker, and glory is God. The just man that Plato foretold, the divine teacher that Socrates predicted to his pupil Alcibiades, has come, and taught the nations, and died upon the cross, our ransom, and has risen from the grave, our first-fruits; he pleads before the throne our Prince and our Intercessor; and he will come again in intolerable glory and receive us to himself, that where he is there may we be also. A light shines upon us clear and level along the whole of our path through the world that now is, and it forsakes us not at the portals of the grave, it gleams along the dim valley of the shadow of death, and is reflected on the uplifted eyes of the pilgrims of God, from the towers of the heavenly Jerusalem. Blessed, oh! blessed be God, and would that we felt it deeper still, for that sunrise upon the hills of Palestine, eighteen hundred years ago.

This holy light possesses a peculiar character, which the light of mere science, literature, or secular knowledge has not and cannot have. The light that is purest from the schools of earth is snow light or ice light, dimly revealing distant, cold, and unapproachable realms; but the light that gleams from this divine page is living light, warm, genial, inspiring, rejoicing. Mount Sinai, to take another contrast, is the lightning, scorching, blasting the world; but Calvary, or Christianity, is the sweet light of the day, opening the folded buds, — waking the earth to a sense of the approaching summer, — falling so softly that a blade of grass is not crushed by it, — yet with such power, life, and force that the earth beneath its touch bursts into blossom, and the hills are covered with corn, and the valleys shout for joy, they also sing.

The light of science, of literature, and of this world, has excellences, but not the chief excellency. The light of this gospel, which Christians see, not only supplies what the arts and sciences cannot; not only solves the deepest problems the intellect fails to reach; not only contrasts in its gentle, productive, and blessed effects, with the light of this world; but to the light of Christianity, the light that comes from the cross, we are indebted for all our best social, charitable, and national blessings. Hospitals, dispensaries, charitable institutions, never existed in heathendom; they were not merely imperfect, but they scarcely existed at all. The poor now, amid all their degradation, occupy a place in the thoughts of the rich and the arrangement of statesmen, they never held in ancient times. The chains of the slave are now melted by the beams of Christianity shining upon our native shores; the horrors of war have been prodigiously mitigated. With all the criminalities of modern warfare, it has few of the atrocities of the wars of ancient times. Our soldiers and our sailors are not serfs; they are treated as men; provided for as men, spoken to as immortals, and instructed in the knowledge of the Prince of Peace. The soldiers that fought at Marathon and Thermopylæ were mere helots; the fields that are the pride of ancient days and the shining recollections of the present, were fought by slaves let loose from the mills and looms of their tyrant masters. Our soldiers and our sailors are now more than ever independent and respected, and wholly through the indirect light of the gospel of Christ. Commerce is not now what it was — a system of chicanery and gambling; but a dignified, elevating, and ennobling employment; so that the merchants of our country rank with the princes of the earth. Polygamy and social immorality are now extinguished, or if they exist they must go to the dens and dark places of the earth, and hide their heads from the light of the gospel of Christ. What a revolution, produced by the successive steps of a reformation, has the light of this blessed gospel created among mankind!

And since its dawn, even those bright things that were proposed as substitutes for it, this light has seized and made handmaids to it. Literature, and science, and art, and painting, and poetry have been urged, even in this century, as they were worshipped in ancient times, as substitutes for Christianity. This religion no sooner shone upon them than it gave them their true place, it lifted them from the grovelling level they occupied in the academy, and taught them to grow up the handmaids of the gospel; not the obscurers, but the reflectors of the light that shines from Gethsemane, and Calvary, and Paradise. Christianity in the middle ages, even under the terrible eclipse that overshadowed it, originated an architecture peculiarly its own. Christianity has inspired the richest music, and the noblest productions of the most celebrated painters are associated with great Christian truths: and if they had not been controlled by the apostasy that professed to encourage while it really corrupted them, there had been less the taint of Rome upon the canvas, and more the true rendering and definition of the truths of the Bible. Cast your eye at this moment along the vista of the ages, and what do you find? That this religion, the light of this religion, instead of being hostile to science and literature, as some in their folly assert, has been, as it really is at this moment, the greatest patroness of it. We shall find in the world at the present day, that the nations that are greatest in literature are greatest in the knowledge of the Bible, and in the Christian religion. Modern heathen nations are a dead sea; Mahometanism at the present moment is, as far as literature is concerned, a stagnant marsh. In Christendom alone the purest churches have around them the noblest temples of science; and the most enlightened philosophers are the willing servants of the gospel of Christ Jesus. Nor need we wonder at it. Science in the hands of scepticism becomes a hard, cold, and freezing thing, without warmth, or love, or hope; and the few and far between incidental excellences that appear, are like the flowerets and the mosses that grow in the rents of a rock, owing not to the rock, but to the particles of Christian soil that have got between. Painting as the creation of infidels is sensual, debasing; poetry, in the hands of a Byron and a Shelley, is not as poetry should be, full of hope, inspiring joy, but earthly, carnal, defiling. And science wielded by Voltaire and D'Alembert, and the men of the academy of former days, was a hard, heavy, clumsy weapon, with which they struck fiercely, but struck in vain, at the fortress of the gospel of Christ. Not only does this light reveal what science, and literature, and the arts cannot reveal; but it takes up the arts and the literature of the world, and consecrates them to its own benign and beneficent purposes.

There are two tendencies abroad in the present day extremely to be deplored. One is expressed by spiritually minded and truly genial Christians, who seem to think that their only business upon earth is to wend through this world as quietly and quickly as they can to heaven, caring no more about painting, poetry, music, and science, and literature, than if they were positively and absolutely proscribed. I cannot think that this is the mind or the meaning of our blessed Lord. He says, Ye are "the lights," not of a *coterie*, not of a sect, but "the lights of the world." And that would seem to me to teach that, as long as there is a world to be aroused, and a church to be sanctified, we are bound to be on that account in that world. We must seize and hold the world for God. If we give up these things, Satan watches to seize them, the Pope stands ready to desecrate them, Infidelity waits to welcome them. But why surrender them? Every bit of this world is meant for God; let us not resign an inch of it to Satan; tell him and his emissaries that all that is in the world — its poetry, its painting, its music, its architecture, are meant to be the handmaids of religion, and ought not to be desecrated to the service of that which is corrupt, or to the support of that which is antichristian. This blessed religion of ours does not teach that we should pass through the world just as a skater would go over thin ice — as rapidly as possible in order to get to another part, looking neither on one side nor the other. We are meant and wanted for this world as well as for the next; and that school education which does not train the young for this world as well as for the next, is therefore defective. Religion is meant to regulate, to inspire, to comfort, to strengthen, to encourage in this world; and we are summoned to do its duties, fulfil its obligations, while we make ready for a better, a brighter, and a nobler land beyond it. Our blessed Lord did not say, "I pray that thou wouldest take them *out* of the world." Yet, the instant that a man is a child of God he is fit for heaven. Why then is he left in the world? Because the world needs him, because he will be of use in the world. And when our Redeemer prayed, he said, "I pray not that thou wouldest take them out of the world" — which condemns the monkish and anchorite idea — "but that thou wouldest keep them in the world from the evil of the world." What intense common sense is in that book, the Bible! The more that one reads it the more wonderful that blessed book appears, and the more it commends itself to that which is, after grace, no common gift, that strong, good, common sense which is deepest in the heart of mankind.

On the other hand, there are others just as far wrong, who take the opposite idea, and insist upon the divorce of science and religion. I fear that the polarity of the present day is very much in this direction. Many seem to think now that education is merely a preparation for this world. This is just going off in the opposite extreme. It is not a preparation only for this world, but a preparation also for another. Suppose a man has to go a journey, say of a thousand miles. The mere secular educationalist would say to him, Take food with you for five hundred miles, and make the best of your way through the remaining five hundred that you can. The traveller would drop and die. The other we have spoken of would say, You have a thousand miles to go; take nothing with you, but walk, — an impossibility, — and therefore he also will perish. But the Christian way and the common sense way is, if you have a thousand miles to travel take food for all the way; and then you will run the race set before you; run, and not be weary; walk, and not be faint; looking to the bread of life, the author and the finisher of your faith. We must not attempt to divorce science from Christianity. Common things, as a nobleman very justly said the other day, ought to be taught rather than fine things, and along with sacred things. To try to divorce common things from Christian things, secular education from religious education, is to act like the false mother of old, who preferred to divide the living child in twain rather than suffer the true mother to be the possessor of it. The two were made and meant to go together; and what God has joined, man should not put asunder. And there is a reason for this. Mere science, or literature, or earthly knowledge is so busy in its own department, that it forgets every thing else. Just as men constantly executing very delicate engravings, or tracery, through a powerful microscopic lens, ultimately cease to be able to see many feet beyond; so those who are constantly dealing with the things of science or of literature come under a tendency to forget that there is any thing above, or other things beyond. They are so busy investigating creation, that it comes to take the place of the Creator. At that moment Christianity beautifully steps into the school-room, or the college class room or lecture room, and says to the scientific man, I admire these beautiful links that you have struck out, constituting a long and illuminated chain; and I, Christianity, just add to the chain the link that fixes it to the staple that is in the throne of God, the Maker and the Governor of all. One can see clearly that without religion science or literature is very defective, and often ends in the idolatry of the creature; and wherever the divorce has been attempted the consequences have been most disastrous. Let us not forget as a warning the German universities. Some of their Professors are Jews, some Roman Catholics, some Protestants, and many sceptics; and the only way they can live together in decent harmony is by excluding religion from the university altogether. The result is, that Germany has given birth to that hard rationalism, which borrows its splendor from the intellect instead of, as of old, borrowing its splendor from the senses; and has become the source and the hotbed of the most deadly and mischievous Pantheism, Atheism, and Infidelity, that have ever existed among mankind. I will allow the statesmen of the world to make our laws in parliament, if they will allow me to take in my hands the education of the young. I care not what laws statesmen make, if I can only see in our schools, not theologians, but religious men, saturating all education with religious truth, and letting the light that shines from the pulpit radiate from the schoolmaster's desk, and fill the whole place with its imperishable splendors.

We cannot exaggerate the importance of these two being connected together. No science or philosophy can be a substitute for religion; yet we do not propose to resign to Satan, to sin, and to the world those things which are in themselves good. It is of vital importance that everywhere true religion and true science should go together. We do not dread science; the more it shines the better; we do not shrink from secular education; the more it prevails the better; but woe to that country that separates the two, or rather adjures one! woe to that nation that, in its national provision for the education of the people, leaves out of its atmosphere its oxygen, from its system its lifeblood, its vitality, and its nutriment!

Having seen the light itself, let us notice now what is the more practical part for us — that Christians are the bearers of this light into all the ends of the world. Kindled from the Sun, they are to go forth and cast their light upon the world. A man is made a Christian that he may Christianize. A candle is lighted just that it may be luminous. We receive just that we may give. The monk, the nun, the anchorite, if lighted at all, which is questionable, goes each into a convent, or nunnery, and thus hides his light under a bushel. The Christian, who is lighted, goes forth into the world, and lets his light so shine in daily life, that others seeing his good works may glorify, not him, but his Father who is in heaven. The believer is to be a light, and the light of all the world. And the world shone upon by such light, will cease to be a mere workshop in which man gains his bread, and will rise to the dignity of a porch and a vestibule of heaven, in which he is educated for God and for glory.

If we be lights, and if Christians we are so, we are not responsible for the elevation at which we are placed. We are each a light, but God gives the candlestick; in one it may be a very high one, in another it may be a very low one; what we are responsible for is, not the place where God in his providence has set us, or the elevation at which God in his wisdom has placed us, but for filling the sphere which we hold with the light we are. If we be lights, our mission is to enlighten the sphere in which we are placed;

this is our only responsibility. Whatever be the sphere of influence you are in, or the element of power you have, if you be light, that sphere will be filled with its beams, and every available element of power will be worked for God and for good. Have you in your hand that most powerful engine of modern times, the press? No words of mine can express the gravity of your responsibility. If the Apostle Paul were living in the nineteenth century he would take the command of the press, if he could, as truly as of the pulpit. I know no engine of greater power in daily life than the daily press. How dreadful when it reflects the baleful lights of superstition, when unbaptized it toils in the drudgery of Satan, when without the fear of God it is worked only for the ruin and demoralization of mankind! But on the other hand, what a blessing, what a gigantic blessing, when it is inspired by the truth, consecrated by grace, helps pilgrims to their country, exiles to their home, prodigals to their Father, and children to their God! Are you, on the other hand, in possession of the pulpit? It is, if not perhaps above, certainly equal to, the press as a focus of intense light. The pulpit in the present day, it has been thought by some, falls behind the age; we fear it does so. But if there be any spot upon earth where apathy is guilt, where negligence is a crime, and where want of success is to be attributed not so often as it is to the absence of a blessing, (and that blessing is of all things the most vital,) but to the want of our fitness for it, it is here. What an awful state of things in the last century, when a gentleman said, I have a son; he is not fit for being a soldier or a sailor — make a clergyman of him! How shocking! what an outrage upon all that is holy and good! If there be a place upon earth where the greatest genius, power, piety should be concentrated and combined, and poured forth in inexhaustible fulness, it is from that spot where overtures are distributed that will rise either in the sweet echoes of the songs of heaven, or in the reverberating crashes of the wails of the lost. If there be one spot upon earth that has awful responsibility it is surely the pulpit.

I read somewhere of a traveller at Calais going one dark and stormy night to the light-house there. Whilst standing looking on, the keeper of the house boasted of its brilliancy and beauty, observing there were few such lights in the world beside. The traveller said — thoughtlessly it may be, "What if one of these burners of yours should go out to-night?" "What!" said the keeper, "go out, sir? Oh, sir," said the light-house keeper, "look at that dark and stormy sea. You cannot see them, but there are ships passing and repassing there to every point of the compass. Were the light to go out from my inattention, in six months news would arrive from every part of the coast, that such ships and crews were lost by my neglect! No, no! God forbid such a thing should ever occur. I feel every night as I look at my burner, as if all the eyes of all the sailors of the world were looking at my lights, and watching me." He for an earthly, we for an heavenly. If such was his care of lights, the extinction of which could lead only to temporal catastrophes, oh! what should be ours!

"Far sadder sight than eye can know,
Than proud bark lost or seaman's woe,
Or battle fire or tempest cloud,
Or prey bird's shriek or ocean's shroud,
The shipwreck of the soul."

Are we watching the burner in the light-house on which God has placed us? He built the house, and placed us in it; it is ours to let the light so shine that the white-winged doves of commerce, as they move from sea to sea and from shore to shore, or rather as the pilgrims of eternity wend their way to an everlasting haven, they may never have to criminate us for culpable neglect.

# CHAPTER XIII.

## UNCONSCIOUS INFLUENCE.

"Is it Christ's light is too divine,
We dare not hope like Him to shine?
But see, around his dazzling shrine,
Earth's gems the fire of heaven have caught."

"Ye are the light of the world. A city that is set on an hill cannot be hid. Neither do men light a candle, and put it under a bushel, but on a candlestick; and it giveth light unto all that are in the house."—MATT. v. 14, 15.

EVERY figure used to describe a Christian is essentially aggressive. It teaches us that no man is a Christian in order to enjoy a monopoly of blessing for himself. Being made a Christian, his very first function is to go forth and Christianize others. Some talk of proselytism as a sin, and denounce it even as a crime. Proselytism to a sect is most obnoxious, proselytism to the truths of the gospel is the duty of every man that knows them. Some persons play upon words, and do not distinguish things that differ. They make you suppose by their remarks that your first and primary duty, to bless others by having been blessed yourself, is a sin, a crime, a scandal. Every figure used to describe a Christian indicates his duty to Christianize. "Ye are the salt of the earth." What is the nature of salt? To give savor to the substance with which it is mixed, or in contact, and to preserve that substance, if needs be, from corruption. An idea involved in salt is something transmissive of virtue; and if you, therefore, are the salt of the world, your part of the world will be touched by the savor of what you are, and so be benefited and blessed. Ye are the "light of the world." A lamp is lighted for diffusing light; and if it do not diffuse light, it is because it is not light. A man who is not a missionary, is not a Christian; he that does not seek to promote what he has, feels in his conscience he has nothing worth promoting. You may have a choice of these two figures. Some would prefer to be the lights of the world; to illuminate with a visible splendor that men can admire, rather than to act as the silent, hidden salt of the world, that penetrates the mass, and is not seen, but felt. But one or other you must be, except you choose to be what a Napoleon and an Alexander preferred — not the silent, penetrating *salt*, not the quiet and beautiful *light*, but the rending and crashing *lightning*, that blasts the world, not blesses it and does it good.

From the expression, "Ye are the light of the world," we learn how truly catholic Christianity is. The church that boasts emphatically to be catholic is the most sectarian of all, for she believes there is no Christianity without her own pale. That is sectarianism. The really catholic Church believes there are Christians everywhere, whom she hails as such. She can forgive ritual peculiarities because of the living religion that underlies them. This religion was meant to be universal. "Ye are the lights," not of a country, nor of a century, nor of an age, but of the wide world. You are to be satisfied with nothing less than the world for your sphere, and no fewer than all mankind for your brethren in Christ Jesus. Christianity, it is true, was once restricted to a few, but it was then in its infancy; as soon as it was grown enough to be exhibited to all, the conviction of a few became the creed of mighty and powerful nations: and now wherever the prince of the power of the air has left his footprint behind him, wherever sin has tainted the earth with its poison and its trail, wherever the human mind is in darkness, the human heart depraved, the human will in chains, the human soul without a Saviour, there, irrespective of caste, of clime, of color, the angel of the everlasting gospel goes and preaches the opening of the prison doors to them that are bound, sight to the blind, freedom to the slave, and blessings high as heaven and wide as the universe to all that wait and are willing to accept them.

But in looking at the world let us not dissipate by any excessive generalization, if I may use such an expression, our own daily duties. Some men are so charmed with the magnificent that they have no time to attend to the minute. Some who are splendid advocates in parliament for liberty to all, are the greatest tyrants in their own homes. Some who are every thing benevolent abroad, seem to have so expended their stores upon all mankind that they have not one flash of sunshine for their own firesides. We are very apt so to think of the grand, that we overlook the instant, and the more practical and personally minute. "Ye are the lights of the world." Your world is your shop, your warehouse, your counting-house, the parliament, whatever place God in his providence has placed you in, that is to you for all practical purposes your world: and before you feel such an absorbing interest in the enlightening of the wide world, just see if you have put your light under a bushel in that little world in which for six days of the week from morning to evening you must move. "Ye are the lights of the world." We are not answerable for the sphere we are in: we are only responsible for letting our light shine in it. If

God has made you rich, powerful, illustrious, great, that is his sovereign act; over that you have no control. Your personal duty is to do well the work that is assigned you, in the sphere in which God in his providence has placed you; never to dream that what you want in order to do better is to get a larger sphere. Many people make excuses to themselves for not doing better in the little sphere in which they are, by saying, Ah, if I were only in such a sphere you would see how I would shine. Now if you do not shine in a cellar, depend upon it you would not shine in a palace; if you do not shine in the shop, depend upon it you would not shine if you had the command of her Majesty's fleet. Your duty as light is to irradiate the sphere you are in; and when you have done that well, God, who placed you there, and sees you are able to fill a higher, will say, "Come up higher."

This very thought, that "we are the lights of the world," whatever that world may be to us, implies that we are constantly in that sphere to keep and to carry our Christianity with us. You are never to merge the Christian in the tradesman, but always to unite the tradesman to the Christian. You are not to merge the Christian in the member of parliament, but always to remember that the Christian is to govern the senator, not the senator to govern the Christian. Christianity is not a religion confined to consecrated tiles, and holy places, and holy days, but a religion that treads with as beautiful a foot life's lowliest floor as it walks in grand procession in the noblest cathedral of Europe. Our religion is not a beautiful robe that we must lay carefully aside upon Sunday night, lest it should be rumpled by the rough wear and tear of the weekday; it is a religion that we are to carry with all the splendor of its first kindling into life's highest, and life's lowest, and life's universal places, knowing it is fit to sanctify all, and make us shine as the lights of the world in all. And if you cannot be where God has placed you *sunlight*, you may always be *light*. We do not expect that there will be all the splendor of a martyr's testimony behind the counter, but we do expect that there will always be the quiet every-day life of a Christian's character there and everywhere. And you know quite well, writing for many who are in trade and in business, that every-day proposals are made, offers come before you, plans are mooted, schemes are suggested, which constantly bring into demand or play your Christian character; you must either, when these proposals are made, put your Christianity away, and deal with them as tradesmen, or you must take your Christianity with you, and let it control, direct, give tone and force to every thing you are and every thing you do. Therefore the conclusion we come to is this, that the man who is a Christian is not to cease to be a tradesman, a physician, a lawyer, a senator, a judge; but to be a Christian tradesman, a Christian lawyer, a Christian senator, a Christian judge. The monk and the suicide, who belong to the same category; for the one runs from society to escape its perils, and the other runs from society in order to escape its burdens; both fly from duty, the one to escape danger, the other suffering, and yet neither succeed. We ought to be in the world, not of it. The ladies who go into a convent, if they be lights, thereby go and put their lights under a bushel, whereas, if true lights, instead of putting them under a bushel, they ought to let them shine, that the whole house may be better for it. When it is urged that men should go into monasteries, and women into convents, because they are so holy, so pure, that they would be contaminated by the world, they should recollect that if they be so holy and so pure, of all people upon earth the world has the greatest need of them. If all the good that is in the world were to leave it, the world would go to corruption and ruin. Just because, as they say they are so holy, so good, and so pure, therefore, instead of deserting as cowards the banners of the force they belong to, they ought as good soldiers of Christ to remain in the world, conquering the world for Christ, and for his glory, and for his people.

But every man, whatever his character, a Christian or not, a light that burns, or a lamp that has been quenched, has everywhere and always a continuous influence upon all that are around him. Some think that by not professing to be Christians they escape the responsibility of their duties towards those that are around them; but this is impossible, for what man is exercises as powerful an influence as any thing that man does or professes. There is in the human body, voluntary action and involuntary action. When I move my hand, or my tongue, or my legs, that is voluntary; I can stop, or I can go on; but my heart and my lungs go on in spite of me; they are involuntary movements: so in the human character there are two influences; there is the voluntary influence, as when I go out and speak to a person in order to convince him, or appeal to a person in order to make him better; I am then exercising a designed and a voluntary influence upon that individual; but there is an involuntary influence, in my character, my conduct, my temper, when I think no man sees me, though many may be seeing me; all these without my volition, and in spite of my volition, are shaping the character, and giving tone and temper, and it may be everlasting colors, to the souls of mankind. In other words, it is impossible to be in the world and not in some shape to influence the world. What we say may not proceed from real conviction, but what we are is always before the world, the symbol or sign of what grace has made us, or what sin has left us. No child walks along a street without learning lessons. Every sign board teaches, every random exclamation teaches, every fugitive look on the human countenance teaches. The fact is, we are constantly under teaching to the latest moment of our lives; and what we come into contact with, is moulding and shaping our character, it may be for ever. It is very difficult to persuade men that it is so, because they have the idea that there is only power where there is noise, bustle, excitement. But it is really not so. All the forces in nature that are the most powerful, are the most quiet. We speak of the rolling thunder, as powerful; but gravitation, which makes no noise, has no speech, utters not a syllable, yet keeps orbs in their orbits, and the whole system in its harmony, binding every atom in one orb to the great central source of all attraction, is ten thousand times ten thousand more powerful. We say the red lightning is very powerful; so it is; when it rends the gnarled oak into splinters, or splits the solid battlements into fragments; but it is not half so powerful as that gentle light, that comes so softly from the skies that we do not feel it, that travels at an inconceivable speed, strikes and yet is not felt, but exercises an influence so powerful, that the sea is kept back by it, that the earth is clothed with verdure through its influence, and all nature beautified and blessed by its ceaseless action. The things that are most noisy are not the most powerful; things that make no noise and make no pretension, may be really the most powerful. An eloquent speech will never have the effect of an eloquent life. The most conclusive logic that a preacher uses in the pulpit will never exercise the effect that the piety, the consistent piety of character, will exercise over all the world. And in many congregations the preacher who may have few to hear him, and where, if we heard him, we should say that he has not the power of expressing clearly and intelligibly the great thoughts that he feels, may be comparatively dumb and ineffective in the pulpit, but in his walks amid his flock, his beautiful and holy character, may be spreading an influence around him, that will tell more upon the destinies of souls than if he had wielded all the thunders of Demosthenes, or pleaded with the persuasive eloquence that flowed from the lips of Cicero.

It is not what we intend to do that strikes the most, it is what we are. It is not beautiful words in the pulpit, but the beating of an earnest heart heard under the preacher's simplest words. It is not Christianity on the lip that is eloquent, but Christianity in the life that is holy, that tells most upon the character of mankind. And the secret of the failure in the case of the hypocrite is, that if he were to speak like an angel, or reason like a metaphysician, we know that the background will not bear inspection. A person who is not sincere, let him speak with superhuman skill, will produce no effect. And hence, as we know in political and in ecclesiastical matters, the man who is gifted with the greatest eloquence, but who has let out undesignedly the secret of his insincerity, may be admired as a specimen of intellectual power, but he is despised and worthless as an instrument of good among mankind. Thus what a man is, rather than what a man says, tells. Our blessed Lord spake, it is true, as never man spake; but it was rather the dignity, and yet the lowliness, the grandeur, and yet the humility, the holiness of heaven, and yet all the sympathies of earth radiant from that spotless character, which left its deepest and most permanent impression upon mankind. Jesus made converts as much by what he was, as by what he said. You may be serving in a shop, behind a counter; you do not think you can be doing any moral good there; you are quite mistaken. The quietness with which you serve, the gentleness with which you reply, the simple, unpretending, and therefore appropriate, remark that you make, all are telling. There is not a face that does not almost repeat itself. In the modern discovery of the daguerreotype, rays coming from an object paint that object on the sensitive surface which they touch. It seems as if character radiated from the human countenance, painted itself on the characters of those it touches. What a man thinks, the very look of the countenance, the very thought that flashes through the eye, the very feeling that plays upon the lip, all are influencing others. There is not a mistress whose looks are not telling on a servant; there is not a master whose silent looks are not making somebody beneath him worse or better for it. It is impossible to go through the world without exercising influence; it is only possible to have that influence dipped in the fountain of light and life, and to have it so baptized and consecrated by a heavenly baptism, that wherever you are, you shall walk through the world an ambassador from God, a benefactor of all mankind. And what a solemn lesson is here for all teachers in schools, and parents acting in the presence of their children. The most susceptible creatures upon earth are children; and I do not believe that we give them credit for the intensity of their sensitive and susceptible nature. A child looks in your face and distinguishes your meaning long before you have given utterance to it. A child watches your countenance, and picks out your temper, your taste, your sympathy, long before you have audibly expressed it. And very many parents look things and say things, and when they think the child has detected what they did not mean the child to know, often in a very bungling way, as indeed all attempts at deception must be, they try to do away with the mischief they have done by suddenly turning a corner in the conversation, and launching on another subject. Do you think the child did not see that? He saw as clearly as you; and that act of yours has left upon that child a conviction of crookedness that may live in his memory, and fill up his character throughout the rest of his pilgrimage upon earth. To children we cannot be too direct, too straightforward; we cannot be too childlike in our intercourse with them, yet we must not be childish. Daily life is more powerful than Sunday life. The face as a dial cannot too purely, too truly reflect the innermost thoughts and imaginations of the heart. Be Christians, and your voluntary and involuntary influence will be Christian also. Be salt, and the savor will necessarily be good; be lights, and the influence that radiates from you will necessarily be light. What we want to be is not to look Christians, or to pretend Christians, or to profess Christians, but to be Christians. You need not then so carefully guard yourself, you need not be on the ceaseless watch what you do. Take an anagram; read it from the right or from the left, or from the top or from the bottom; it reads the same thing. Take a Christian, look at him at one angle, or look at another angle, look at him in any light or in any direction, and he is a Christian still. The great secret of getting rid of a vast amount of trouble and inconvenience, is being a Christian; and when you are a Christian your eye will be single, your body will be full of light, and all influences, sanctified and blessed by the Holy Spirit of God, will be sanctifying, and will bless all that are connected with you.

How responsible a thing is daily life!

## CHAPTER XIV.

### THE CHRISTIAN.

"Yon cottager who weaves at her own door,
Pillow and bobbins all her little store:—
She, for her humble sphere by nature fit,
Has little understanding, and no wit,
Just knows, and knows no more, her Bible true,
A truth the brilliant Frenchman never knew,
And in that charter reads with sparkling eyes
Her title to a treasure in the skies.
O happy peasant! O unhappy bard!
His the mere tinsel, hers the rich reward;
He praised perhaps for ages yet to come,
She never heard of half a mile from home;
He lost in errors his vain heart prefers,
She safe in the simplicity of hers."

"And the disciples were called Christians first in Antioch."—ACTS ix. 26.

THE character of which the name Christian is the exponent, or representative, has been found from the beginning. Adam was a Christian without the name; Judas was a Christian without the character. The followers of Christ in the earliest days of the Christian dispensation, were called by their enemies "Nazarenes," "Galileans," "Jews," "people who turned the world upside down." They were called by themselves "disciples, believers in Jesus, saints, brethren"

— brethren from their love to each other, saints from the holiness of their character, believers from their trust, and disciples of Jesus from their manifest and unswerving obedience to him. But in Antioch they were called by a name, — new, as a sound, but old, as a reality; and they were called so, not by themselves, nor yet by their enemies, but, as the word really implies, by God himself. They were called by themselves disciples, brethren, saints; they were called by their enemies Nazarenes, Galileans, Jews; but this name I think was a baptism immediately from God himself.

The Greek word which is translated in Acts xi. 26, "called," is not the usual word so translated. For instance, "Many are called" — κλητοι from καλεω, "to call." Again, "The called in Christ Jesus," where the word is κλητοι. But in the Acts, a new Greek word is introduced, namely, Χρηματιζω; and the question is, in what sense that word is used throughout the New Testament? It is always, or nearly so, used in the sense of a heavenly call directly from God himself. The first instance occurs in Matt. ii. 12, "And being warned of God in a dream." The Greek word translated "called" in the Acts is translated in this passage, "warned," and such warning was directly from God himself. In the 22d verse of the same chapter, "Notwithstanding, being warned of God in a dream." That is the same Greek word, and it means there a Divine warning or call. We find the same word used in Luke ii. 26, "And it was revealed unto him by the Holy Ghost." That is the same word, again used in the sense of a Divine call, only the person calling here is the Holy Ghost. It occurs in Acts x. 22. "And they said, Cornelius the centurion, a just man, and one that feareth God, and of good report among all the nation of the Jews, was warned from God." That is the same verb translated "called" in my text. Again, in

Hebrews viii. 5, we find an instance of its use, "Who serve unto the example and shadow of heavenly things, as Moses was admonished of God." That is the same Greek word translated "called" in the Acts. And lastly, in Hebrews xi. 7, "By faith Noah, being warned of God." That also is the very same Greek word. Now, in every instance, the word which is rendered "called" as applied to Christians, is used to denote an admonition, a voice, or command, from God himself. And therefore, we might translate the passage from the Acts, "The believers were first divinely called Christians in Antioch."

If this be not a name originally pronounced in scorn, as some have supposed, nor a name assumed by the Christians themselves to denote their relationship to the Great Founder, Author, and Finisher, of the faith, but one that was bestowed, not as a brand, but as an honor, a beauty, and a glory, directly and immediately from God himself, we are all very much to blame in adding to our generic, distinctive, and noblest name, even a Divine one, so many human additions as those into which the visible Church is so sadly and unhappily split. The first name, pronounced from heaven, was "Christian," and we may depend upon it it will be the last; for just in proportion as we grow towards the beautiful original in character, in the same proportion will those assumed human names — Presbyterians, Independents, Baptists, Episcopalians, Churchmen, Dissenters — drop off. Just as Christ is in a Christian's heart, all and in all, so, when that inner influence becomes an outer life, "Christian" will be in a Christian's vocabulary all and in all, also.

We will not dwell longer upon the direct evidence, though we might adduce further proofs, that this name was divinely bestowed. Let us notice what seems a hint of the future new nomenclature given in ancient prophecy. In

Isaiah lxii. 2, "And the Gentiles shall see thy righteousness, and all kings thy glory: and thou shalt be called by a new name, which the mouth of the Lord shall name." Again, in Isa. lxv. 15, it is said, "For the Lord God shall slay thee, and call his servants by another name;" that is, that the name "Hebrew," or the name "Jew" from Judah, or "son of Abraham," should be lost in the new name, that of Christian.

What is meant by this name? It is often misapplied. It is often diluted. We read of geographical Christians, ecclesiastical Christians, and we call all who are baptized, and profess the gospel, Christians. But all who are baptized are not Christians, and all who profess Christianity are not Christians. The name has a deep and precious significance. As a name, it can have no value; as a life, it is precious indeed. What does a Christion denote? First, it denotes one who is said in Scripture language to be "in Christ." "There is no condemnation to them that are in Christ Jesus." "I knew a man in Christ." And again, says the apostle, "that I may be found in Christ." Is not this a strange expression? Its very peculiarity indicates that there is some deep meaning and relationship in it. We never say that a Stoic is a man in Zeno, or that a Peripatetic is a man in Aristotle, or that a servant is in his master, or a pupil in his teacher. People would smile at such expressions. They would outrage common sense, and the fair and proper usage of language. But in Scripture nothing is more common than to find that very phrase, which is inapplicable to every relationship upon earth, constantly, and without the least explanation as if it were strange, applied to our relationship to Christ Jesus. It must mean, therefore, that there is something in a Christian's relationship to Christ, deeper, closer, more real, if I may use the expression, than in a pupil's relationship to his teacher, a servant's to his master, a philosopher's to the founder of the school to which he belongs. We go to Scripture and look for similitudes and explanation; and we find it compared to the branch in the tree, the limb in the body, the wife as related to the husband. All that indicates close, near, endearing connection, is seized and exhausted to denote a Christian's connection with Christ, and his relationship to him. Only all these similitudes fail. The branch may be severed from the vine, the limb may be torn from the body; but who shall separate us from the love of God which is in Christ Jesus our Lord?

A Christian means in Scripture one having the unction or anointing of the Holy Spirit of God. "Ye have," says the apostle, "an unction from the Holy One;" "The Spirit will show you things to come;" "If any man have not the Spirit of Christ, he is none of his." The word Χριστος comes from a Greek word which means "to anoint;" and when we call a person a Christian, we call him an anointed man, a man having a Divine unction. Well, what is that Divine unction? Ancient priests had oil poured on their heads when they were consecrated to their office. Ancient kings were anointed with oil when they were elevated to their thrones. The very phraseology and usage that belonged to ancient official dignity is applied to the true Christian. A Christian is a king and a priest unto God. He is an anointed and consecrated person. He is set apart from profane things to holy and Divine purposes. He has a destiny of everlasting happiness before him, a consecration directly Divine upon him. He is an anointed person, a Christian. When you, therefore, are tempted to do what is wrong, your feeling and recollections must be, I am an anointed one, I am set apart for another purpose, for another mission, for a very different function, as I am reserved for a very different destiny.

A Christian means also one who is the property of Christ. "Ye know that ye were not redeemed with corruptible things, as silver and gold, but with the precious blood of Christ, as of a lamb without blemish and without spot." "Ye are not your own." "Know ye not that your body is the temple of the Holy Ghost?" Therefore whatever I have is not mine. It is mine for use by me; but it is God's, because to be used to his glory, and in obedience to his will. My talent, my influence, my money, are all in my possession; but they are in the possession of a steward, who must use them after the prescriptions of him who has conferred them, not in the possession of an absolute king, who may do what he will with his own. We are not our own, we are bought with a price. Therefore let us with our souls and our bodies glorify God.

A Christian is one who delights and strives to obey Christ's commands. "Ye are my disciples." He himself says, "if ye keep my commandments." And again, "If ye love me, keep my commandments." It does not imply that a Christian will perfectly keep every law, or that he will keep all God's laws. He may fail, he may fall; but the constant beat, desire, and disposition of his heart will be to do what conscience, enlightened by God's word, proves to be his will, and in all things and on all occasions to do what he can discover from God's inspired word to be the will of his Master who is in heaven.

A Christian is one who feels deeply interested in the cause of Christianity. One may judge what one's interest in this cause is, and how far one has the inner spirit of a Christian, by the sympathy that we feel with it throughout the world. Are we grieved when Christian people suffer for Christ's sake? Are we delighted when Christianity gains new speed, achieves new victories, and covers the dark and desert places of the earth with a new and expanding glory? Are we rejoiced and ever anxious to hear tidings of the triumphs of this kingdom? And is it the prayer that we can breathe from the heart, "Thy kingdom come?"

A Christian would seem to me to be one who, openly and publicly, on all proper occasions, professes, and is not ashamed to profess, his attachment to the Redeemer. I do not mean that in his trade, if he be a tradesman, he should be constantly saying, "I am a Christian;" or that in the place he occupies in this world he should try to make people believe he is a Christian. This would be pretension; it would make one rather suspected than otherwise. He is to let men know that he is a Christian in trade, in a profession, in his duties in the world, in daily life, not by speaking Christianity, but by doing Christianity; so that the world, taking notice of him, will soon infer the Master he serves, the cause wherewith he is identified, and the spirit that sustains, informs, and actuates his life. If he be not a Christian, he need not try to persuade the world that he is. If he be a Christian, he need not say it to the world; for the world is acute enough to see the broad and palpable distinction between him that serveth God and him that serveth him not. But at baptism, if you are adults, you profess your attachment to the Saviour. If children, you are brought forward and dedicated to him. And at a communion table you are to say, (and I think it is one of the main lessons which the world may learn by seeing you there,) "I am not ashamed of the gospel of Christ." The communion table is the sacrament — the *sacramentum*, the ancient oath that a soldier took to his sovereign and his country. And when you come to that table you say, "I am not ashamed of Him whom the Jew hates, whom the Gentile does not know, whom the sceptic denies, but whom I hold, and hereby solemnly declare that I do hold, to be the wisdom of God, and the power of God, and the only Name given among men whereby I can be saved."

A Christian will ever look for Christ's return. The attitude of the church of Christ throughout the whole of revelation is that of the bride looking for the bridegroom, or the widow looking for a coming husband. This being so, the Christian will be constantly looking for Christ. His rest will be upon the cross, but his hope will stretch onward to the crown. To them that look for him will he come the second time without sin unto salvation. Waiting for the coming of the Lord, is one of the features laid down by the apostle as peculiar to a Christian. Christ is spiritually present throughout all this dispensation, but he will one day be personally present. The Christian cannot be satisfied with any substitute; he looks beyond all that attempts to be a substitute, and cries, "Come, Lord Jesus."

A Christian is one who departs from all iniquity. The apostle lays this down very distinctly, "Let every one that nameth the name of Christ depart from iniquity." A dishonest, a lying, or a drunken Christian is absurd. It is impossible to use such phraseology with any propriety. You can no more speak of a dishonest, lying, or drunken Christian, than you can speak of an ignorant scholar, an honest thief, or a charitable miser. These last would be felt to be contradictions, the moment you hear them, but it is no less a contradiction to say, a lying Christian, a drunken Christian, a dishonest Christian. Men who live knowingly in the practice of sin — knowingly and deliberately in the practice of what they know to be sin — are no more Christians than they are dukes, earls, barons, or marquises. Alexander the Great once said to a coward in his army, who was called by his name, "Either imitate my example, or give up my name." So Christ would say to all who are called Christians, but who do not live the life of Christ, "Either surrender my name, or imitate my example."

A Christian is one who denies himself. "If any man will come after me, let him deny himself, and take up his cross, and follow me." But what is meant by denying oneself? It is denying oneself an enjoyment in order to discharge a duty; or denying oneself something that is perfectly proper, in order to do good to a brother who needs it, or to give an impulse to a cause that faints and fails for want of it. Now do we deny ourselves? Can we give up what we prefer in deference to duty? Can we surrender a pleasure for the sake of doing good in some way indicated in the providence of God, or pointed out by his holy word? If we cannot deny ourselves, if we must indulge ourselves, at all hazards, then we want one of those features that seem to me essential to the Christian character, and we so far fail in giving the clearest and sharpest lineaments of that beautiful and Divine stature.

If you be a Christian, you will love all your fellow Christians just because they are Christians, and for no other reason. I do not say that you may not prefer the man of taste to the man who has none. You may prefer talent to the absence of it. You may have your preference of one peculiarity, tone, or temperament of mind to another. But there will always be this grand feature in your predilections — you will prefer an ignorant Christian to an accomplished worldling. You will prefer a true Christian without taste, to a man of fine taste without character. You will prefer the humblest and most plebeian child of God to a marquis or an earl who is but a gambler, and a wicked and profane profligate. You may have your preferences of many things in this world justly and properly; but you will surrender all preferences, and sacrifice all prejudices, on the altar of a common Christianity, holding and feeling that men may be this, but they must be that, to have communion and fellowship with you. And you will love a Christian, too, in spite of much in him that makes him sometimes very unlovely. Christians are not in this world perfect. There are sometimes Christians who have very bad tempers, there are Christians who have many oddities, and much in their character that you do not admire; but you will love them, not because they are passionate or odd, but in spite of their being so, and in spite of their having a bad taste, just because they are Christians, the sons and daughters of the Almighty, and the followers of the Lord. You may dislike dissent, because you are churchmen; or you may dislike the church, because you are dissenters; and you may have your own views and your own predilections on these subjects; but you will love the Christian in spite of his dissent, or his churchmanship; you will forgive him all his defects, if he only hold fast Christ and him crucified, as all and in all, in his heart, his hopes, his faith, his life, his walk. I do not forbid any to have preferences; I only ask all to subordinate them to that which is higher than all, that name which was first, that name which will be last, the name of Christian.

It is as Christians that we are to come to the Lord's table, and in no other capacity whatever. What is the central object, and what ought, therefore, to be the weightiest thought, at a communion table? What is it spread for? What do we approach it for? The answer is, to show forth the death of Christ until he come again. There that one thought ought to be supreme. The love of Christ ought so to fill all the interstices, and cells, and nooks of the human heart, that there shall be no room left for Luther, Calvin, Knox, Latimer, or any other, however worthy or excellent. It is not "Do this in remembrance of" John, or Paul, or Peter; or in remembrance of Luther, or Ridley, or Calvin;

but it is "Do this in remembrance of" One only. And therefore, as you turn over the leaves of memory at that table, that one Name ought to be first, last, all, and in all. As you look into your heart at that table, that Name ought to be engraven upon it, as on a precious gem, indelible forever. To that table Christians only should come. Leave your ecclesiastical robes at the door, put off your sectarian shoes at the threshold, and come in shod with the preparation of the gospel of peace, wearing robes that have been washed and made white in the blood of the Lamb, which alone are worn in heaven, and on which there is no stain, and because of which alone the choirs of the redeemed stand before the throne of God, and serve him day and night without ceasing.

Are we Christians? This is the great question. You are not responsible for being rich, noble, royal. These are providential distinctions, which involve no guilt on the part of those who are strangers to them. But you are responsible for being Christians. It is your own blame if you are not Christians. The whole guilt of not being so lies at your own door. You are summoned to embrace this noble dignity, to put on this grand name, and to feel in your heart, by believing with your whole mind, that Christ is your Prophet, your Priest, your King, your all and in all. Is the religion of the New Testament the religion that you want to know? Is the Bible the rule of faith that you love to study, the rule of life that you prefer to follow? Do you open the Bible, not as critics, or scholars, or admirers of beautiful poetry, rich eloquence, or fine writing, but as wayfaring men, seeking to know Christ, the way to heaven? Do you come into the house of God, not as critics, in your own minds or with others, to discuss the preacher's sermon, but as hungering for living bread, thirsting for living water, and desiring to get strength in life's weary walk, and courage amid life's arduous and corroding trials; so that refreshed, as from one of the springs in the valley of Baca, you may go on your way rejoicing, and appear before God at length in Zion?

Are we Christians? To ascertain this, let us inquire what we are when alone? In society we may wear a mask; before the church we may seem what we are not; but alone with God we appear exactly what we are. When alone, free from the harassment of business, and the world, and its cares, do our thoughts ever instinctively turn to Him who is their strength, their inspiration, and their hope? The flower follows the sun, and the Christian's heart, when left to itself, will lean instinctively and by its very nature towards Him who is its trust, its hope, its strength, and its joy. The first thing that the heart, left to itself, gravitates to, is its chief thing. If it be money, learning, home, or stores, or treasures of any sort, these you love more than God. It is a very admirable way of ascertaining what we are, to watch where the heart naturally gravitates, towards whom and what is its instinctive polarity, on whom it leans, of whom it thinks. Does the thought of God ever spring up in your heart without the preacher's voice awakening it? Does the idea of eternity ever come into your mind without its being suggested by a sermon? If so, this would indicate that your heart has affinities beyond the horizon, that rest and terminate only in Him who gave them their birth and their being, the Lord Jesus Christ.

Let us look at the Christian in his home. This is the first place where he is seen by others. He is not perfect anywhere, and there his imperfections will be seen most clearly and most fully. What are you in your home? Are your counsels based upon Scripture? Is your example originated and directed by it? Is family worship not so much a duty as an instinct, not so much a performance that you must go through, as a necessity without which you feel you cannot happily live, or justly act? Is your home a sanctuary? Are its inmates as Levites? Is it your desire that it should be like a vestibule of the sanctuary, participating, in its influence, and consecrated by contact and communion with it?

Let us look at the Christian in the church, that is, in the assembly of God's people. Do you come to hear, not what pleases the fancy, but what will enlighten the mind and impress the heart? Do you come to hear merely because it is habit; or because the newsroom is shut upon the Sunday, and the church only is accessible? or do you come to the sanctuary really hungering for bread, longing to hear something that will refresh you after the weary toils of the week, and give you new strength, vigor, and inpulse to undertake the duties that are before you, and to go through them, and be more than conquerors through Him that loved you? Is church-going an earnest matter, or an old inveterate habit merely, that you do not feel much pleasure in, but that you cannot easily lay aside? It is well if it be a habit, but it is not enough if it be a habit only. Coming to church is not the duty done; it is only a step towards the discharge of the duty by embracing the privilege, and learning all the words of everlasting life.

Let us look at the Christian in daily life. What are you in business, in trade, in traffic, in all the transactions with which you come in contact, and in which you take a part, in this world? Very many, I fear, carry the world into the church; but it is the few who carry the church into the world. To bring the world into the church is to desecrate the church; to bring the church into the world is to consecrate and elevate the world. We ought to gather, as on the sabbath day, not only manna for our maintenance on the weekdays, but also courage, inspiration, motive, for boldly and distinctly letting the world see that our church-going is not a form, but a power; and that what we hear on the Sunday does not make us more morose, gloomy, or destitute of courtesy, or adverse to all the reciprocities of social life, but gives us a patience, a content, a gentleness, a meekness, and yet a fixity of purpose, as well as purity of motive, which the world is altogether a stranger to. Do you then seek to have the world's sunny places made brighter by the influence of heaven, and the world's dark and shady places enlightened by the truths of the blessed gospel? and can you take your place at your desk, or behind your counter, or in the post and place of duty, with a sense of responsibility almost as sacred and solemn as that with which you take your place at a communion table. We have a bad habit of saying, This is holy work, and that is worldly work. The fact is, to a Christian all work should be holy, all days should be Christian, and all life should be a ceaseless sacrament. A Christian comes to the sanctuary, not there to be the Christian on the Sunday, and then to go out into the world on the Monday, and there to be the worldling, just as if he had never been in the sanctuary at all. The sanctuary is the ward in the hospital, to which he comes to receive the prescription that can heal him, whence he goes forth on the Monday, the lame leaping like the roe, the deaf hearing, the dumb speaking, and all living so that the world may see that they have received on the Sunday that which has made them stronger and better on the Monday. The sanctuary and the Sunday are the time and the place for receiving light; the counting-house, the parliament, and elsewhere, on the Monday, are the places for radiating that light. You are not to receive all your light upon the Sunday, and leave it in the pews you have left empty behind you; but you are to take it with you, not in order to say to the world, See what the gospel has made me, but so to act, that the world will be constrained to take notice of that man, that merchant, that senator, as the Jews did of Peter and John, that they have been with Jesus.

Let us look at the Christian in different circumstances of personal experience. In adversity is your lot perhaps. If you are a Christian, your conduct will there appear beautiful, decided, unmistakable. When a worldly man suffers, he is deeply depressed, he sinks into despondency, or he altogether despairs; or, if he be a stoic, he is insensible to it; or, if he be an ascetic, he flees from the world, hoping to avoid its trials by getting some sheltered nook where he thinks he will have perpetual sunshine and uninterrupted peace. But a Christian man in adversity prays; he looks up to Him who has told him that trouble comes not from the ground, that whatever a believer suffers is an expression, not of penal wrath from a judge, but of paternal affection from a Father. Such a one receiving affliction, merely feels that he is put in Christ's school, or, like fine silver, in God's furnace; and that in either case he is laid there, not by hate, but by love; and that he will be kept there, not so long as the devil would like, nor for so short a time as he would prefer, but precisely as long as God in his infinite wisdom sees to be good for him; and during that adversity, a believer, instead of desponding, or despairing, will exclaim, in language that in pitch rises far above the human, "Although the fig-tree shall not blossom, neither shall fruit be in the vines; the labors of the olive shall fail, and the fields shall yield no meat; the flock shall be cut off from the fold, and there shall be no herd in the stalls;" that is, if I lose all my property and possessions, and do not see where or whence to get bread for to-morrow, what shall I do? Despair, run away into the wilderness, commit suicide? No; "yet I will rejoice in the Lord, I will joy in the God of my salvation." When a worldly man loses his figs and his vines, his olives, and his herds in the stall, he has nothing to fall back upon; his all is gone. But when a Christian has lost his goods, he has only lost certain expressions of God's love; the God who gave them still remains; and as the fountain is ever full and ever overflowing, he knows that God will either give him other vines, herds, and fig-trees, or he will give him what is as good, an equivalent in his heart that will inspire the conviction, "It was good that I lost them all." Such is a Christian in adversity.

Let us look at a Christian in prosperity. It is much easier to manage adversity than prosperity; and for one that adversity depresses into despair, there are ten that prosperity makes forget God and themselves together. It is a very painful thing to have and drink from a bitter cup; but it is a very delicate and difficult thing to hold a cup that is full to the brim without spilling some of its contents. It is often wearisome to live in the shade, but it is still more perilous to live perpetually in the sunshine. It may often be very cross to our ambition to tread earth's lowly places, but it is still more dangerous to our spiritual safety to dwell in the high places of the earth. It is the loftiest cedar that is first struck by the lightning; it is the highest spires that first fall; it is they who walk the high places of the earth who are the least under the influence of grace, and of whom the fewest enter into the kingdom of heaven. If therefore you are prosperous, be not proud, be not earthly-minded, saying, "I will pull down my old barns, and build new ones;" be not so attached to the gift, that you forget the giver, and when reminded of God, go away sorrowful. Be not self-indulgent, saying, "Soul, thou hast much goods laid up for many years; take thine ease, eat, drink, and be merry." If you be afflicted, as in the last case, pray; if you be prosperous, as in the present case, praise; and let your adversity and your prosperity equally bring you to Him who sweetens the bitterness of the one cup, and gives strength to hold steadily the over full cup of the other. Thus, if a Christian is afflicted, he prays; if he be merry, he sings psalms; and whether in adversity, or in prosperity, he sets his affections upon God, receives thankfully, enjoys with moderation, gives liberally, and recognizes God as entitled to the glory and the praise of all.

Are you, Christian, placed in sorrow? There is a distinction between sorrow and affliction. Prosperous men may be sorrowful, as well as afflicted men. Adversity is a state that occurs in God's providence; sorrow is an experience implanted by God's Holy Spirit. "Blessed are ye that mourn," says our Saviour; "for ye shall be comforted." This sorrow is created by what you see within you. So much felt there that should not be, and so much wanting there that ought to be, constitute truly weighty reasons for that sorrow which the Saviour says is blessed. When you look back at those things you have done which you ought not to have done, and at those things you have left undone which you ought to have done; the long dark catalogue would sink you into despair, did you not see written across it, bright and luminous in the light in which it was written, "The blood of Jesus Christ his Son cleanseth us from all sin." Sorrow also a Christian will feel when he looks around him, and sees how little progress the gospel has made, how little is doing or has been done in order to promote that gospel amongst mankind; and as Jeremiah said, "Oh that my head were waters, and mine eyes a fountain of tears, that I might weep day and night for the slain of the daughter of my people!" and as David said, "Rivers of waters run down mine eyes, because they keep not thy law;" so a Christian cannot see the drunkenness, the recklessness, and the depravity of a world around him, without grieving that it is so, and lamenting that so little is attempted to make it otherwise.

A Christian may be studied in his joys. Joy is distinct from prosperity, as sorrow is from affliction. There is first a natural joy, which is not forbidden; there is a sensual joy, which is very equivocal; there is a carnal joy, which is fiendish; and there is a Christian joy, which is beautiful. A Christian's joy must be something like the joy of his Lord. It is said that Jesus shall see the travail of his soul, and shall be satisfied. And again, it is said, "For the joy set before him" (what was that joy but the travail of his soul, the sinners that should be saved) "he endured the cross, despising the shame." And, therefore, a Christian's joy is very much associated with the progress and the triumphs of the everlasting gospel. When he hears of new districts added to Christ, of new nations recognizing his sceptre and his sway; of distant lands brought under the light of the Sun of righteousness; and of dens and lanes and alleys at his own threshold visited by the messenger of glad tidings, that never were visited before; like his blessed Master, he feels joy, and rejoices in spirit. A Christian ought to rejoice when he hears of the gospel's spread, and he ought to grieve when he hears of obstructions to its progress. In other words, if we are Christians, we shall have the same interest in the gospel that a politician has in the politics and progress of the party he belongs to. If you watch a politician, he says, I move under a certain banner; I am associated with an existing or a deposed prime-minister, and I rejoice that such a one has been elected there, and such a one rejected here. In short, a thorough politician is full of his party. He opens the paper the first thing in the morning, in order to see what his party has gained or lost. His whole heart is in his party. Let us borrow a leaf from his book; let our chief thoughts and affections be in that cause which knows no party, and seeks no partisanship; or if a party at all, that to which all flesh should belong, to belong to which is to be a member of the general assembly of the church of the first-born, whose names are written in the Lamb's book of life.

Let us think of a Christian in that scene in which he must play a part, a death-bed. This is the testing scene. Many things occur in God's providence to test what we are; but this scene will occur in every man's biography, and will thoroughly test what he is. It is the scale that weighs him, the test that thoroughly distinguishes him. It is one, too, that he cannot avert. How shall we feel when we are placed upon that bed? Shall we be able to say, "I have fought a good fight, I have finished my course, I have kept the faith: henceforth there is laid up for me a crown of righteousness, which the Lord, the righteous Judge, shall give me at that day?" Shall I be able to say, "I know in whom I have believed, and am persuaded that he is able to keep that which I have committed to him. I have much to lament, much to seek forgiveness for, but I know that I have committed my soul with its deepest and dearest interests to him; I know in whom I have believed, and I have not the least doubt that he is able and willing to keep that soul which I have committed to his hands against that day?" He who can say so will descend into the deep valley of the shadow of death with unfaltering footstep, because he knows that when he has reached its profoundest depth, he there begins his glorious ascent on the sunlit side that leads to the blessedness and glory of the everlasting and happy Jerusalem. He will die; but because he dies in the Lord, he will see opening before him a pathway to his Father who is in heaven, and to all who have preceded him to the rest that remaineth for the people of God.

A Christian will live in prosperity, in adversity, in his home, in the sanctuary, in the world, as a Christian. This will be the predominating feeling. This will give the tone, direction, and influence to all that he is. And when he comes to die, he who lived a Christian in his daily life, will depart in peace a Christian, and having finished his course, enter on that sabbath life which is the grand feature of the age to come, the blessed hope and unspeakable reward of all true believers.

END.

www.ingramcontent.com/pod-product-compliance
Lightning Source LLC
LaVergne TN
LVHW010227110826
845151LV00004B/1212

* 9 7 8 1 4 2 5 5 2 6 3 7 5 *